John Hurst's
NORFOLK
COASTAL COLOURS

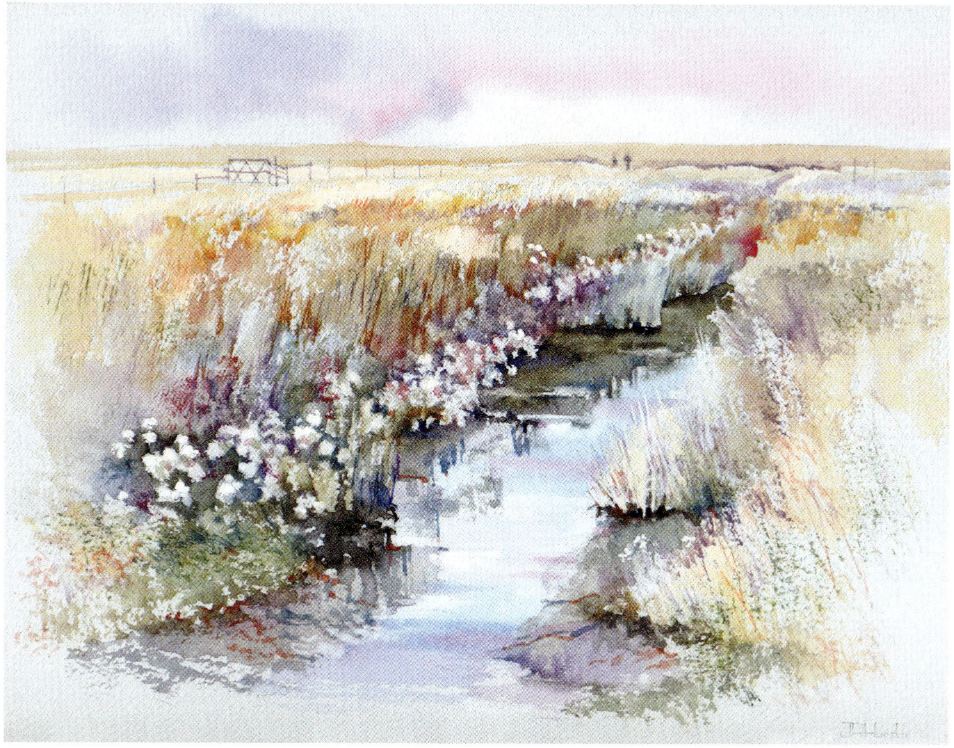

JOHN HURST

HALSTAR

First published in Great Britain in 2010

For further information about the work of the artist please visit www.marshlandarts.co.uk

Unless otherwise stated, all images are 350mm x 255m and were completed during 2009

British Library Cataloguing-in-Publication Data
A CIP record for this title is available from the British Library

ISBN 978 1 906690 22 9

HALSTAR
Halsgrove House,
Ryelands Industrial Estate,
Bagley Road, Wellington, Somerset TA21 9PZ
Tel: 01823 653777 Fax: 01823 216796
email: sales@halsgrove.com

An imprint of Halstar Ltd, part of the halsgrove group of companies
Information on all Halsgrove titles is available at: www.halsgrove.com

Printed and bound by Grafiche Flaminia, Italy

CONTENTS

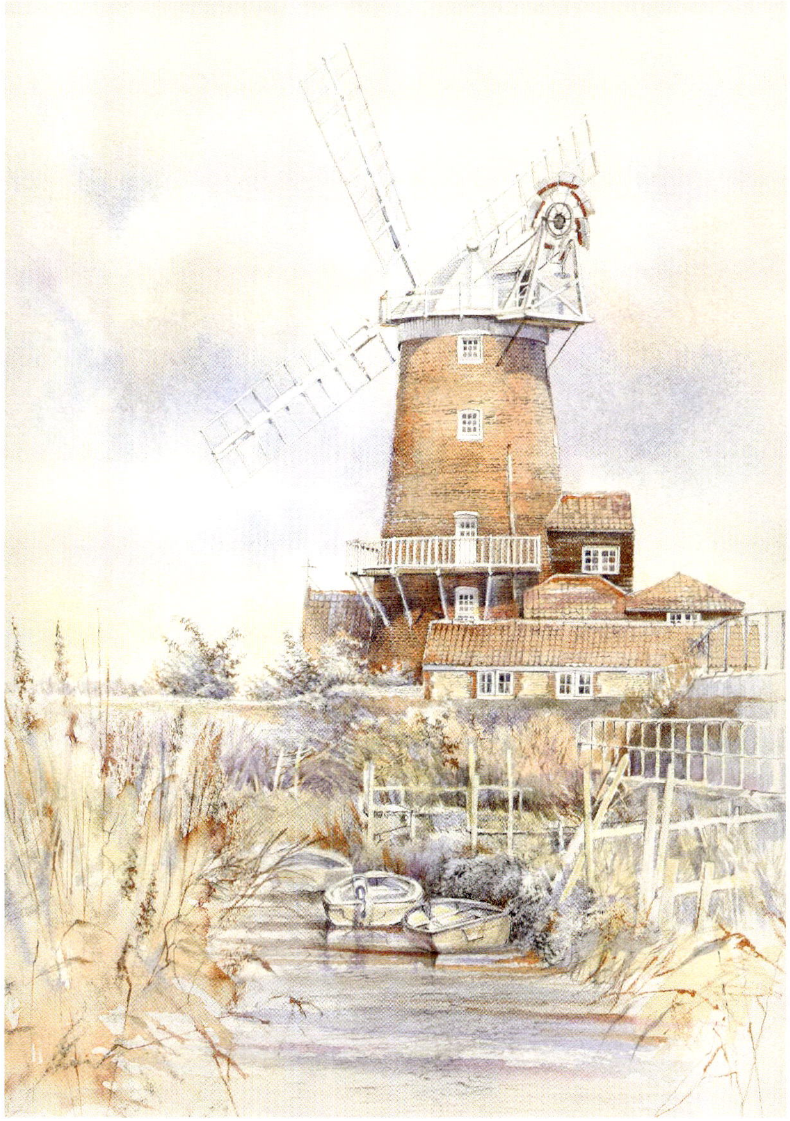

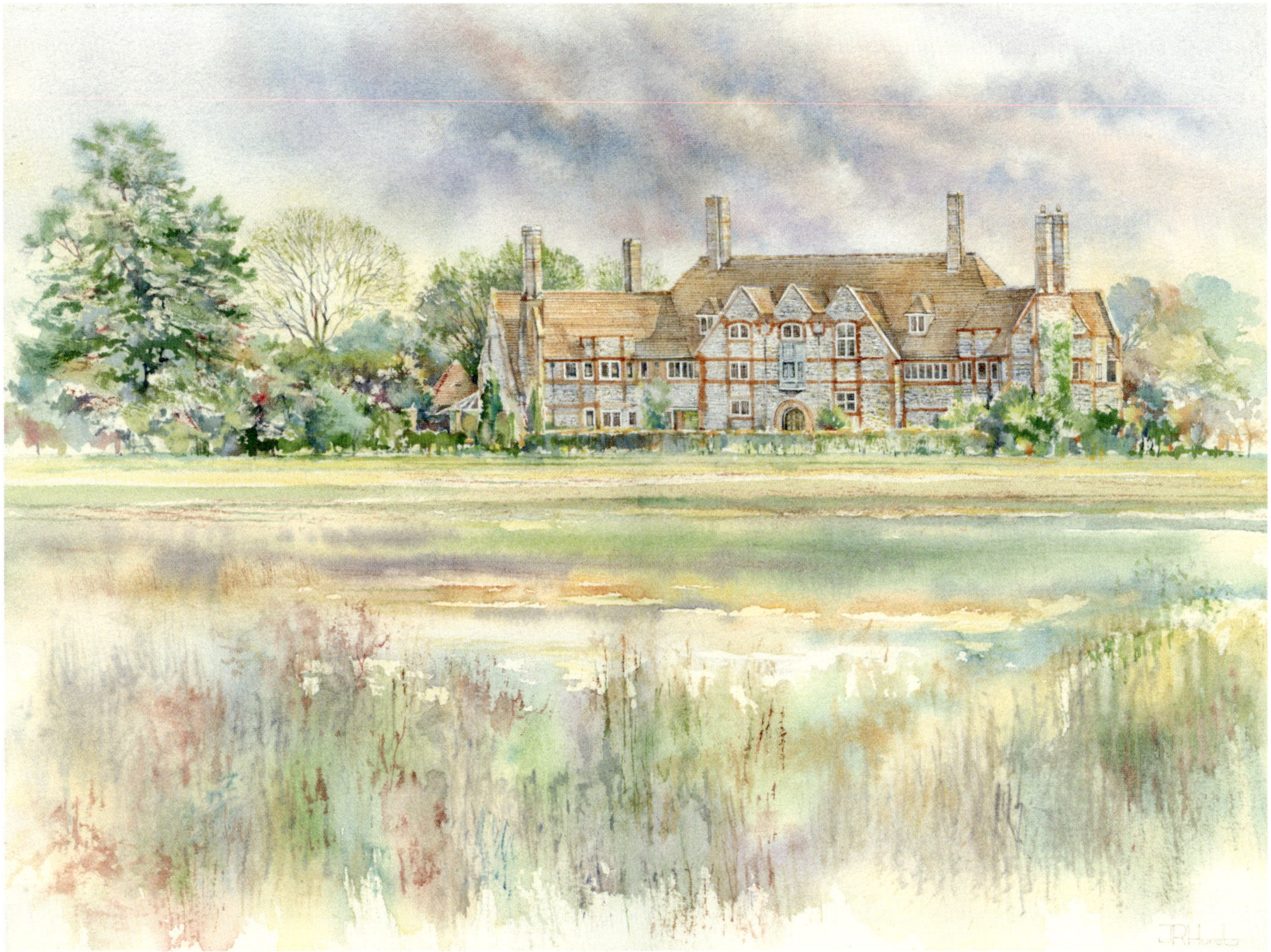

To Shirley and Jimmy

FOREWORD
by Samuel West

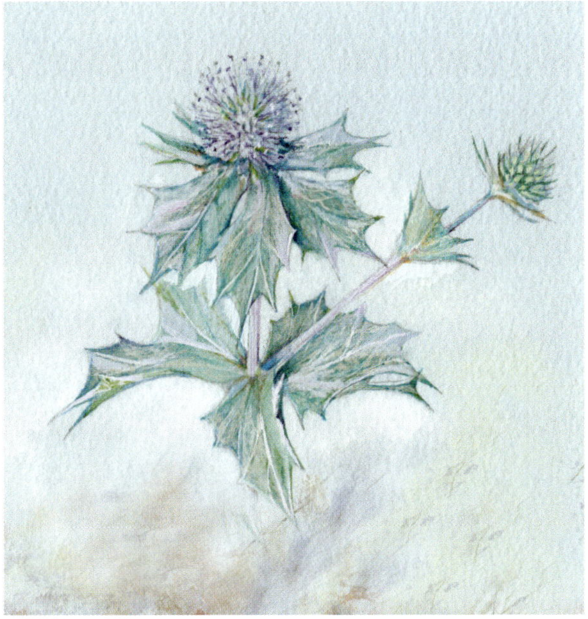

When I first met John Hurst, I'd been a serious birdwatcher for only a year or two. Birding is like any other pursuit: the more hours you put in, the more successful you'll be. So I really didn't deserve, on my first trip to the Isles of Scilly, to meet John on the crossing. I asked for (and got) John's patient help to identify the sea birds, whizzing past and marvelled at his extraordinary keen sight and eye for movement.

Both are qualities that serve him well in these paintings. His lifelong love for nature is not escapist and his work is detailed but never soulless. John's natural curiosity comes across in his paintings; he has as much appreciation of the form and function of a tractor as of a gatehouse, and approaches both with a deep understanding of colour and light. When I look at these pictures, I can imagine the day to come, or the one just past.

And it is passing, slowly. When I ran a theatre in Sheffield, I became concerned that a city which once had made things now simply sold things. Many of the buildings, as they lost their function, were losing their memory. This has not yet happened in north Norfolk. The walls there hum with purpose, and we can still recognise a community, just.

It's important that the place doesn't lose it memory. That's where John comes in.

Samuel West
Actor
January 2010

INTRODUCTION

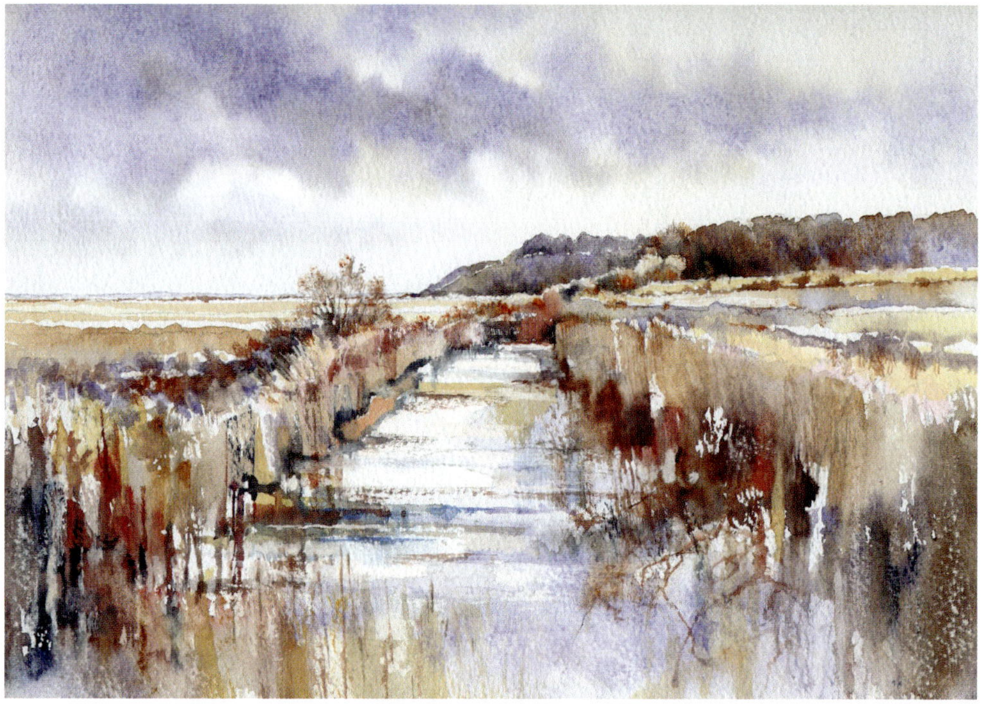

After thirty years of itinerant painting and bird-watching on the vast marshes that stretch from The Wash to the cliffs at Weybourne, I finally made the permanent move to North Norfolk. My many patrons have included enthusiastic tourists, city dwellers with second homes, and the indigenous population, with all of whom I have become very fond. The source of this book started as a commission to paint Wiveton Hall, a beautiful rambling Jacobean house overlooking the marshes near Blakeney. This work was subsequently seen by Shirley Carnt, the accomplished oil painter, formerly of Kelling Hall, who immediately requested as a surprise gift to her husband, Jimmy, a similar study and large number of sketches representing the Kelling Estate.

It soon became apparent that the Deterding family, who were founding members of Royal Dutch Shell, had continued to play an important role in the development of the wider community since building the hall in 1927; their other initiatives including the Blakeney Hotel and The Reading Room in Kelling village. My interest in social history, regional architecture and the natural environment means that I am constantly seeking to record images that have been influenced by location and man's interaction with the landscape.

It is hoped that by referring to these current images, the visitor or resident alike may be reminded of the contrasting beauty of north Norfolk and empathise with those fortunate to work in this unique Area of Outstanding Natural Beauty.

Having been brought up in a close-knit rural community and familiar with its dynamics, I shall always see myself as an 'incomer' with a Lincolnshire accent, and as such wish this collection of words and pictures to be the result of unbiased observations by a neutral observer and one who has a genuine fascination and love for the area in which I now live. It has been a humbling experience to be welcomed into old flint cottages and be told stories of old Norfolk in pure dialect and accent. Some of these accounts are full of typical dry humour, powerful in their illustration of people and place, whilst others are tales of poverty and loss; such is the nature of rural life. I have tried to illustrate the last days of The Deterding family on their beloved estate, capture a working community and record events, people and places as they appear in this celebration, 'a snapshot in time'.

J R Hurst, Salthouse 2010

PREFACE

I have chosen to present the reader of *Coastal Colours* with a journey from west to east Norfolk; recording experiences, completing commissions and telling stories with pen and brush along the way. I took a year out along my journey to study a family estate at Kelling in intimate detail, observing seasonal changes, before exploring a variety of architecture, landscape and habitats towards the east.

Whilst in pursuit of these opportunities, I experienced winter storms, discovered hidden interiors, enjoyed high summer frolics, sensed Edwardian opulence and wandered in autumnal mists. In personal terms, I met many generous local people who were willing to share their experiences and lifelong knowledge, serving as a reminder that, for future generations, this fragile environment is in good hands.

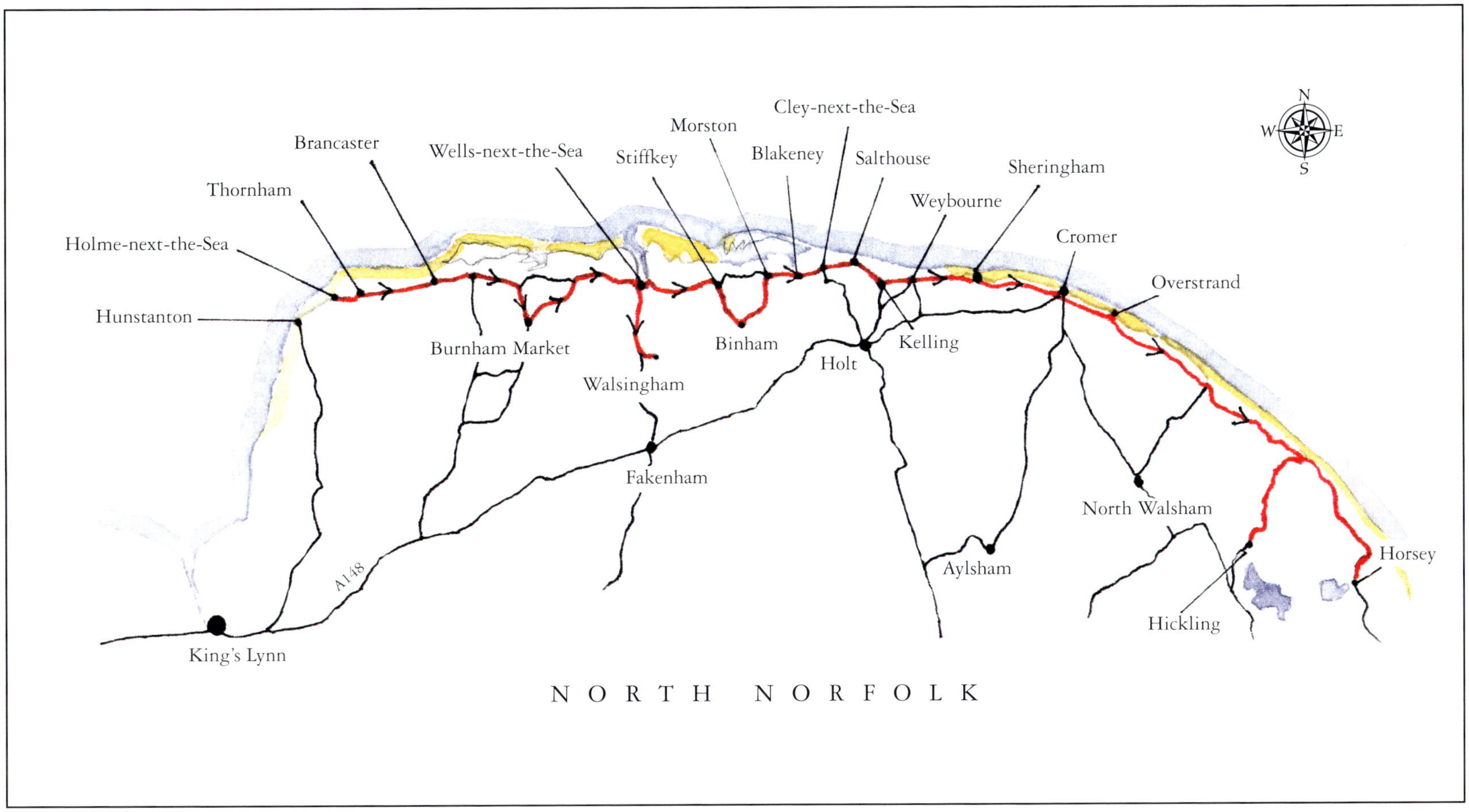

ACKNOWLEDGEMENTS

I would like to thank the following people, without whom this publication would not exist, for giving their time, local knowledge, patience, skills and friendship.

Mr & Mrs J Deterding
Mr & Mrs W Deterding
Kathleen & Bob
Andrew & June
Mr & Mrs B Pope
Mr & Mrs B Slegg
Mr & Mrs Johnson
Mr T Fox
Mr D MacCarthy
Mr & Mrs A Banthorpe
Mr & Mrs R Carter
Mr N Kendal
Mr W Hudson
Mr J Wagstaff
Drs R & S Dawson
Mr Samuel West
Miss Laura Wade
Mr C Sayer
Mr & Mrs J Walker
Mr & Mrs E Edwards MBE
Mr & Mrs D Holmes
Anne Powell
Mr & Mrs C Buxton
Mr & Mrs J Loose
Nick Acheson
Stephen Tuck
Cmdr Roy Francis
Mr G Cooke
Mr C Cooke
Mr K Cooke
Mr G Park
Mr & Mrs J Temple
Mr J Dowsing
Mrs M Dowsing
Mr & Mrs J Martin
Mr J Spalding
Miss Eve Hurst
Miss Mimi Hurst
Mr R Mansey
Mr R Brazier
Mr W Temple
Mr Craske
Mr Middleton
Mr T Holsey
Mr E Wood
P J Scotters
Miss P Alexander
Mr & Mrs P Archer
Rev R Wakelin
Mr & Mrs M Holman
Mr & Mrs J Webster
Mr D Hewitt
Mr & Mrs K Wyatt
Mr & Mrs W Garfit
Drs N & R Sinclair
Mr A Hill
Norfolk Wildlife Trust
Mr & Mrs B Bishop
Mr & Mrs C Large
Mr & Mrs Crossley
Mr C Cobon
Mr S Ayres
Mr & Mrs C Lacoste
Mr & Mrs J Witherspoon
Mr & Mrs G Widdowson
Dr & Mrs N Cary
Goochie Gooch
Sugar Smith
Phil & Gill Murrell
Dr T Irwin
Mr & Mrs J Dowdy
Mr B Riches

With special thanks to Simon Butler and the team at Halsgrove.

With special, special thanks to Jacqui for her graphics wizardry, editing skills and support.

EARLY MARITIME STUDIES

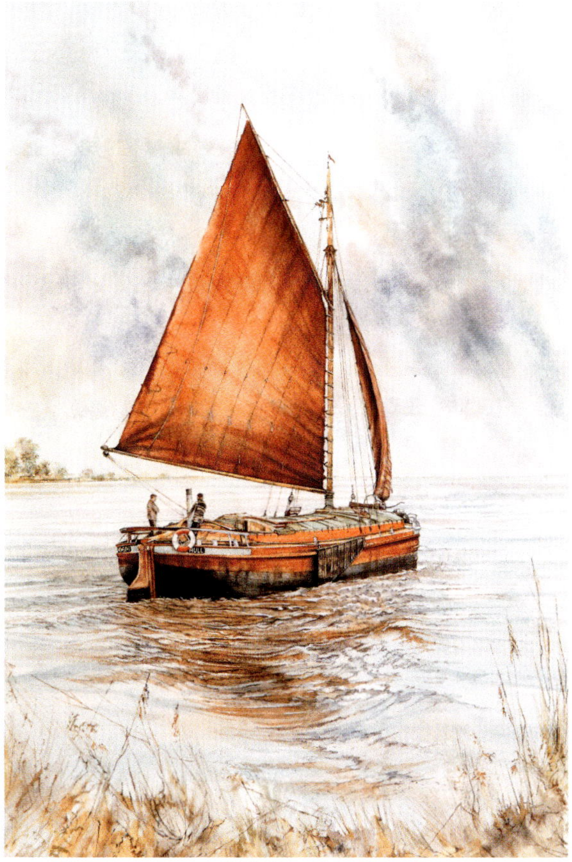

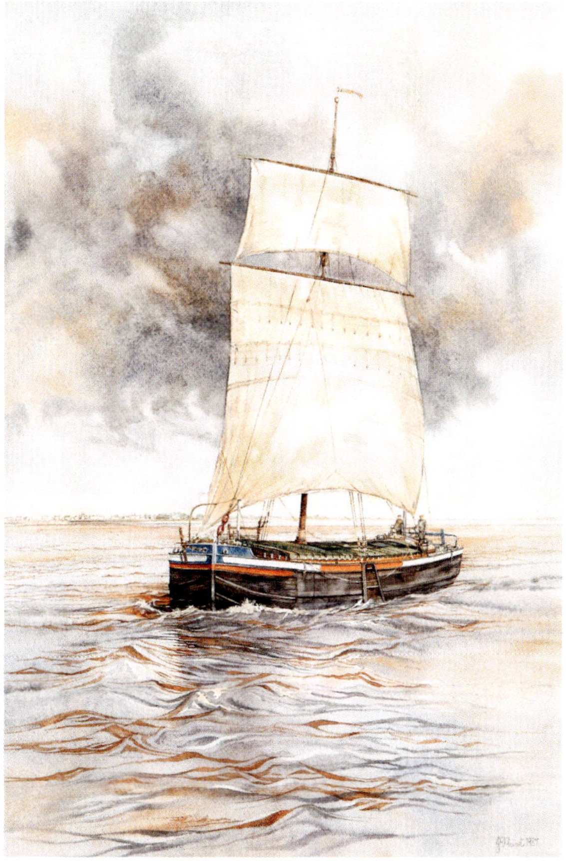

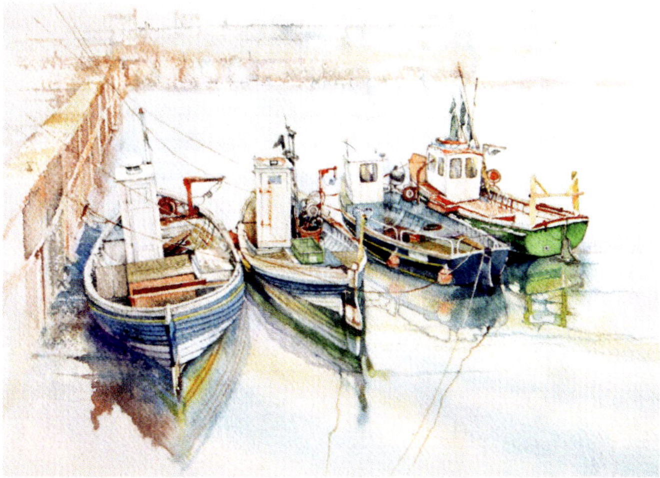

Clockwise from top left:

The Sloop, Amy Howson

360mm x 520mm

The Keel, Comrade

360mm x 520mm

Four Boats

320mm x 270mm

THE DISTANT WEST

Holme and Thornham

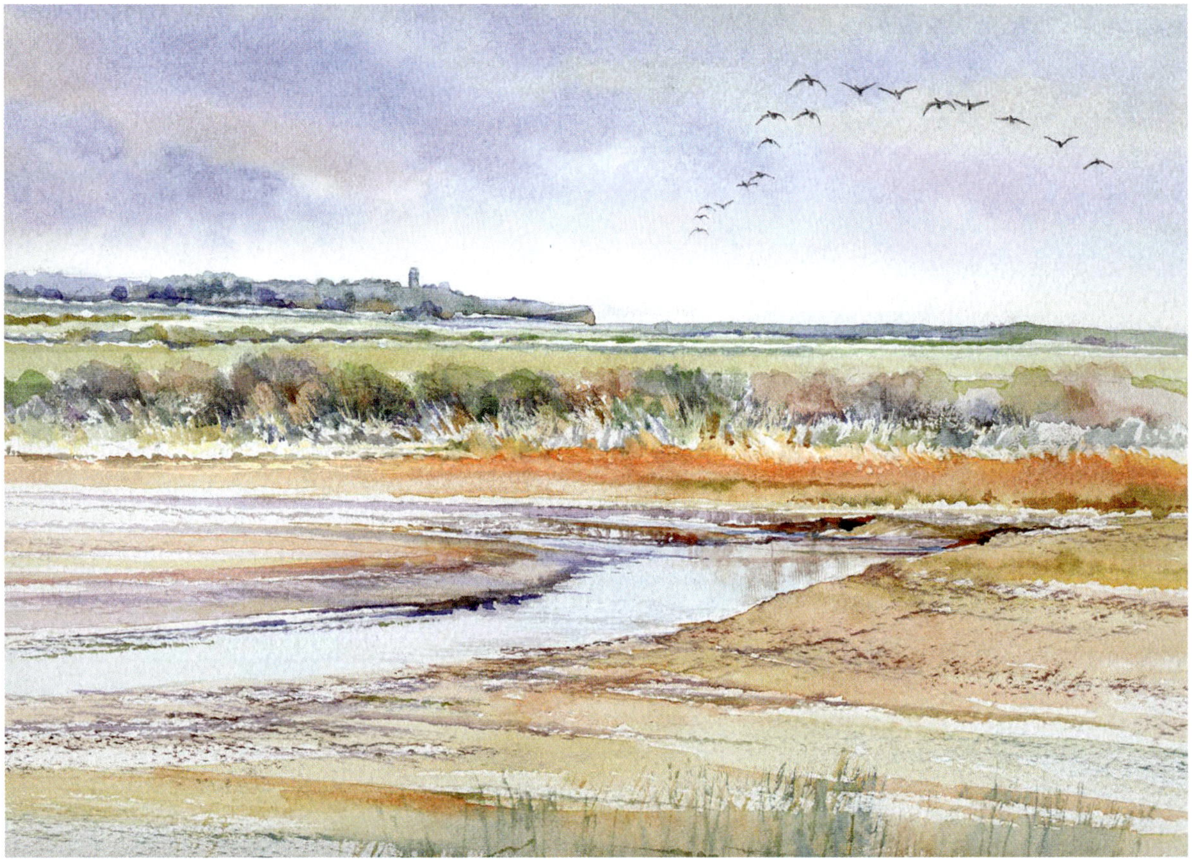

Brents Approaching Gore Point
280mm x 180mm

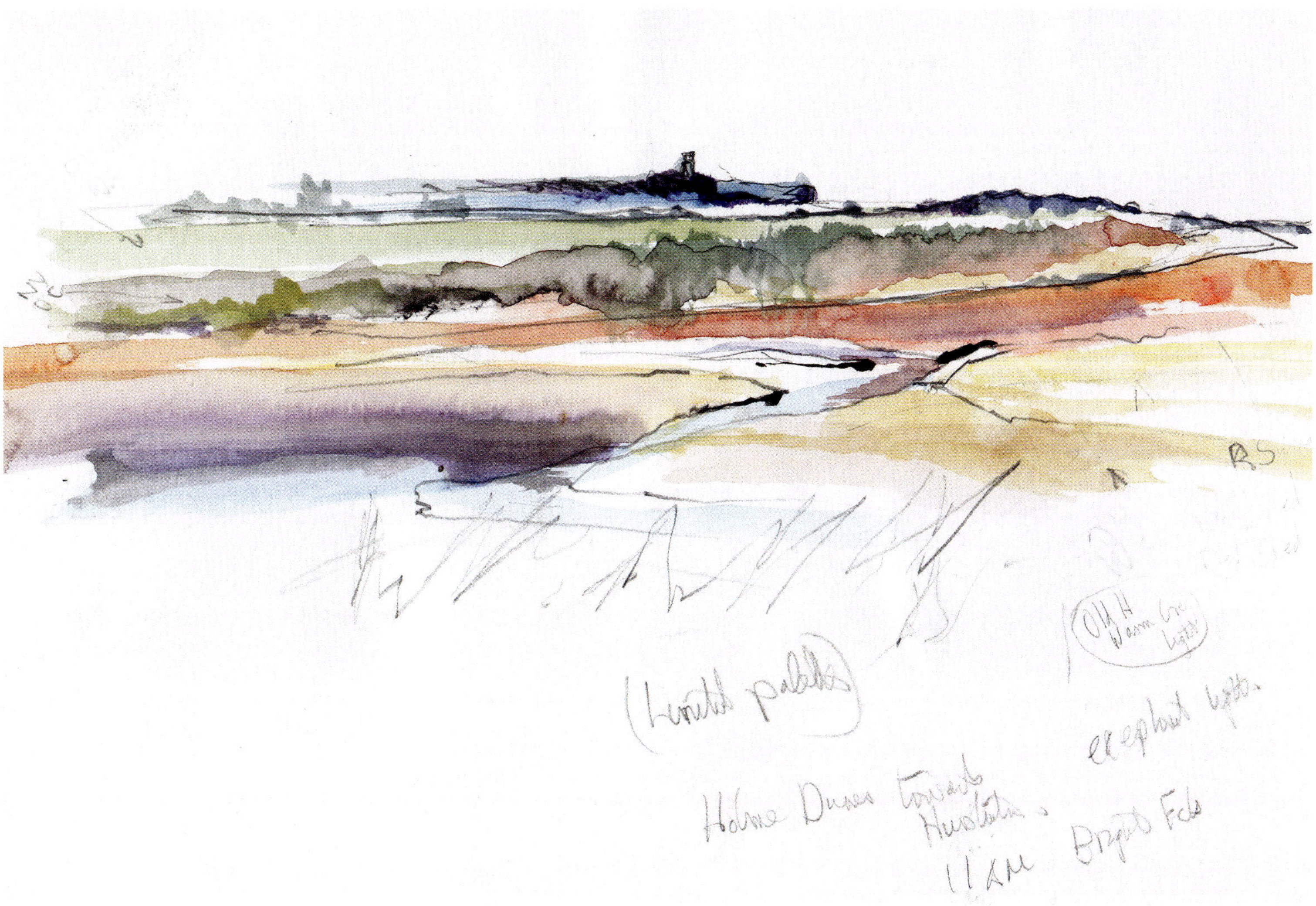

Gore Point Sketchbook Study

This sketch was composed on a bright February morning and shows the strength of colour to be found on the Norfolk tidal marshes. In the distance we see Old Hunstanton lighthouse and in the completed original painting, a skein of brent geese climb over the Suada ridge. The location of this study is the Norfolk Wildlife Trust Reserve at Holme Dunes, an interesting site comprising diverse habitats including salt marsh, dunes, maritime pines, fresh water lagoons, reedbeds and seashore.

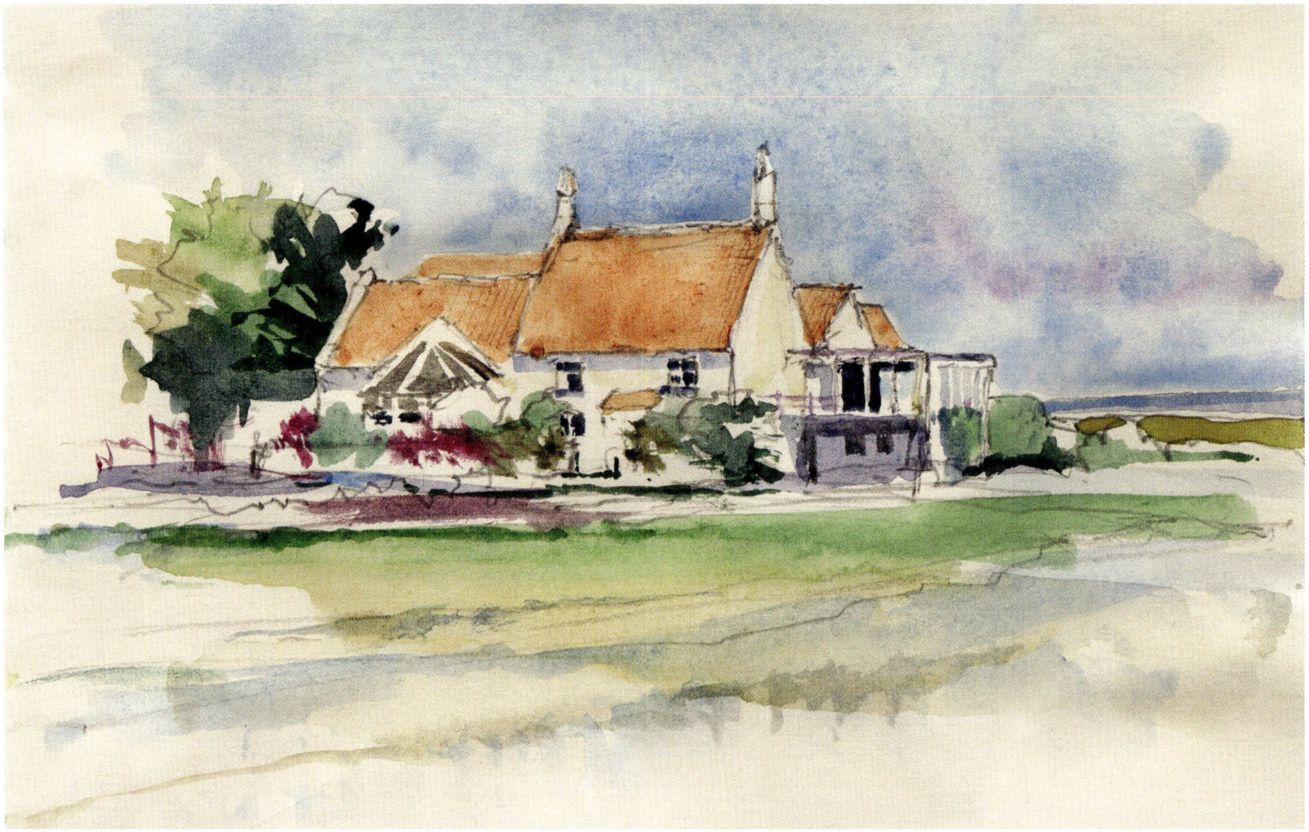

Preliminary Sketch, Coastguard Cottage, Thornham

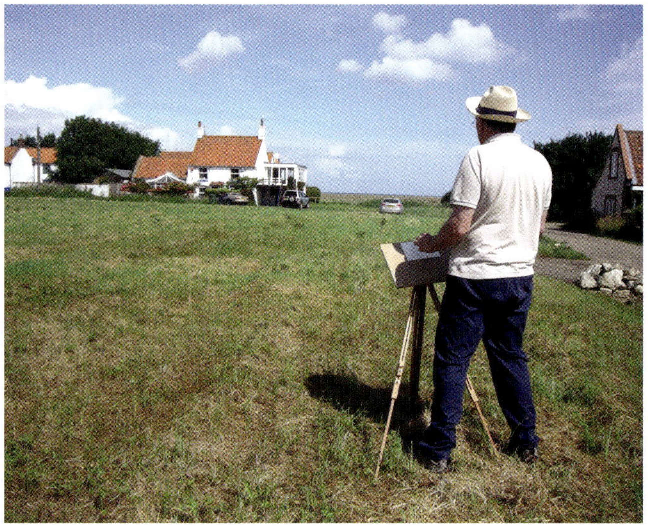

The Artist on Location

This picturesque cottage, standing on the very edge of Thornham marshes, has for many years been the summer home of the painter Shirley Carnt who uses the vast skies and flight of wildfowl as a focus for her distinct oils. Originally a coastguard station, the lookout building was on the left and the watchroom was situated in the cottage on the right. The foreground area of grass is known as The Green and hidden away in a corner was once a pond known rather curiously as 'The Queen of Sheba'.

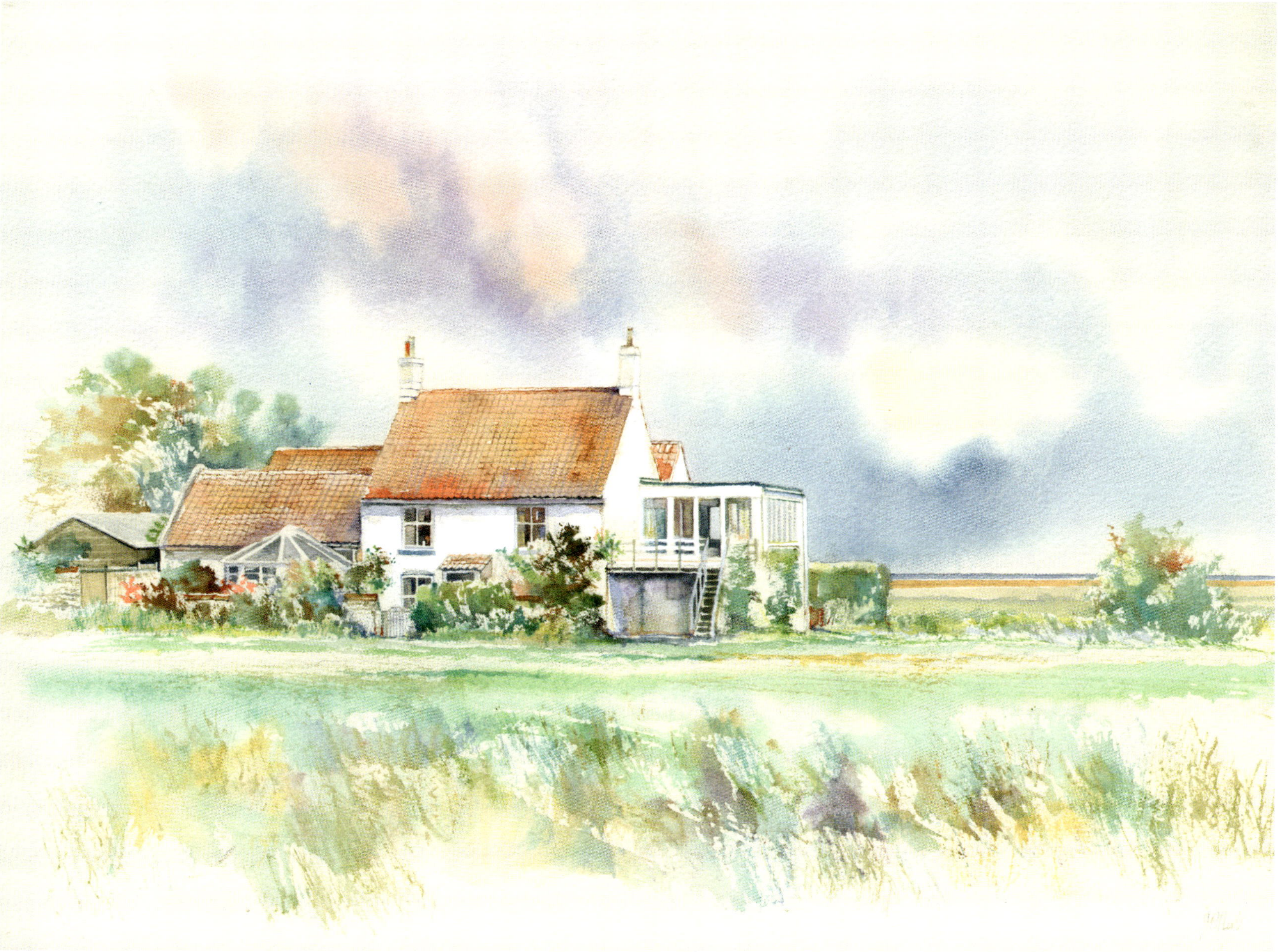

Coastguard Cottage, Thornham
290mm x 190mm

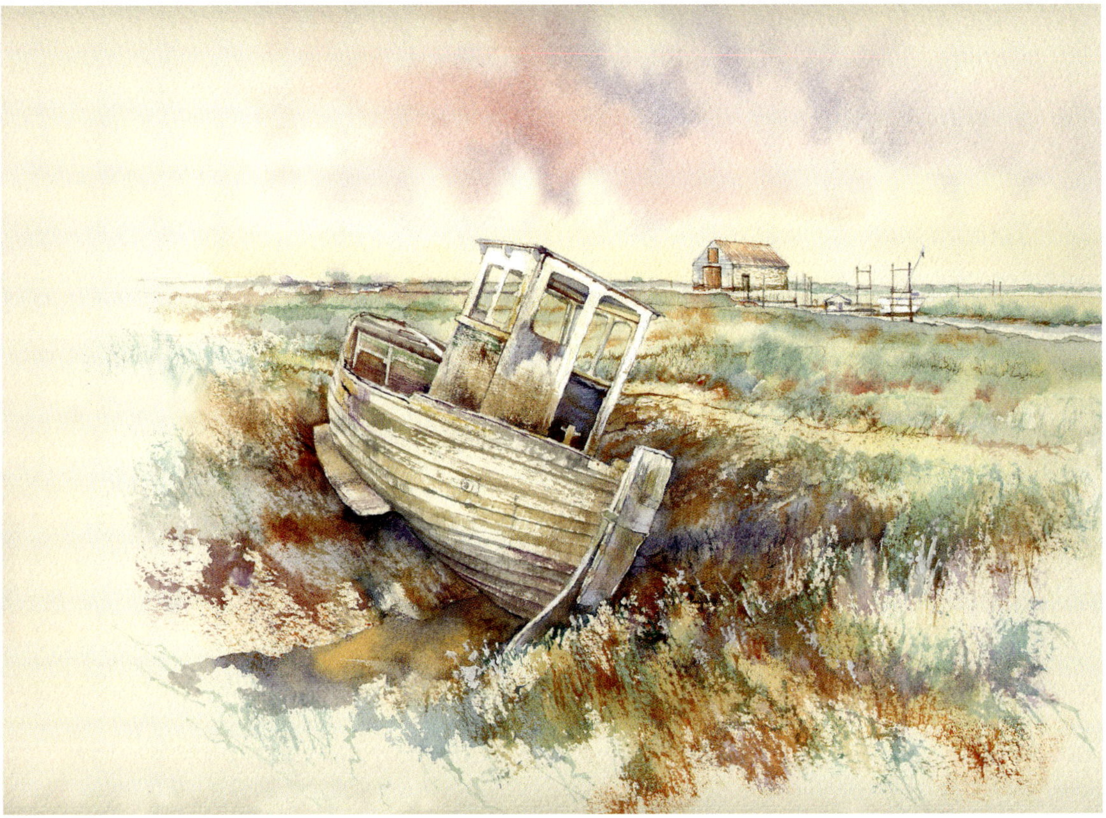

Amberley *Lifeboat*
300mm x 220mm

Jessie Mary, the village's nineteenth century hundred-ton trading ship, served the old coal barn at Thornham Creek for many years. The barn is now the last of three prominent buildings including two granaries that stood further down the inlet. Within living memory, the last one standing which George Hogg built was demolished after the 1953 flood, having sustained damage by 'friendly fire' during the Second World War. In 1996 the coal barn was extensively disguised to become Pip's house for the B.B.C. television's adaptation of *Great Expectations*.

What of the romantic wreck in the foreground? On the second of April 1973, during a Force 10 gale, the collier *Amberley*, in the service of Stephenson Clarke Shipping Ltd, en route from Goole to Shoreham in Sussex, experienced a catastrophic shift of its 2290-ton cargo of coal when four and a half miles off Blakeney Point. The vessel was lost and one of its lifeboats was washed ashore at Sheringham from where it was sold and brought to Thornham. The new owner added timbers to the superstructure along with a cabin, which unfortunately made the boat unstable. Apparently from that day onwards these sad remains have never been out of the harbour, destined to become one more marsh wreck.

Gusting to 65 knots, local mariners still refer to a particular wind on the Norfolk coast as an '*Amberley* breeze'. Three Air Force Crosses, three Queen's Commendations and an Air Force Medal were distributed among members of 22 Squadron Coltishall and 202 Squadron Whirlwind Helicopters, Leconfield, for their epic rescue of the *Amberley's* sixteen crew members.

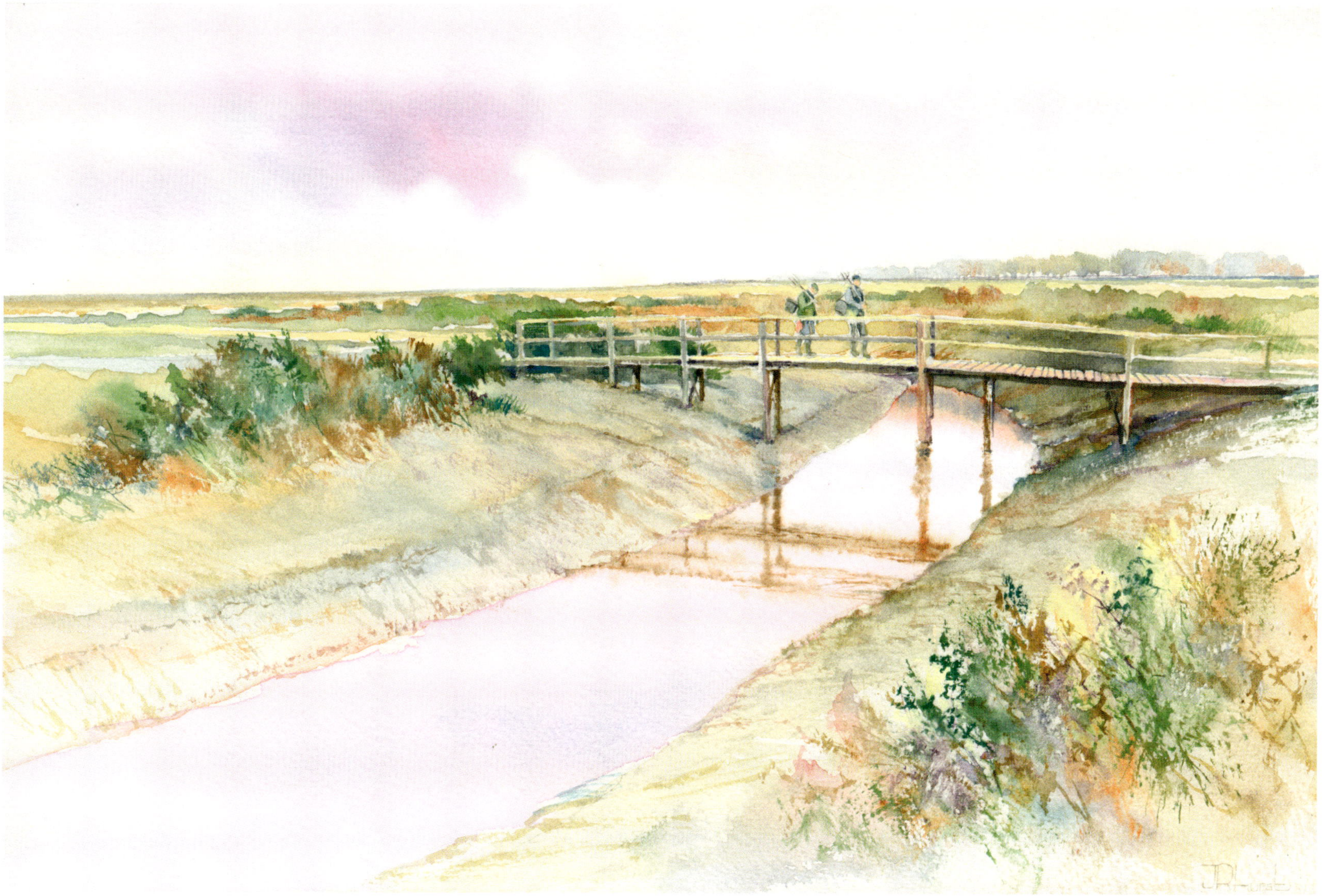

Bait Diggers Crossing a Marsh Bridge
340mm x 240mm

WHELKS AND STAITHES

Brancaster and the Burnhams

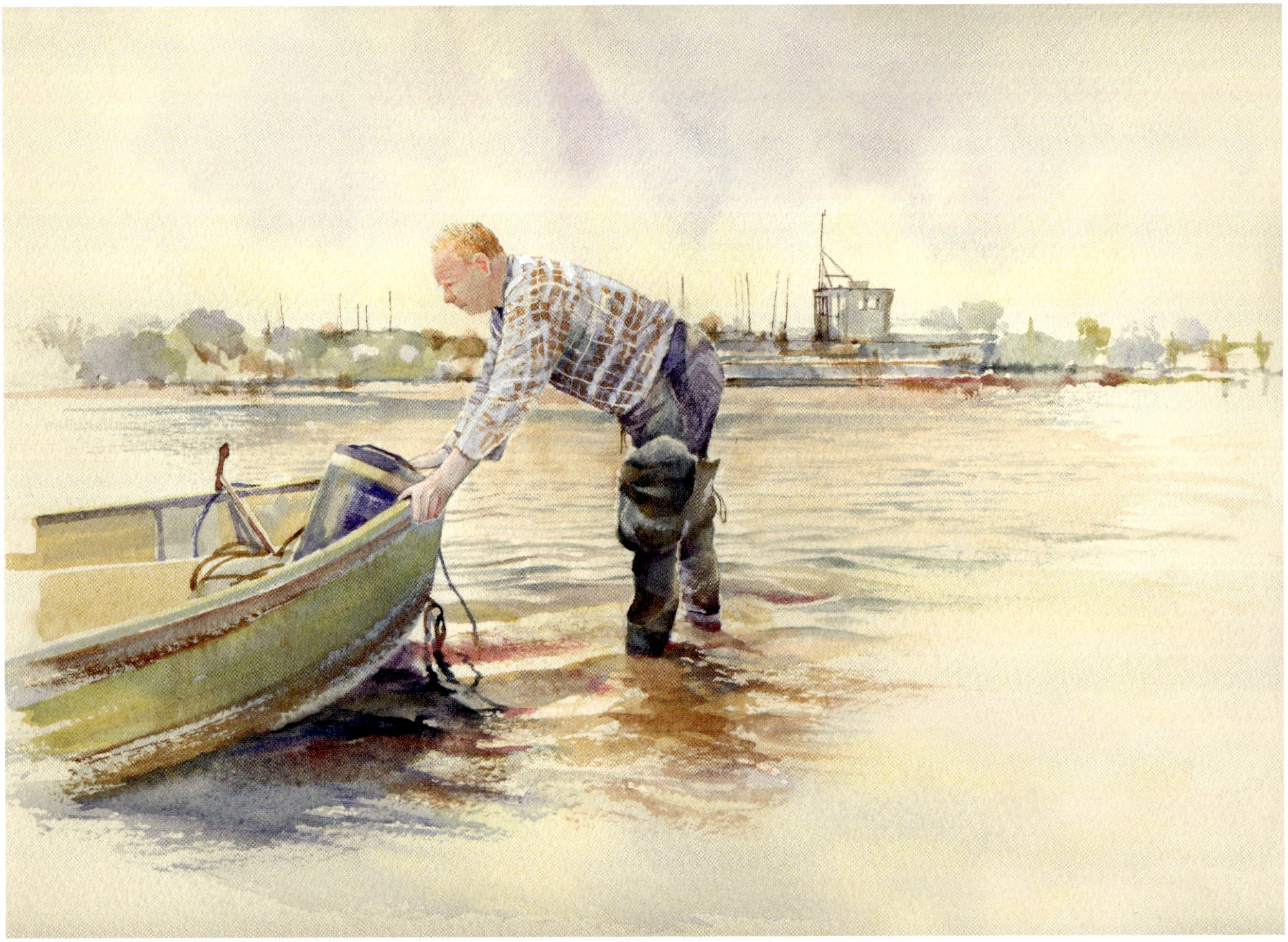

John Loose
350mm x 260mm

I spoke to John Loose on the quay at Brancaster Staithe just to pass the time of day as I hunted for images in the nearby whelk sheds. He stood there in muddy waders having just rowed ashore. With soft voice and sparkling eyes he kindly shared with me the story of *Remus*, the old spratter that is slowly decaying in the harbour. I had painted this boat many years ago as it lay on the exposed mud, finding out recently that it belonged to a near neighbour. *Romulus*, *Remus*, *Cortina* and *Leona* were four boats brought to Wells from Faversham and Whitstable by the Leggett family designed specifically for towing trawls for sprats.

I felt sorry for *Remus* and hoped one day that someone would renovate this old timer as it was taking on water at every tide.

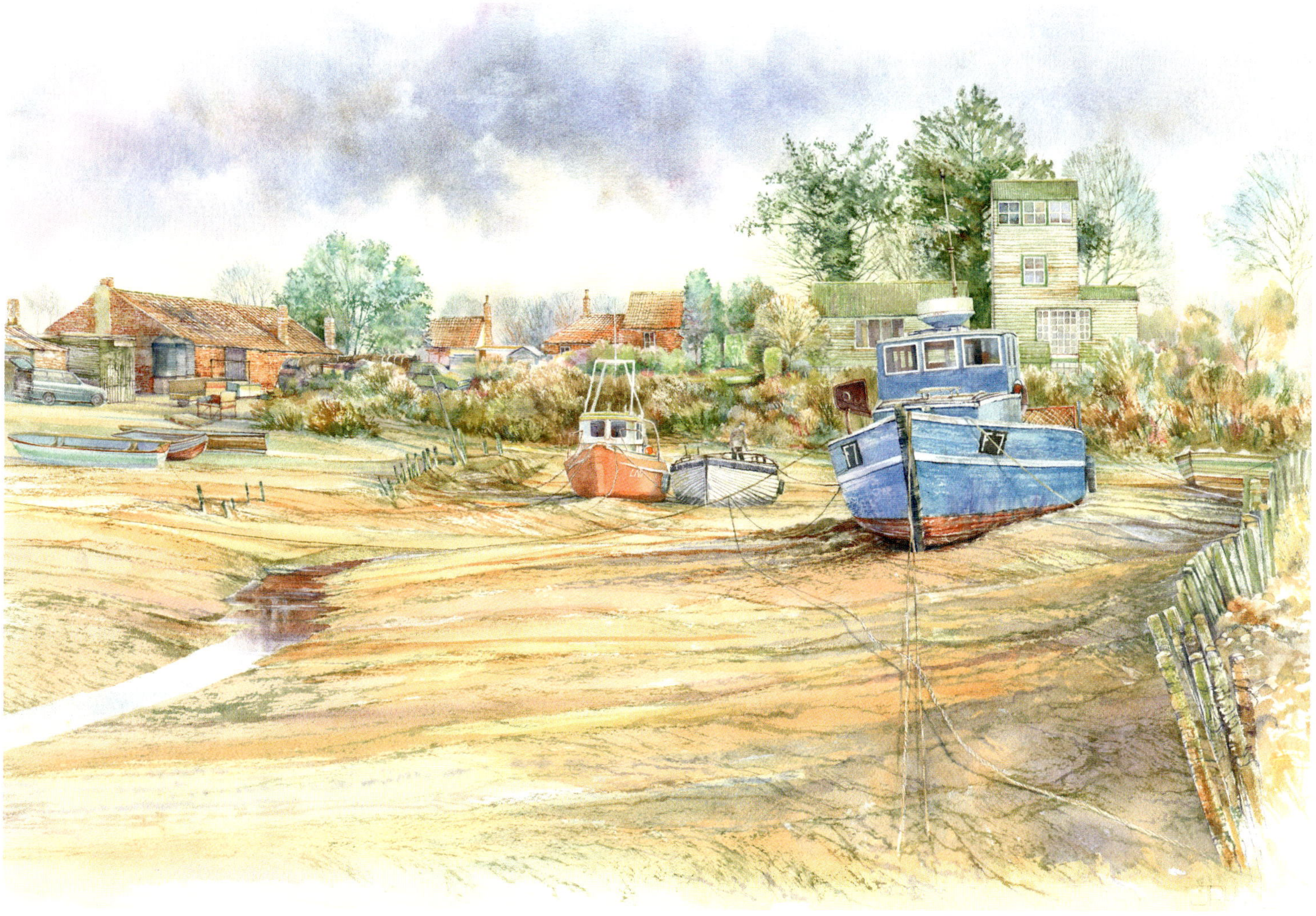

Remus, *The Old Spratter*
580mm x 400mm, 2006

After spending time with John Loose on Brancaster quay, I peered into some semi-derelict sheds along the coast and made studies of their interiors. This still life retains all the elements of a seafaring occupant. Hanging here is a mussel riddle, 'hedge elm' net and a rusting tilly lamp.

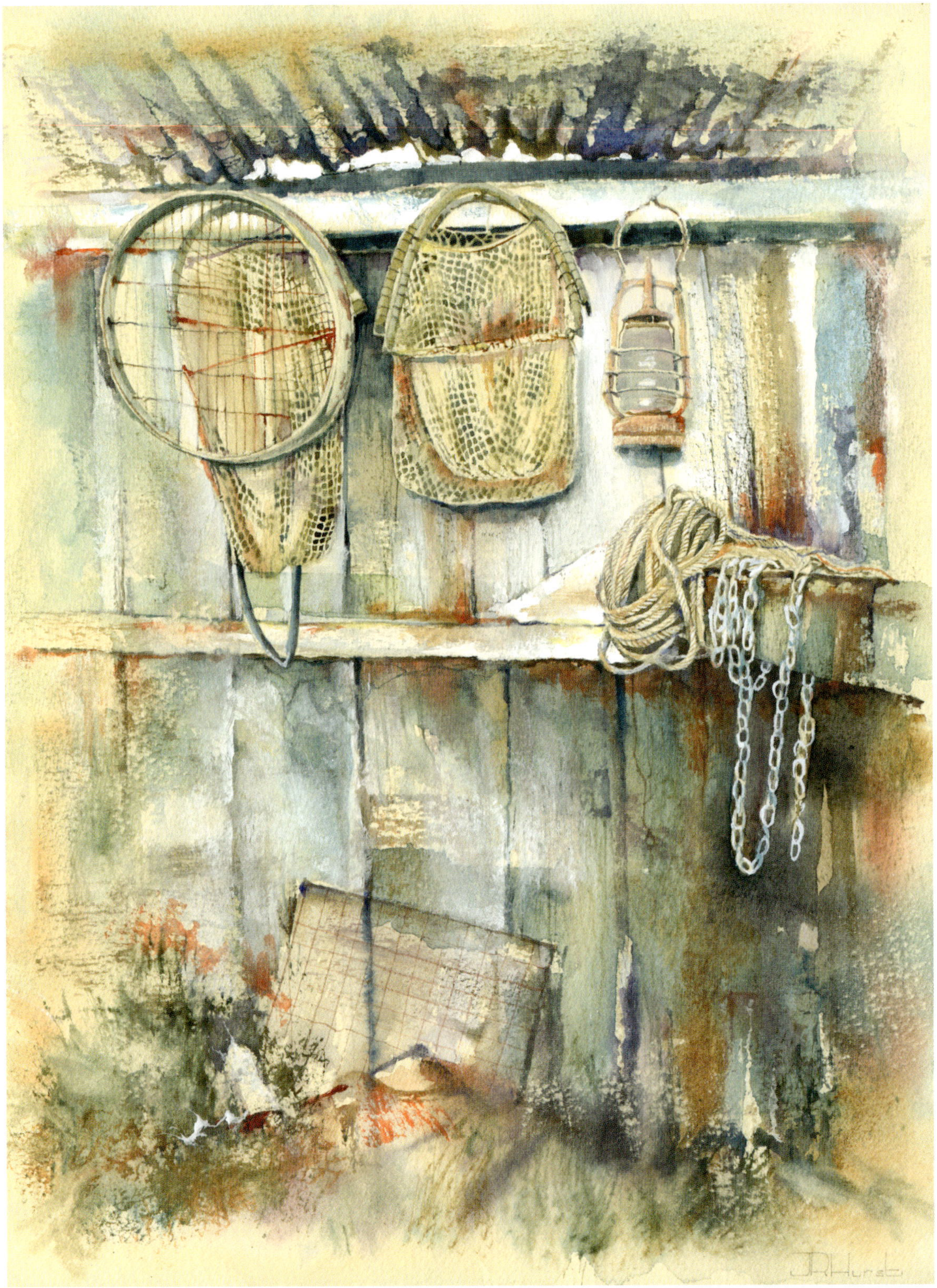

Whelk Shed Interior
260mm x 320mm

When travelling west on the A149 coast road towards Burnham Norton, Burnham Overy tower mill, built by Edmund Savory in 1816, stands on the left before a quaint bridge that spans the River Burn. It worked in conjunction with Burnham Overy lower watermill, until cessation of operations in 1919. Then in 1926 it was bought by H. C. Hughes and presented by him to the National Trust in 1958.

I chose the location of this autumnal study by walking north from the mill towards the marshes. The dismal blackthorns contrast with tints of golden ochre where the rusting sedges are awakened by afternoon light.

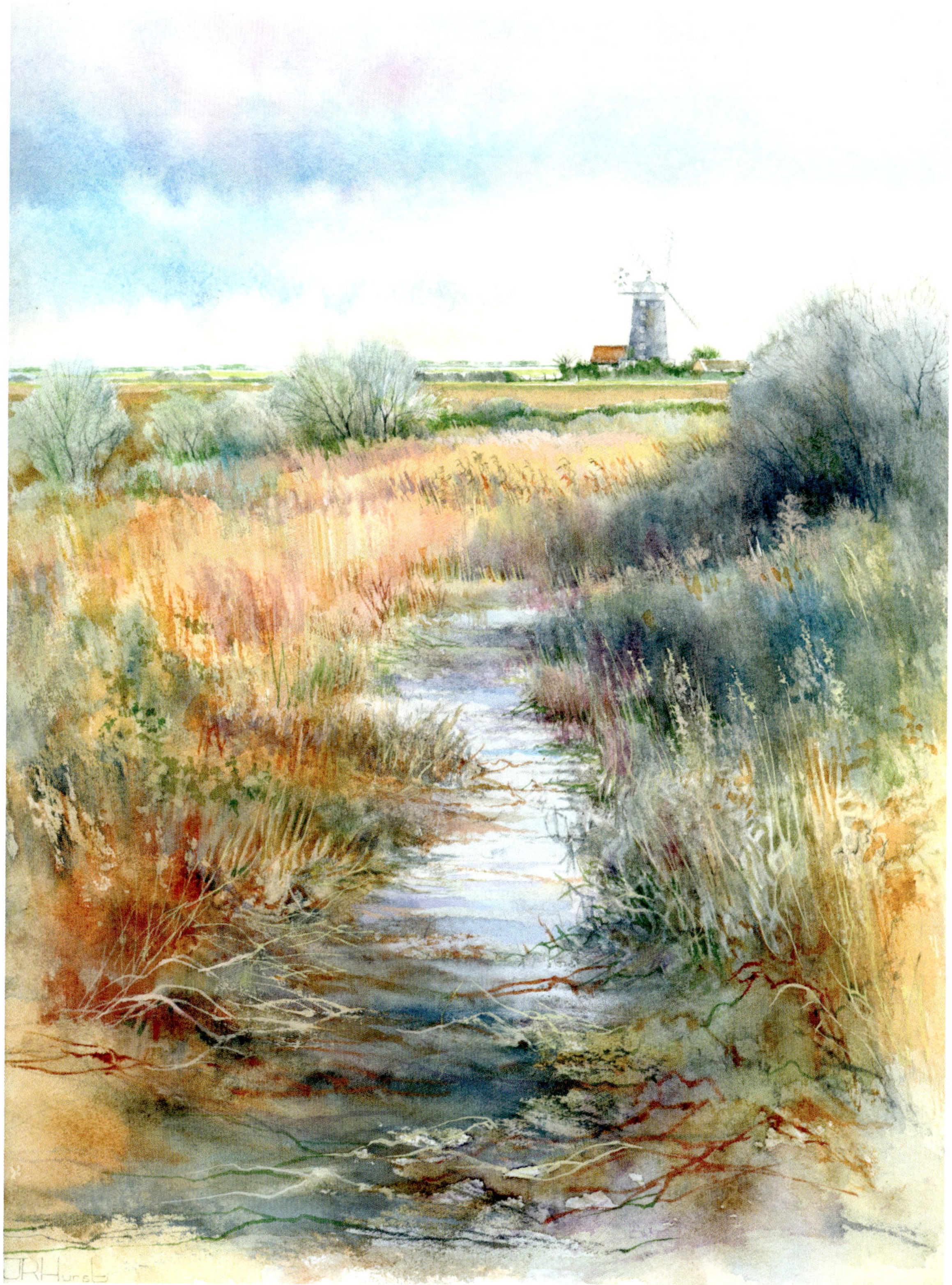

Burnham Overy Mill, Winter Light
260mm x 310mm

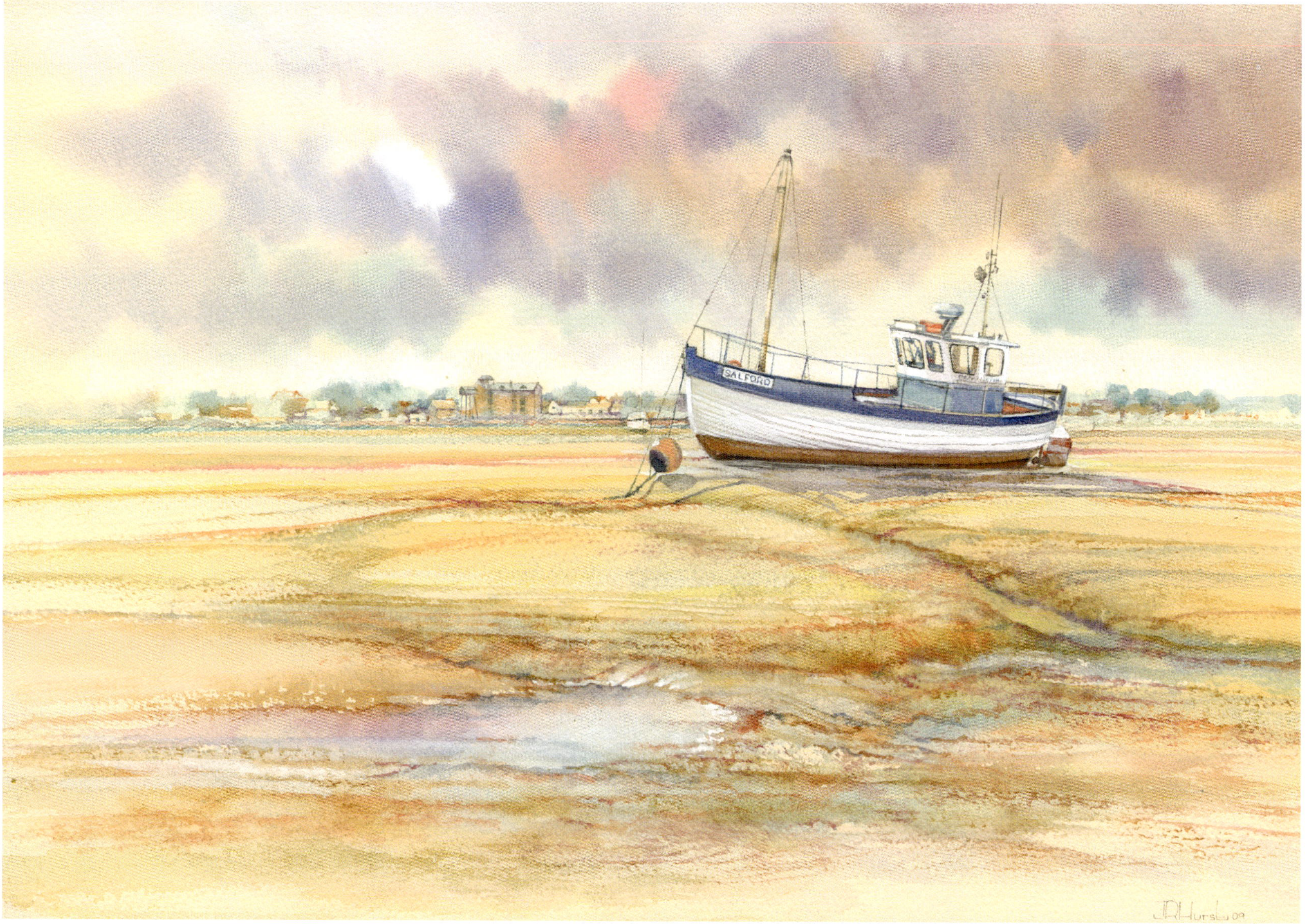

Salford, *Wells Harbour*

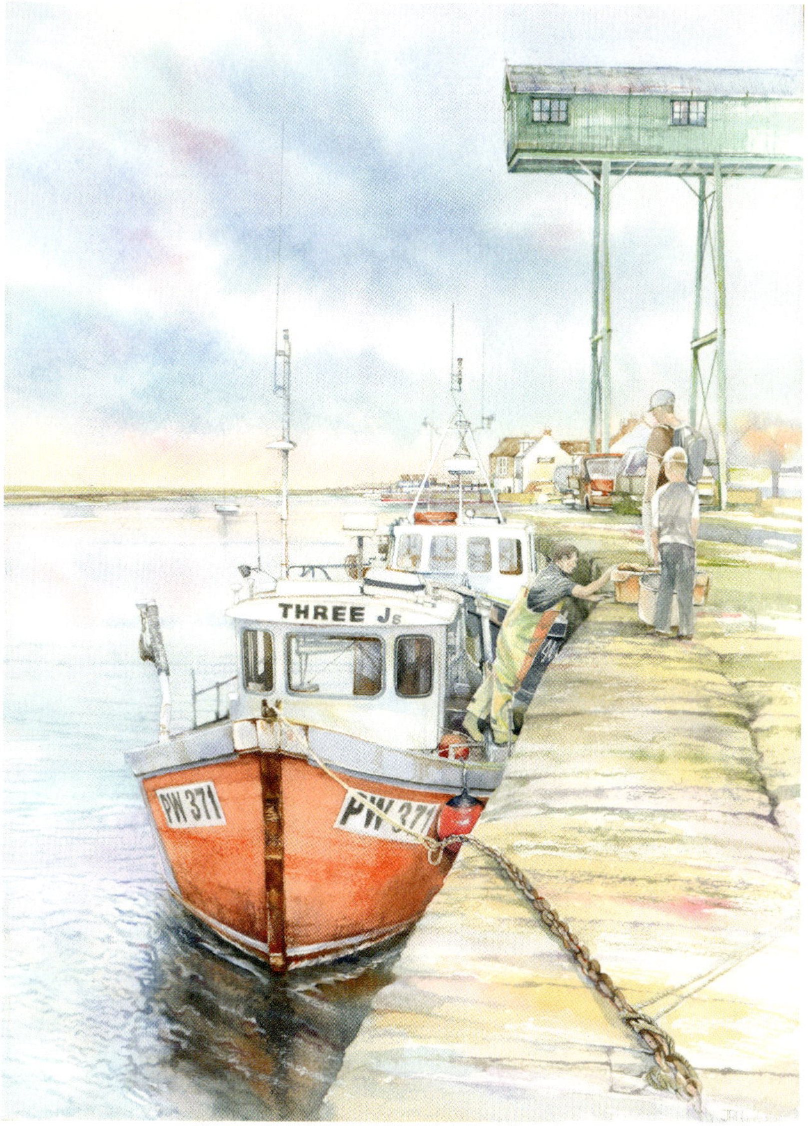

The Three J's
260mm x 310mm

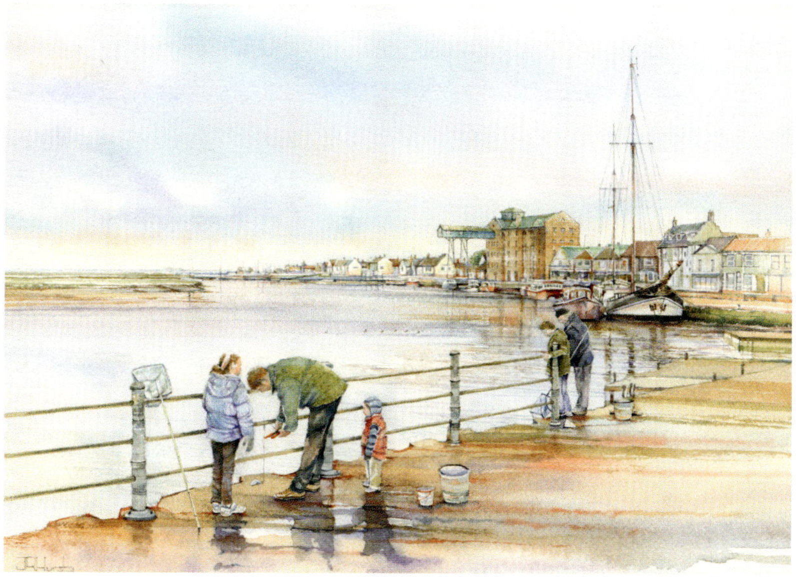

Checking the Crab Line

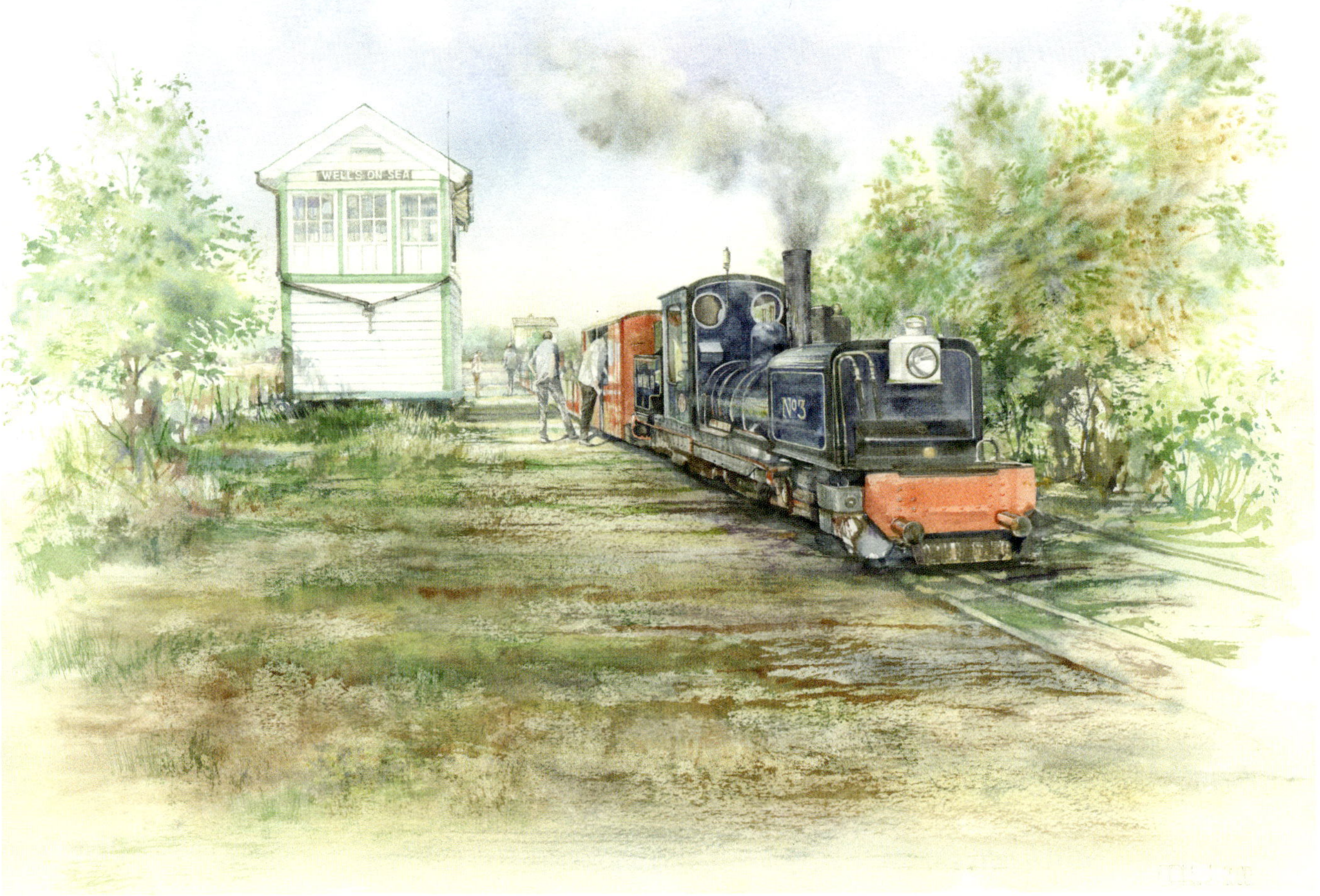

'Norfolk Hero' at Wells

Roy Francis had a dream to build the longest 10¼" narrow gauge steam railway in the world. Over a period of twelve months and with the help of numerous enthusiastic volunteers, the Wells and Walsingham Light Railway was constructed and opened in 1982.

I painted this study because it evokes memories of happy holidays in Norfolk and as Commander Francis says, "The pleasure of our visitors is the main return."

As I write, the eighty-seven year old founder is as enthusiastic as ever and is developing a new 'Garratt' loco similar to 'Norfolk Hero' that currently makes the daily four-mile trip to Walsingham, halting at Warham St Mary and Wighton on demand. Developing a steam pressure of 140lbs per square inch and using three buckets of coal per journey, 'Norfolk Hero' is capable of reaching a cruising speed of 8½ to 9 mph, taking half an hour to cover a journey that traverses pleasant countryside including five bridges. For most of the year the band of volunteers generate enough man power to supply a different driver and guard each day, all enjoying the thrill of being part of this unique operation.

The signal box at Wells station, built in 1886 was formerly operative at Swainsthorpe, south of Norwich on the main London line. It was brought to Wells in 1987, becoming redundant when new signalling technology was introduced.

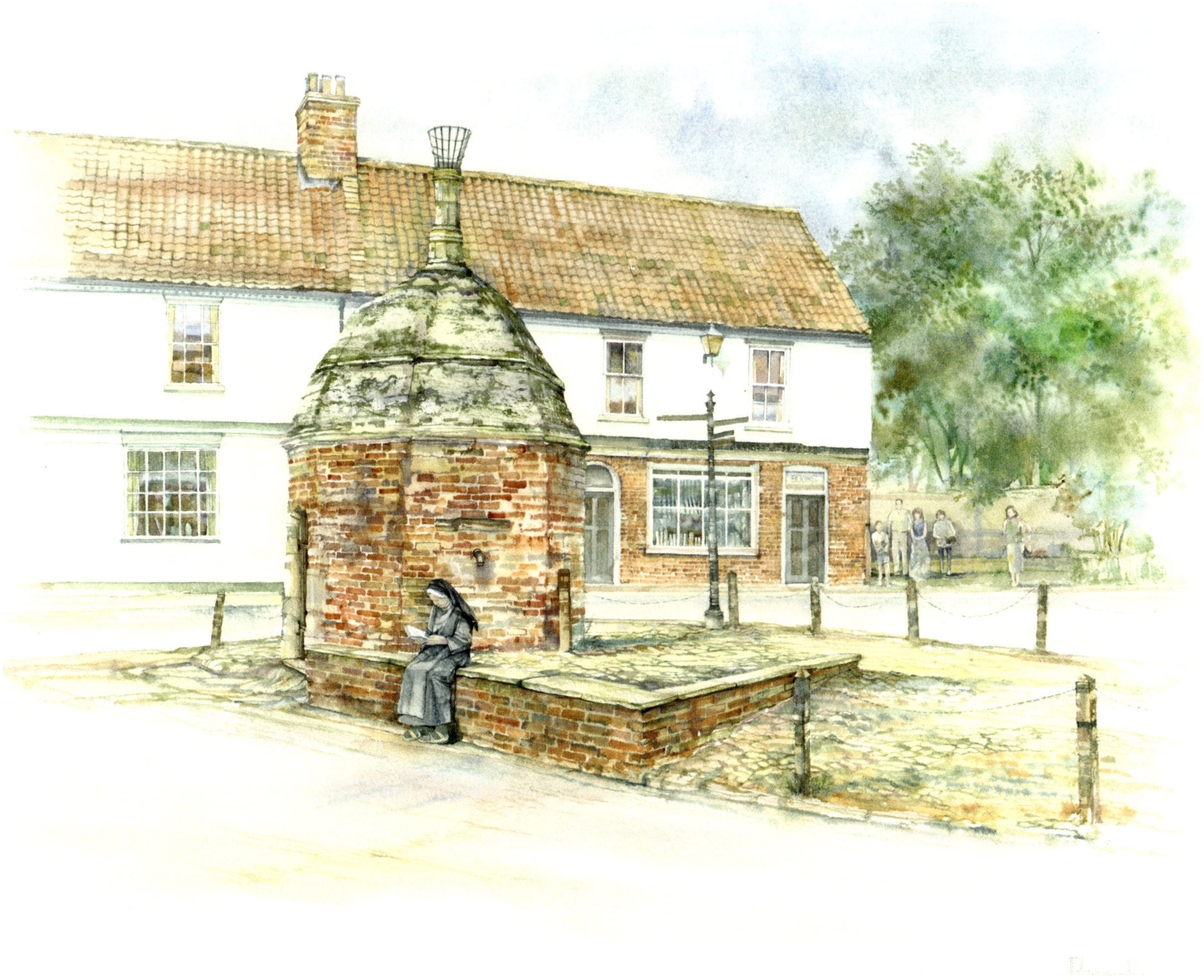

Quiet Reading, Walsingham

After visiting the Anglican Shrine in Little Walsingham village, fondly called 'Little Nazareth', I found myself in an open space named Common Place. Surrounded by 15th and 16th century buildings there stands an octagonal water pump, on the top of which is a rusty iron brazier known locally as 'the beacon', an early source of village lighting.

My attention was drawn to a graceful lady who appeared to be quietly reading. I felt that the reader's presence emulated the very essence of Walsingham, a place of worldwide pilgrimage, great peace and timeless tranquility.

ACROSS THE PIT

Morston to Blakeney Point

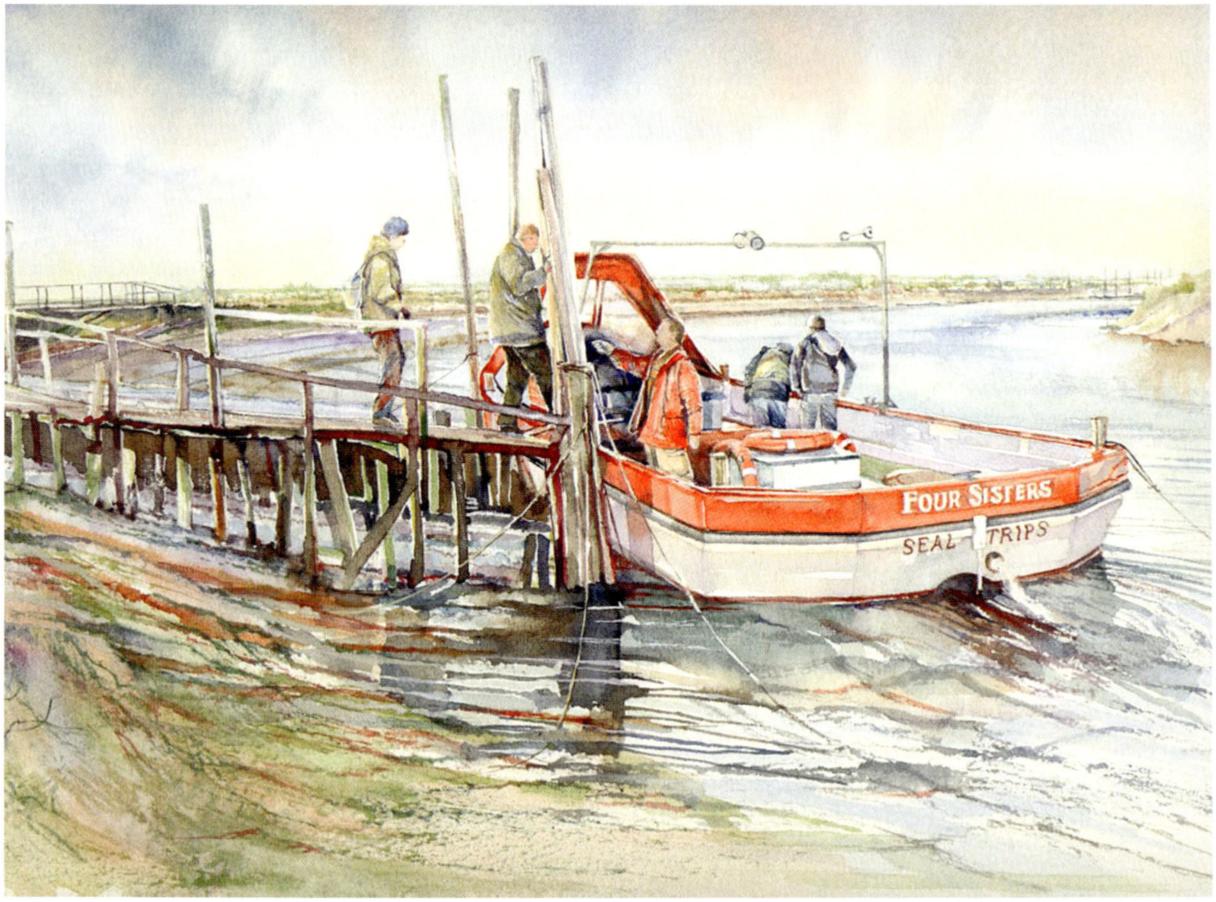

Welcome Aboard
350mm x 320mm

Temple's, Bean's and Bishop's 'tripper boats' at Morston carry daily visitors to view the seal colonies on Blakeney Point. They are very similar to those operating between St Mary's and the outer Isles of Scilly, crewed by sunburnt seafarers who cheerfully cope not only with the vagaries of the weather but also with demands of an enthusiastic public. Seal trips depart from Morston Quay at high tide, negotiating a channel as it meanders through a flotilla of small craft in 'The Pit', their bleached sailcloth fluttering at every tack and turn. Should you visit in summer, as The Point is approached, your attention will be drawn to the distant cries of terns. These 'sea swallows' return each spring from West Africa to nest on the shingle ridge under the watchful eyes of summer wardens. Both common and Atlantic grey seals occupy the far point and adjacent sand bars. Unconcerned big-eyed pups seem to wave a fin of approval as visitors gasp for joy and cameras click.

The Bait Digger and His Dog
160mm x 130mm
Triptych

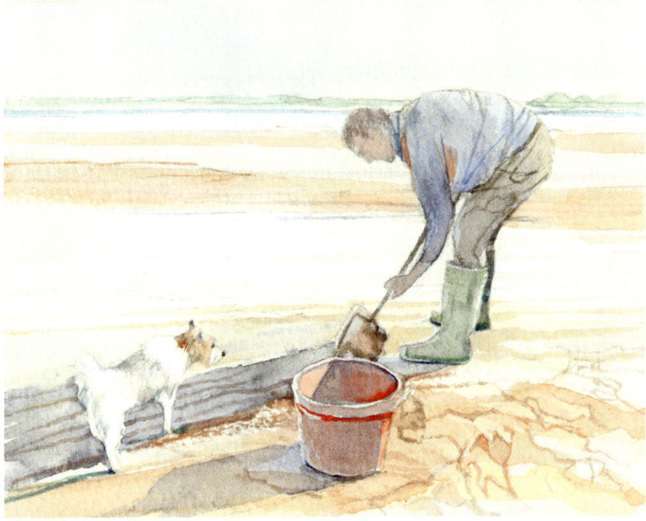

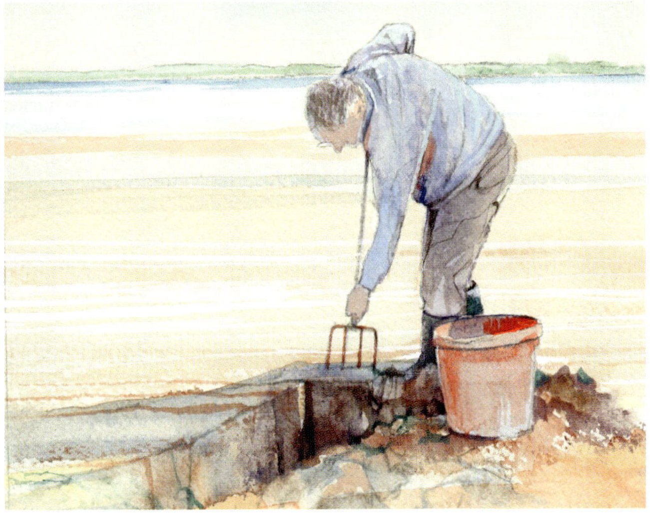

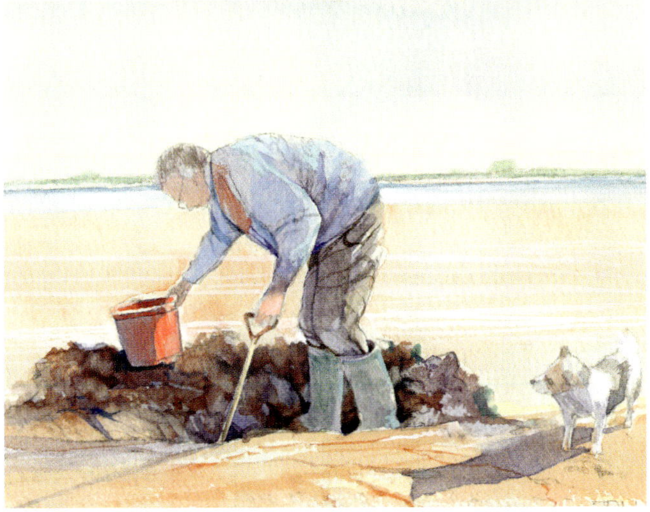

I required the services of a bait digger for my sequence of drawings so who better than Jim Temple whose family are intrinsically associated with the history of Morston. He started digging for lugworm almost fifty years ago as a ten year old along with his brother Bill. They would regularly dig two thousand worms over a weekend on Stiffkey Sands, receiving four shillings per hundred from Bob Cooke of Salthouse. When one considers that a farm labourer's weekly wage was less than ten pounds a week at the time, the boys were doing very well, although Jim recalls one occasion when he 'overdid it'.

"At dawn I dug bait, then ferried passengers to The Point until mid afternoon. As the tide fell I dug again and went out after dark netting sea trout. I don't remember sleeping for three days until waking up on father's boat and realising the tide had come and gone. My passengers were marooned on The Point. There was nothing left to do but row them off. I never did that again!"

Jim explained to me how to identify good lugworm colonies by their casts and his way of working a 'low', or depression in the sand using a dam and the wind to hold back encroaching water. Taking out a trench he then stood in it for the next dig making it easier on the back. Like rubbery fingers, each coated with burrowing hairs the lugworms emerged from each forkful of ooze. Titch, the Jack Russell, looked on inquisitively as shadows lengthened across The Pit and I sketched furiously. Eventually we wended our way homewards to more of Jim's stories. Time had flown like the scattering of tiny dunlin parting in waves before us across the weed-strewn shore.

"I ought to write a book," he joked, while looking through a hole in a stone. "That's good luck!"

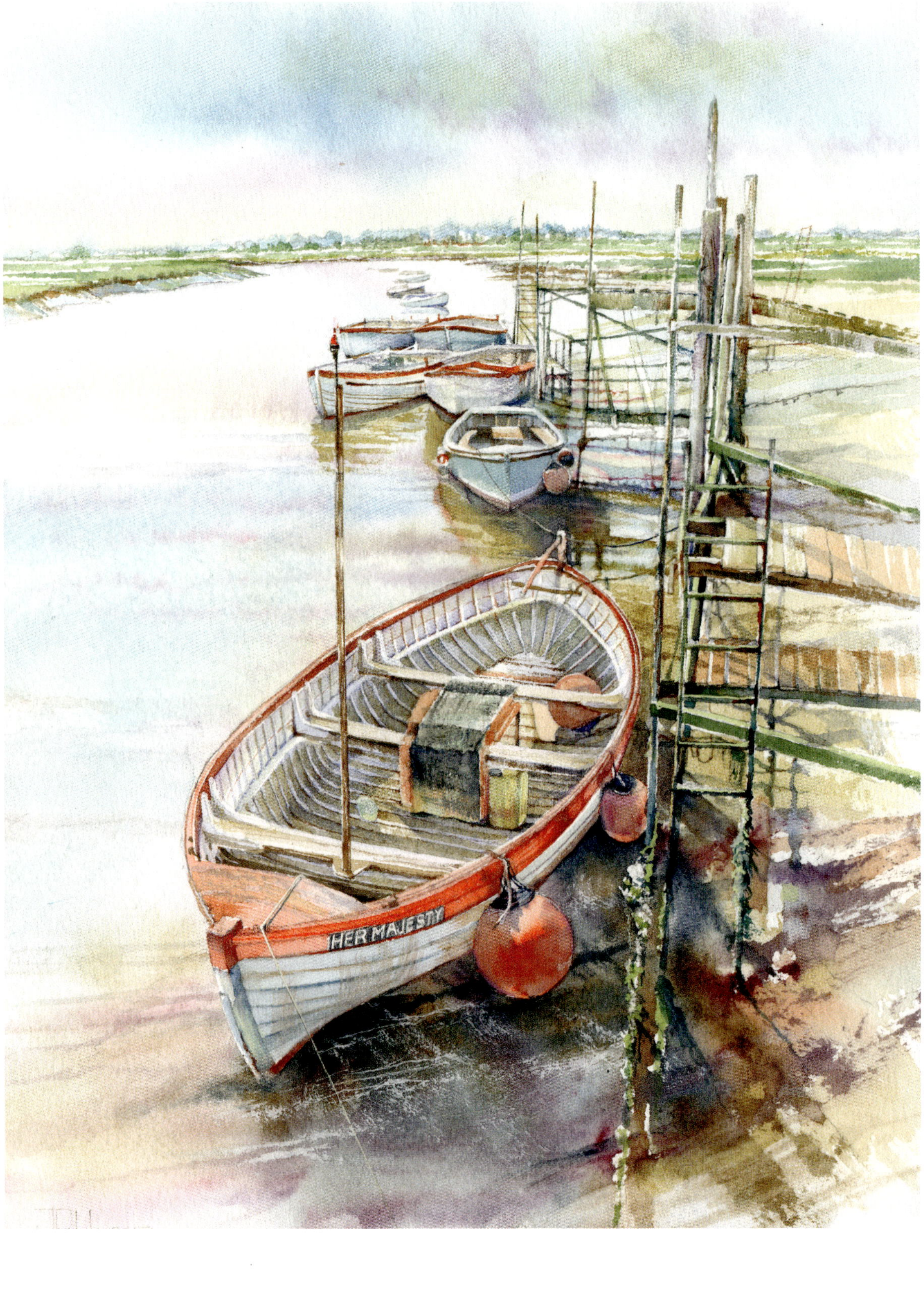

Her Majesty, *Morston*
280mm x 350mm

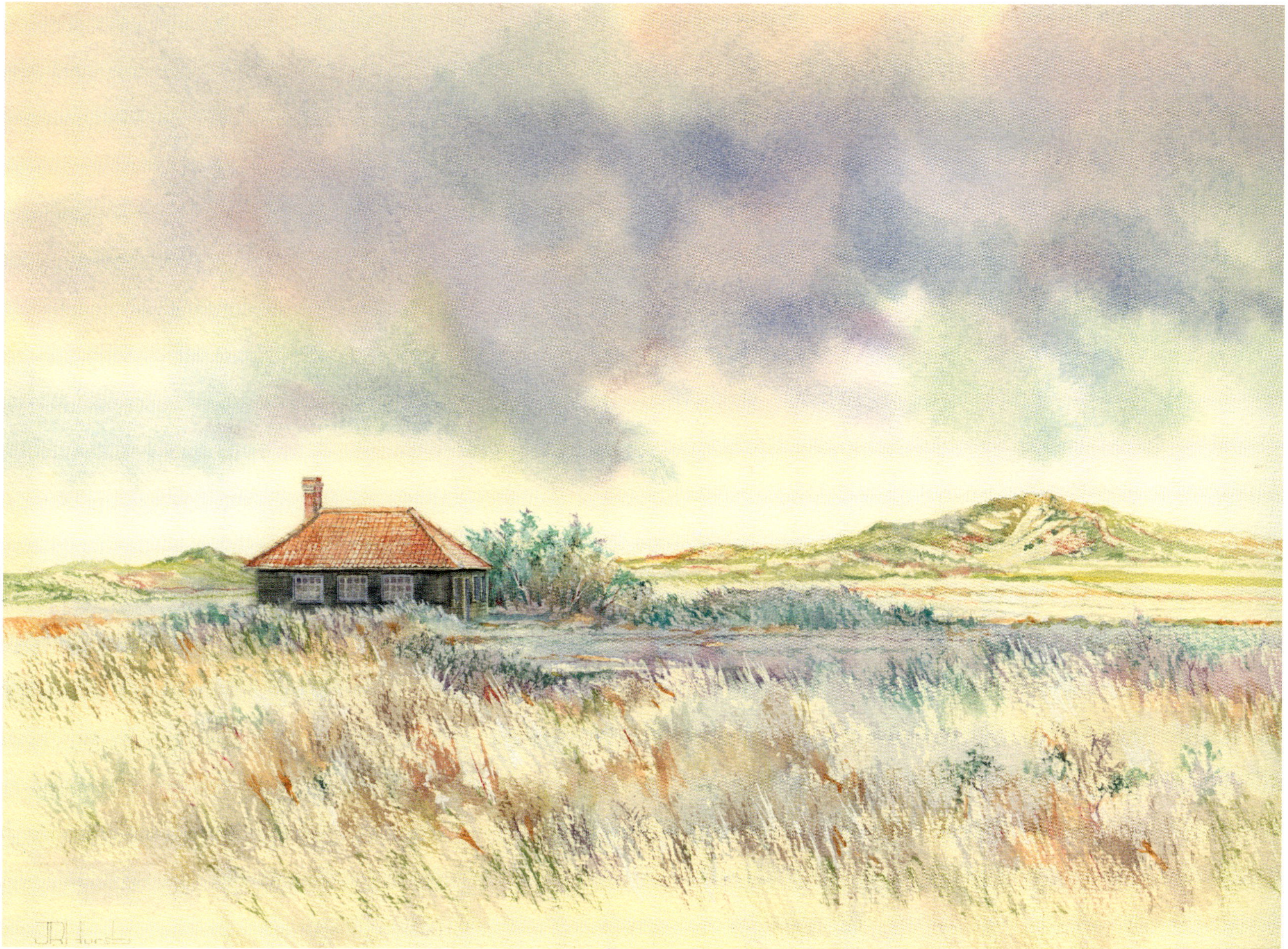

September Morning on Blakeney Point
350mm x 250mm

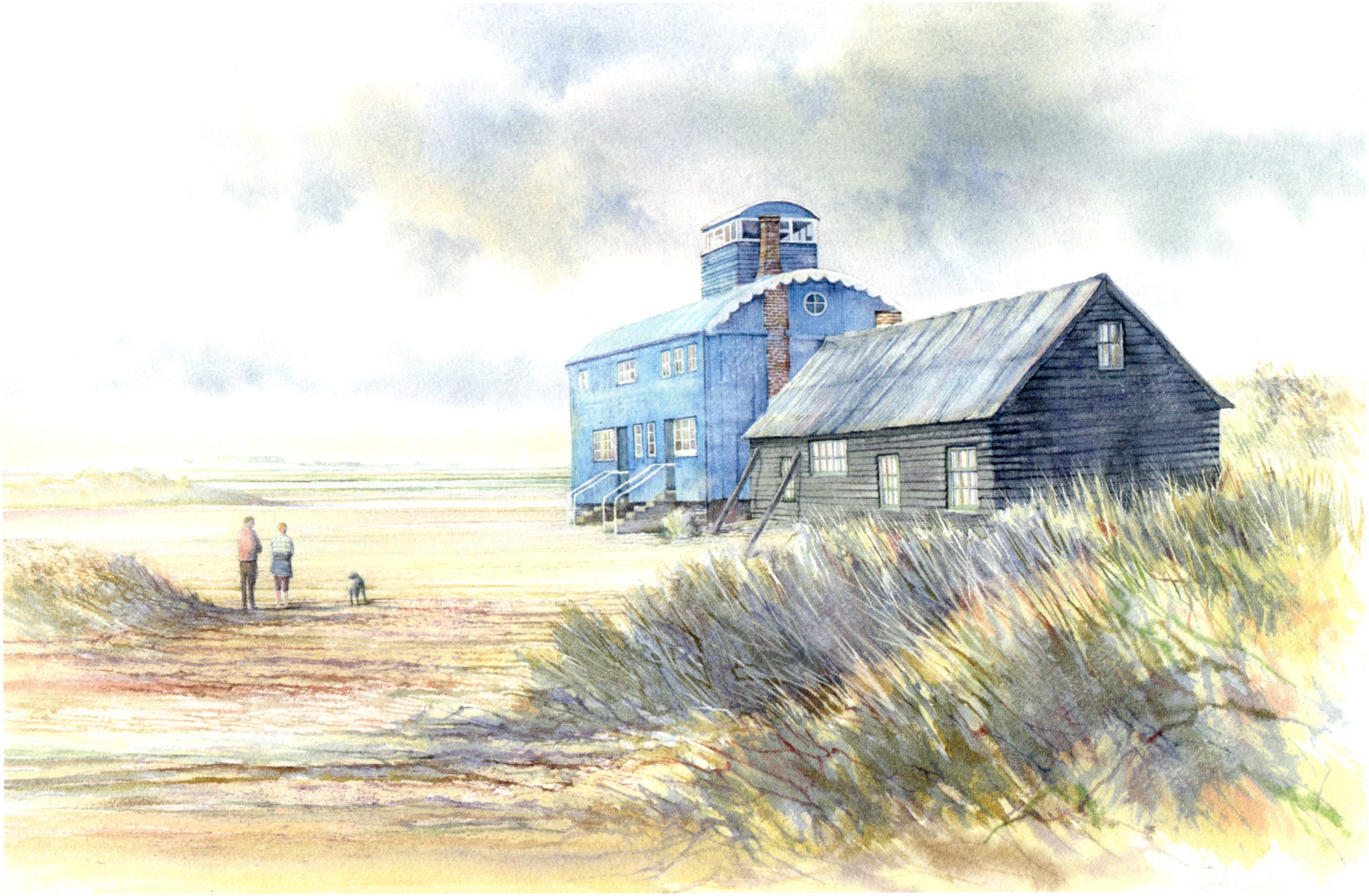

Blakeney Point Coastguard Station
400mm x 280mm

As the riot of summer colour fades, slender pods of yellow-horned poppy seed heads burst to reveal winter food for linnet and snow bunting. The point now becomes another world. Fewer walkers brave the trek, the tern colony becomes silent and grey seals once more haul out to pup on the sands. Wreck 272 continues to undergo the merciless process of winter decay, a beached maritime sculpture exposed to the power of sea and storm. Like the *Yankee* on the next ridge, it is destined to become a passing perch for migrating wheatear, a barely discernable skeleton of rusting metal.

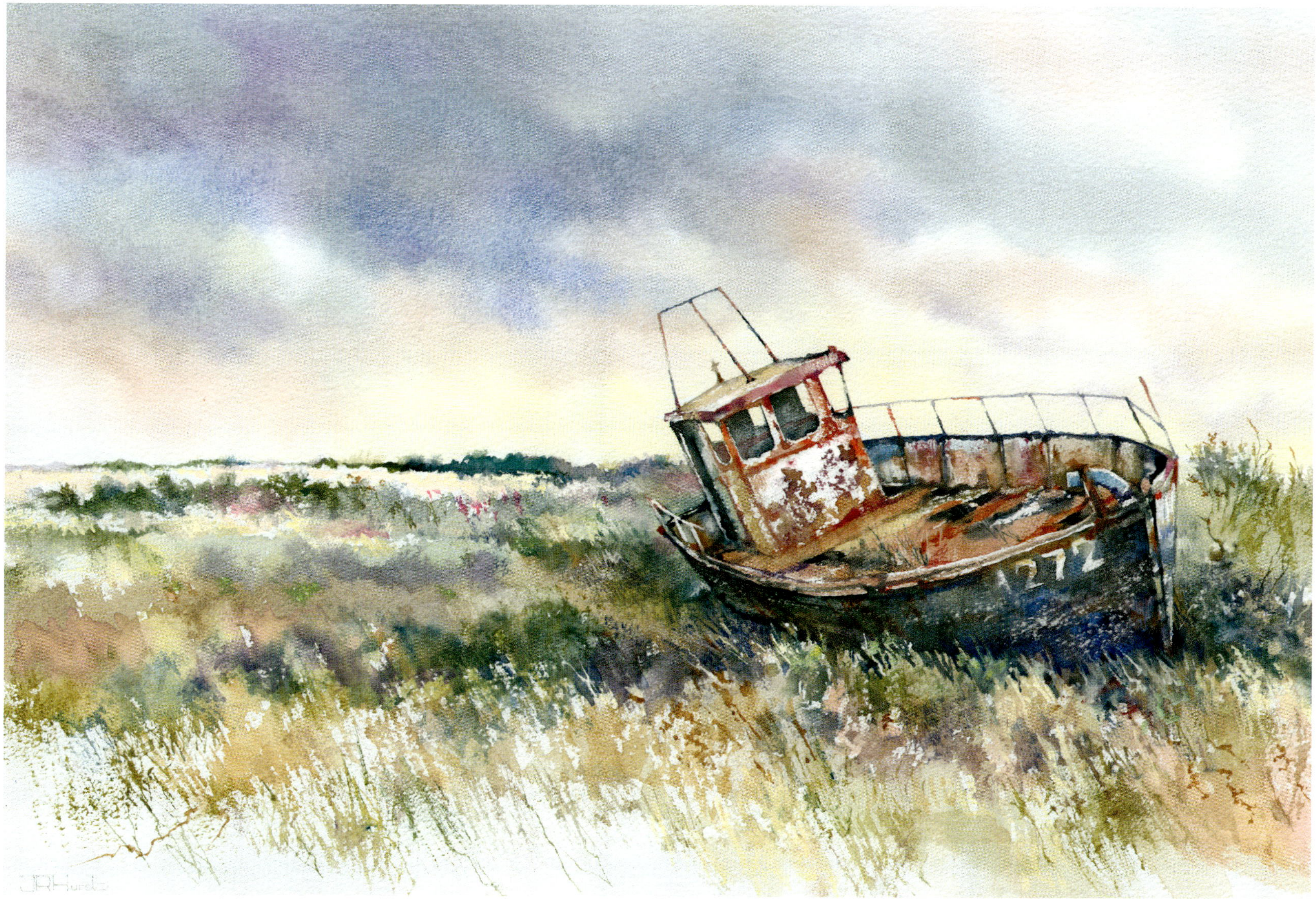

Blakeney Point Wreck
350mm x 270mm

WINTER WIND, SUMMER SUN

Blakeney

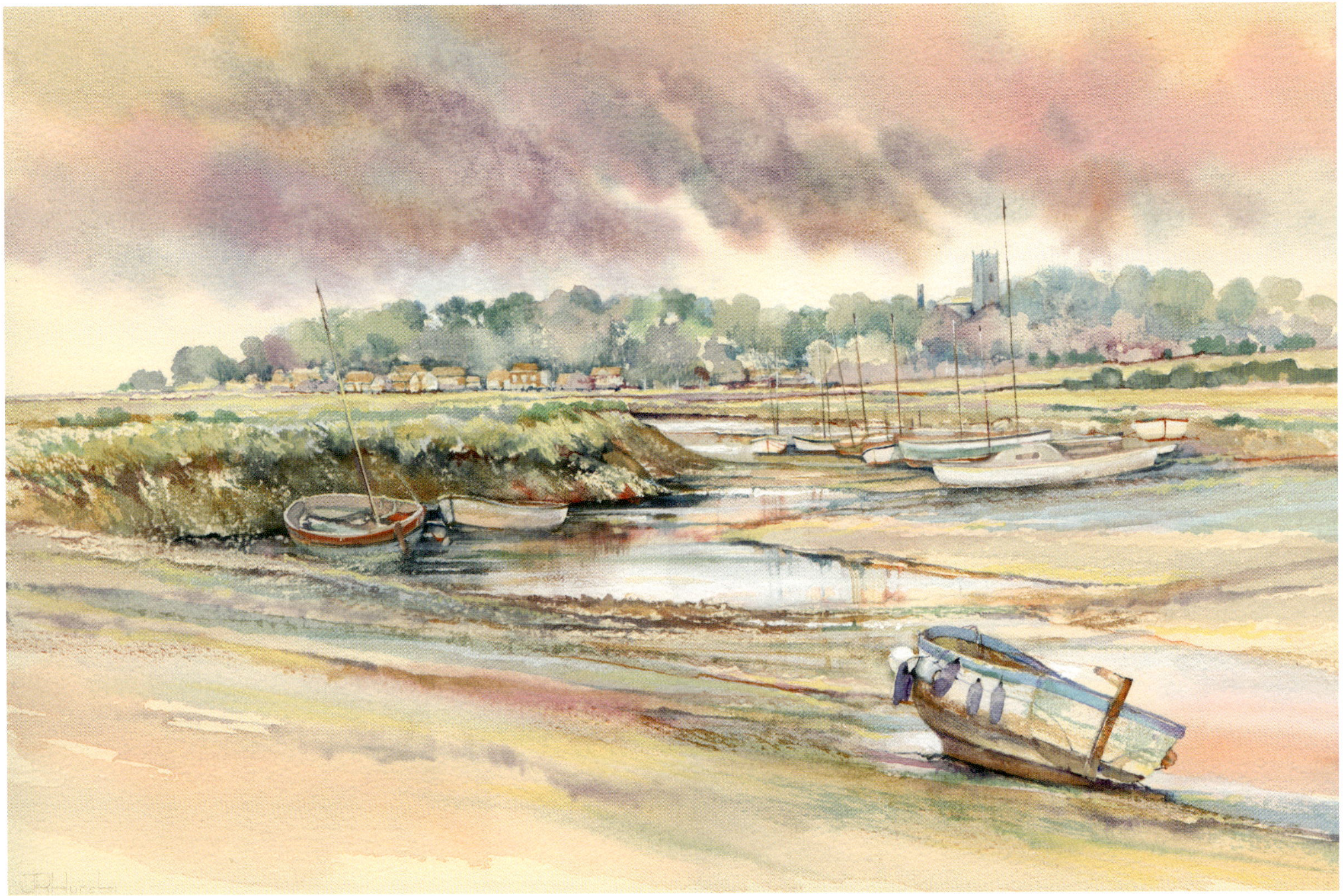

Blakeney from Morston at Low Water
410mm x 250mm

When looking to Blakeney from Morston Quay, a bend in the channel creates the focal point and an opportunity to explore perspective and distance. Using manganese blue and cobalt green hues on cream-tinted paper, my aim at low water was to record changing weather patterns combined with soft foreground light cast across the exposed channel and beached boat.

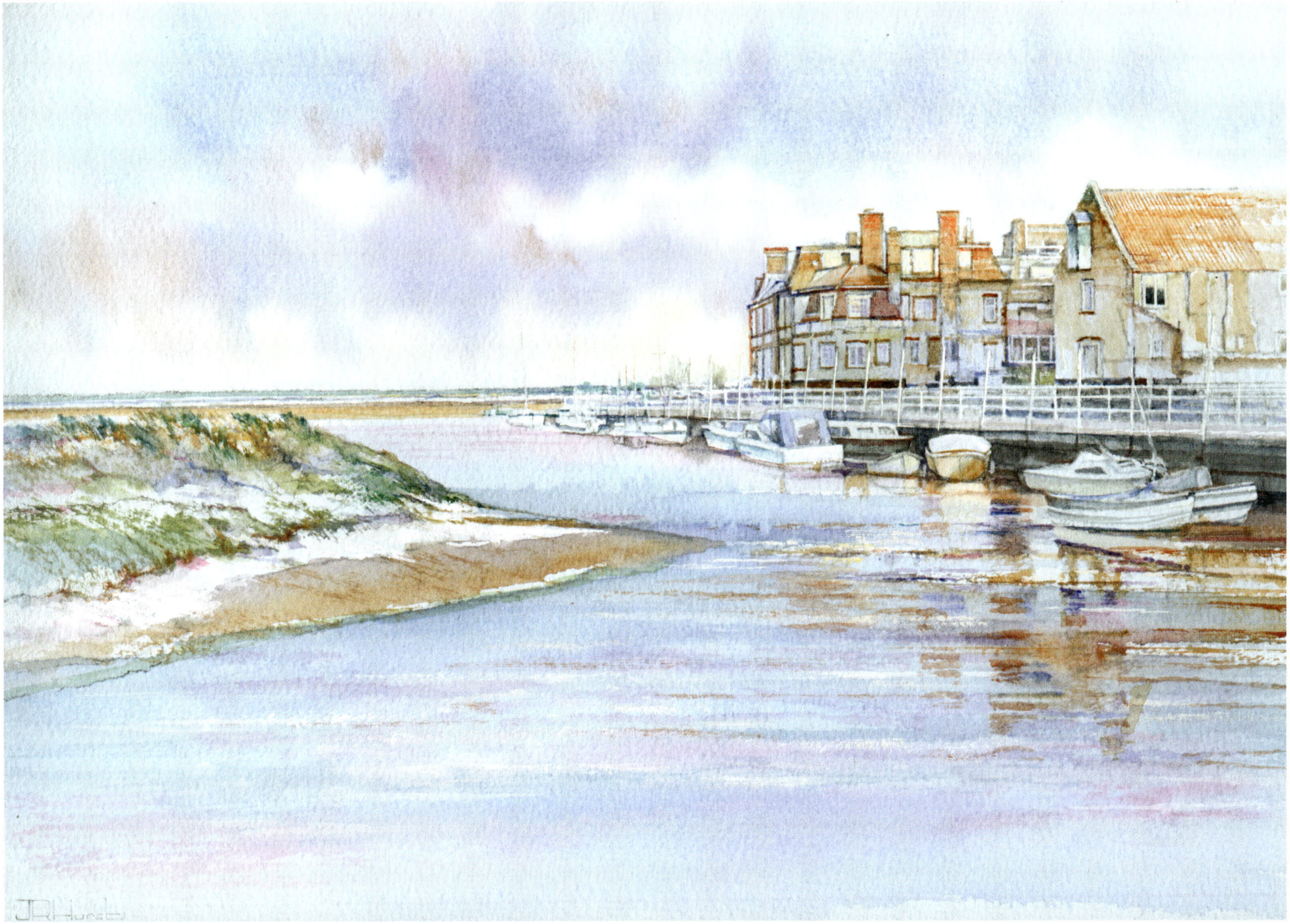

Thaw, Blakeney Harbour
330mm x 220mm

The Deterding family built Blakeney Hotel in 1923, forming part of their establishment of Kelling Estate. The hotel was built for £31,000 on the site of the old Crown and Anchor Inn, nicknamed 'The Barking Dickie'. Local beer was brewed here once a week and sold for one and a half pence a pint. A rapid thaw was taking place as I painted this well known yet now deserted view, a contrast to the busy quayside in summer when excited children fish for crabs and pleasure craft sail on every tide.

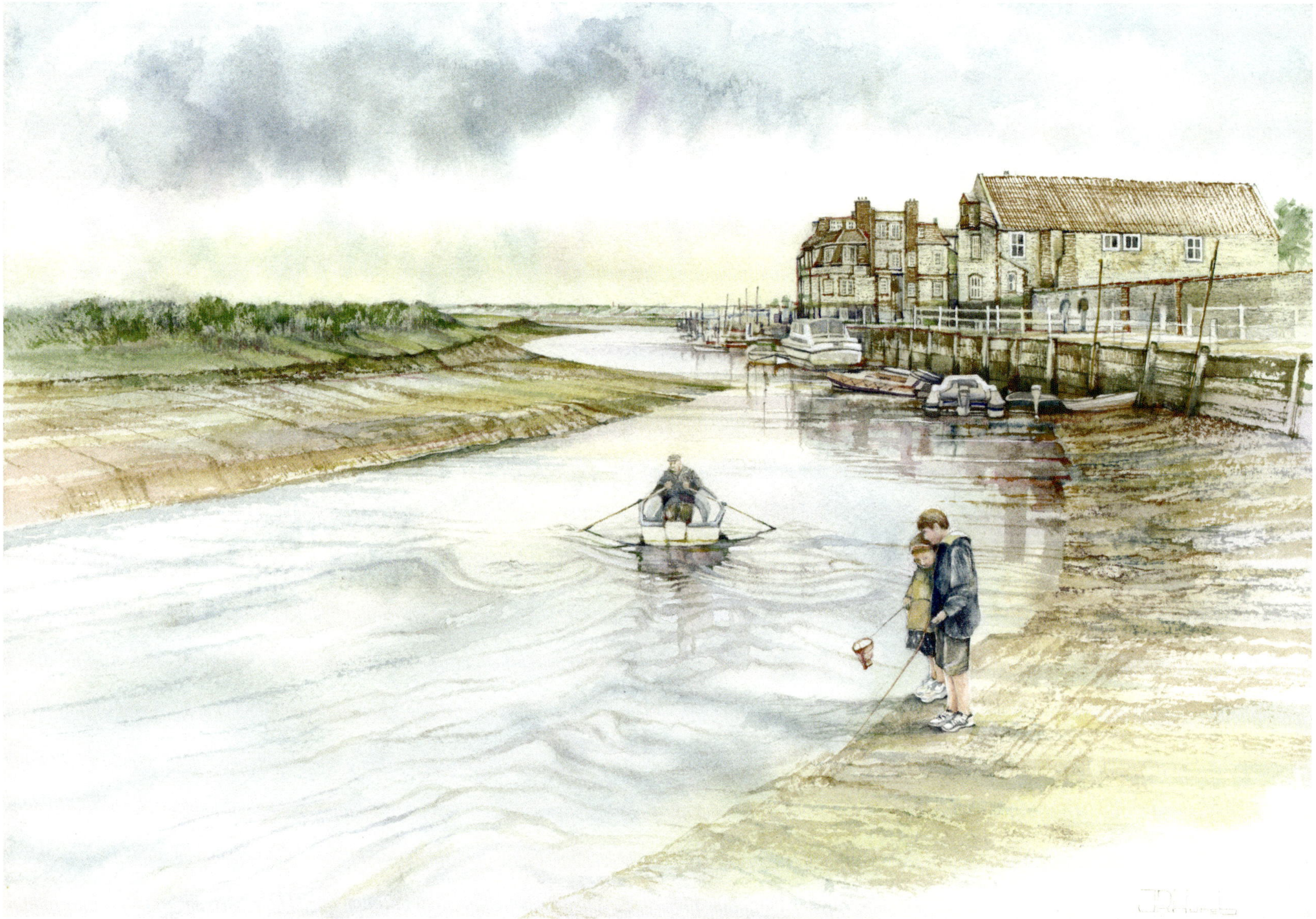

Crab Fishers, Blakeney
350mm x 260mm

Blakeney, as summer breezes toy with the marsh lavender and children dip their nets in anticipation of yet another crab clinging to their bacon rind. During August regatta week, crowds descend to witness a duck race, tug of war and the ever popular greasy pole on which brave contestants gyrate, skid and contort like drunken ballet dancers before hitting the incoming tide with an enormous splash.

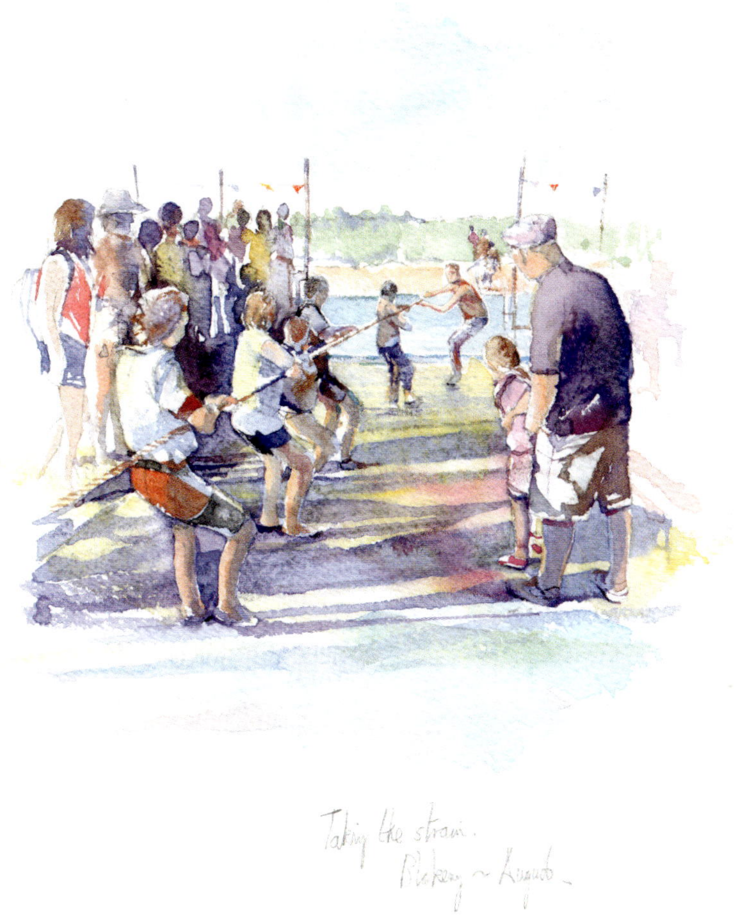

Blakeney Tug-of-War
Sketchbook Study

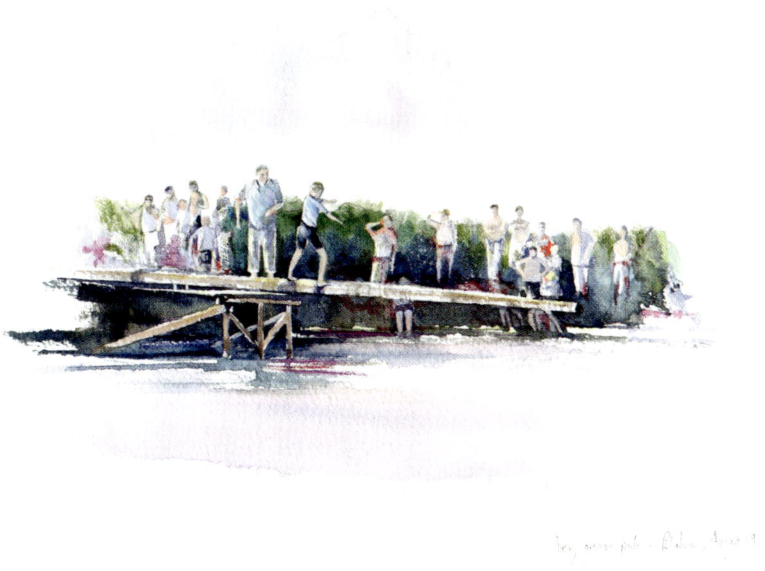

Blakeney Greasy Pole
Sketchbook Study

I painted the house in this composition with one loaded brush of pigment, using the brush as a drawing tool. This can be very pleasing when successful, creating the essence of form. The foreground is painted using the dry brush drag technique in which raw pigment and little water is dragged across the surface of the paper.

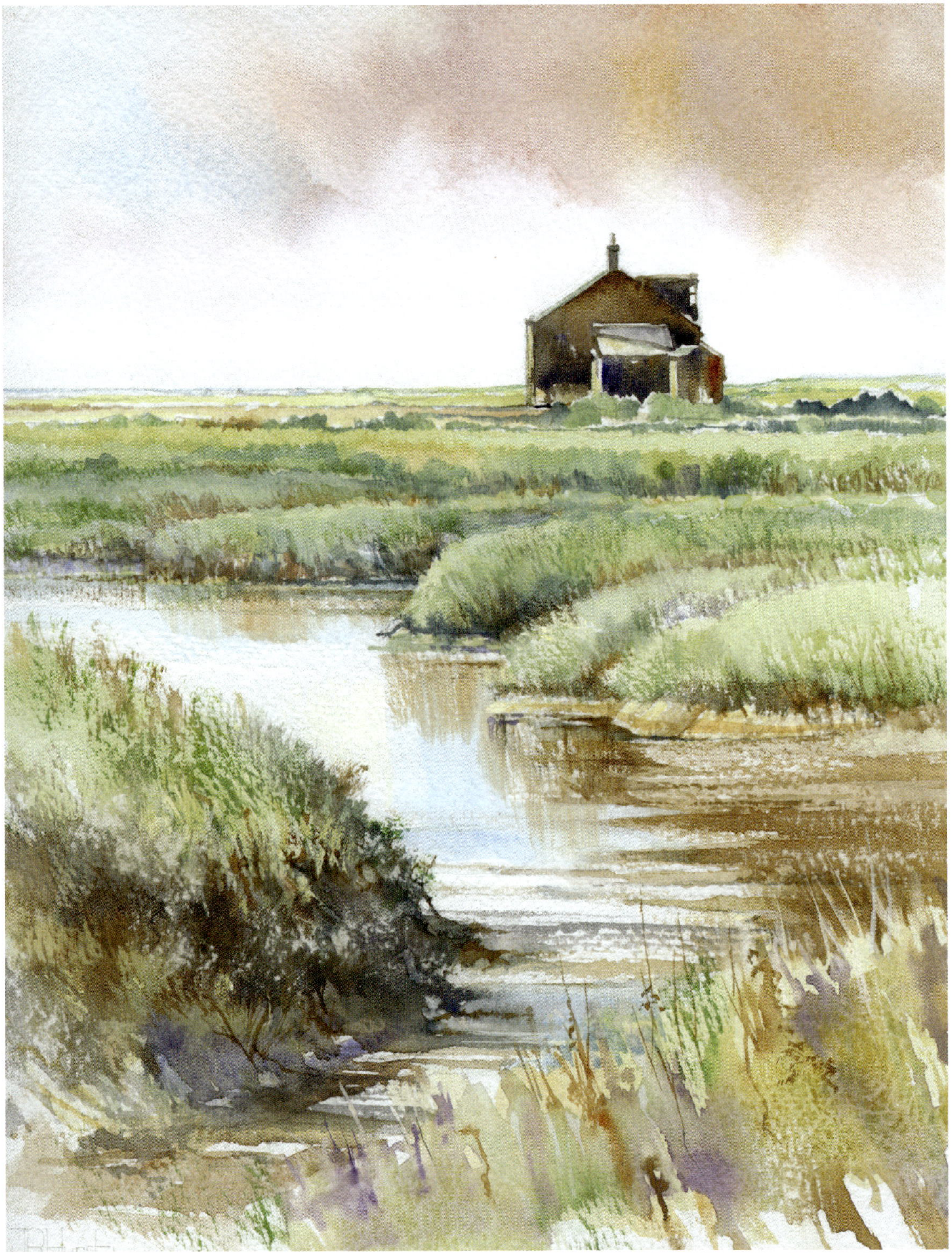

The Watch House Creek
Watercolour and Gouache
330mm x 220mm

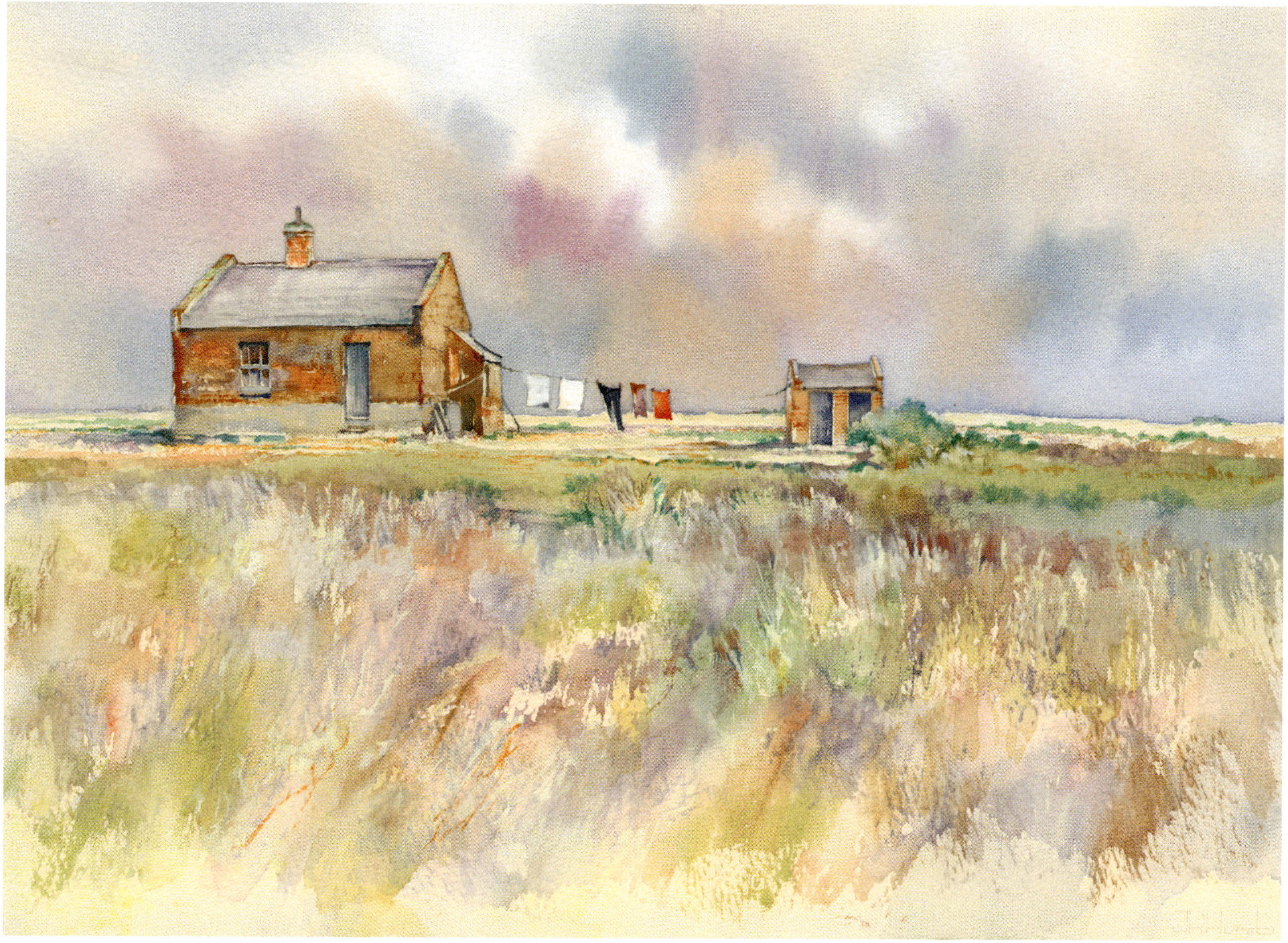

Breezy Washday, Blakeney Point
380mm x 270mm

Blakeney Point has been described as a shingle and dune spit running almost east to west from Cley towards Wells and made famous by the scarce migrating birds that tend to occur there in late spring and early autumn. From the air it appears as a series of elongated fingers, each extending westwards as sand, shingle and dune ridges are built by constant wave action. Far, middle and near Points are the newer deposits, whereas Yankee Ridge and the Watch House Ridge are well established 'Suada ridges' of the last century. Blakeney Point is a place of great seasonal contrasts, ranging from scorching heat to torrential wind driven rain.

The Watch House has always held a fascination for me, built as a coast-guard lookout station in 1865, yet still standing despite exposure to the elements. Accessed by boat or a two mile trudge along the shingle and known by some as a 'hard tent', it is now managed by The Watch House Trust. It may be hired as a holiday destination for those intrepid travellers who wish to haul their own drinking water and wake up to the sound of fishing terns, nesting oystercatchers and shelduck. I was delighted to see washing dancing in the breeze, a reminder that this house may still shelter those who wish to enjoy its remote location.

I was once commissioned to paint a toilet, so chose quite naturally, the one on Blakeney Point that I know to be very remote. The 1950s bucket and spade, a reminder of my visits to the seaside, are actually quite impractical on a shingle ridge where there is little or no sand!

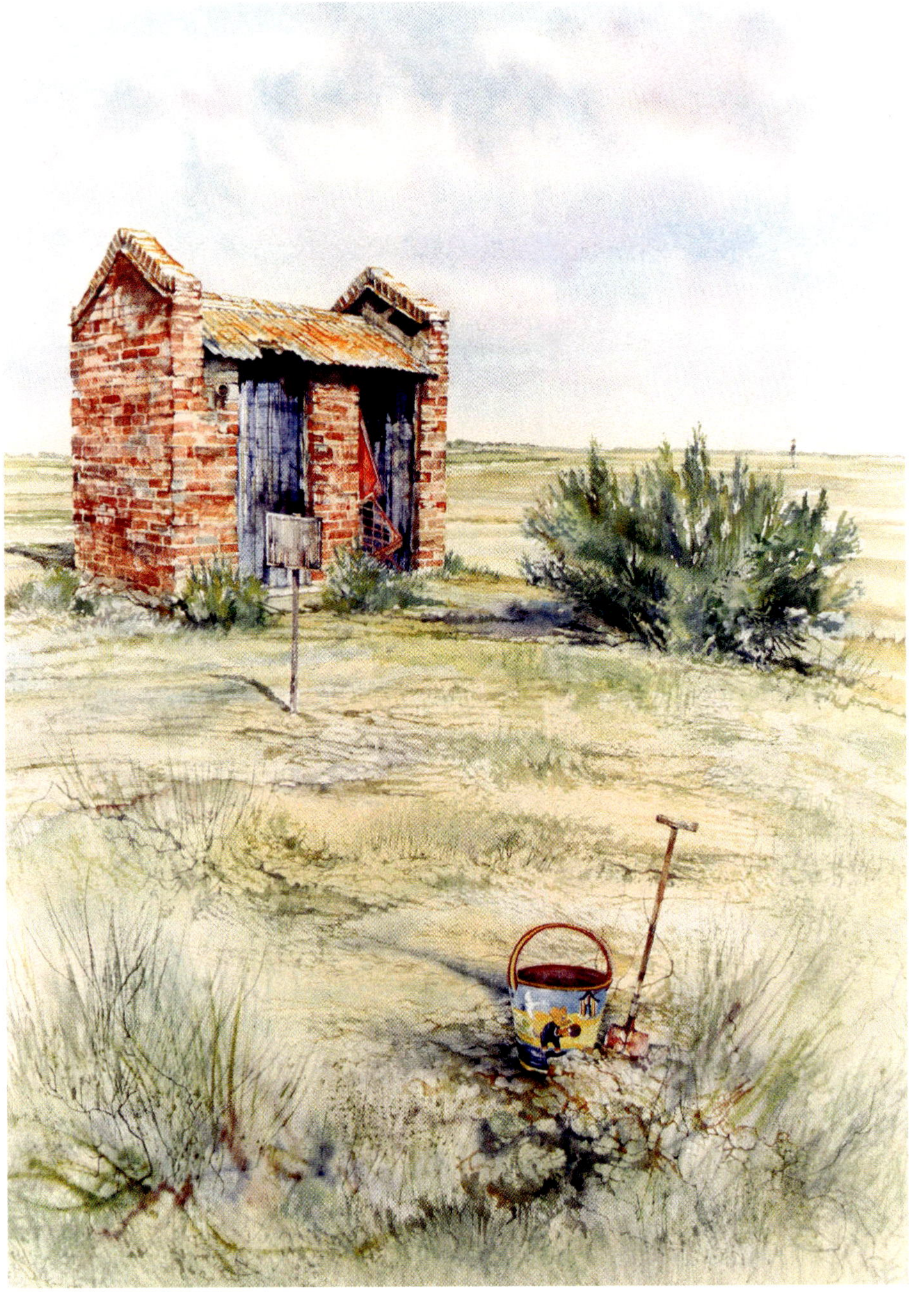

The Coastguard's Toilets, Blakeney Point
300mm x 430mm

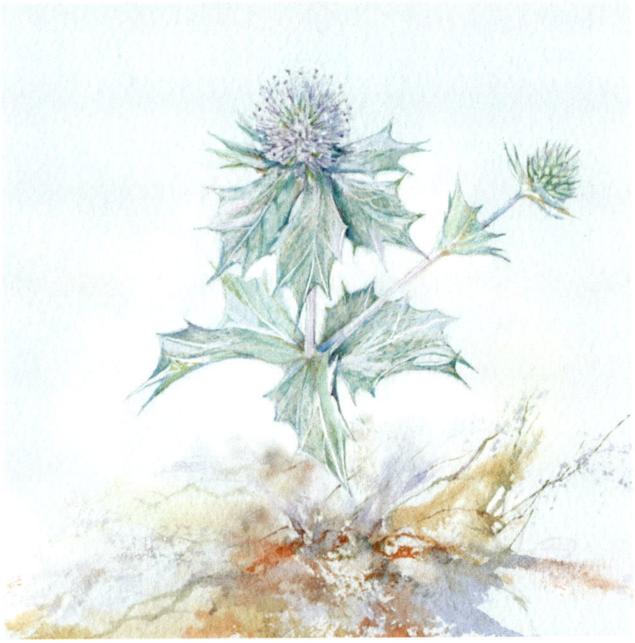

Sea Holly
150mm x 150mm

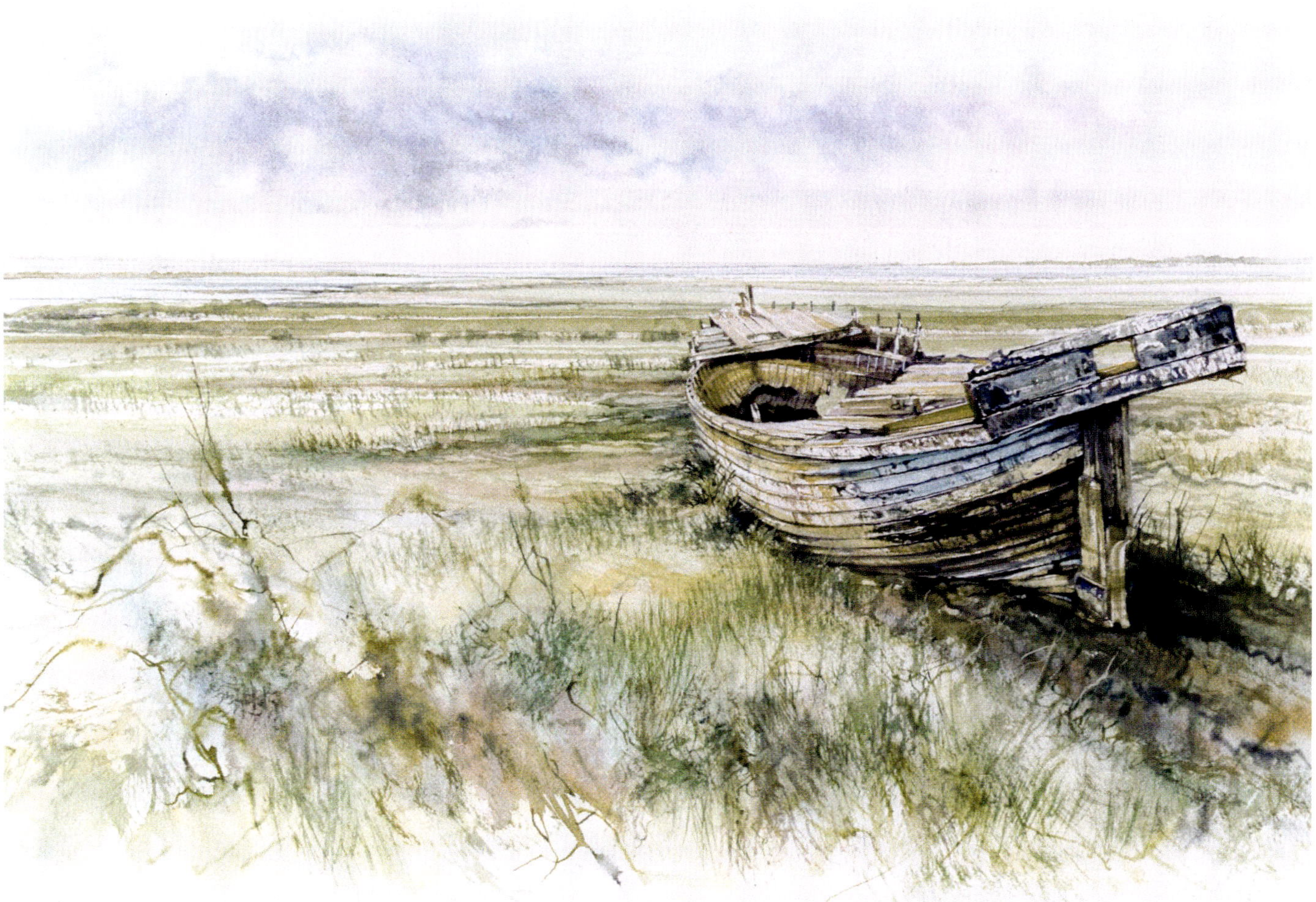

Marsh Wreck, Blakeney
410mm x 210mm

Resting in the last furrow ploughed by its rudder amidst sea blite and alexanders, this wreck lies below the sea wall on Blakeney Marsh. A huge gash on the starboard side exposes ribs like fish bones, bleached white by years of sun and salt. On closer scrutiny the fine carpentry of a shipwright is revealed; each carefully formed timber is placed in perfect harmony with the next.

THE GLAVEN VILLAGES

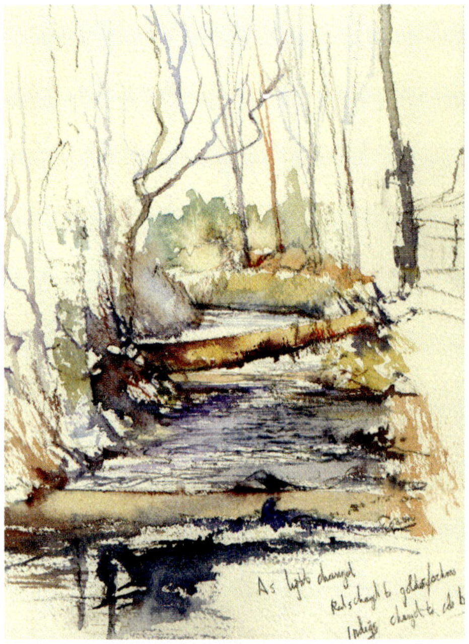

The River Glaven, Hunworth
Sketchbook Study

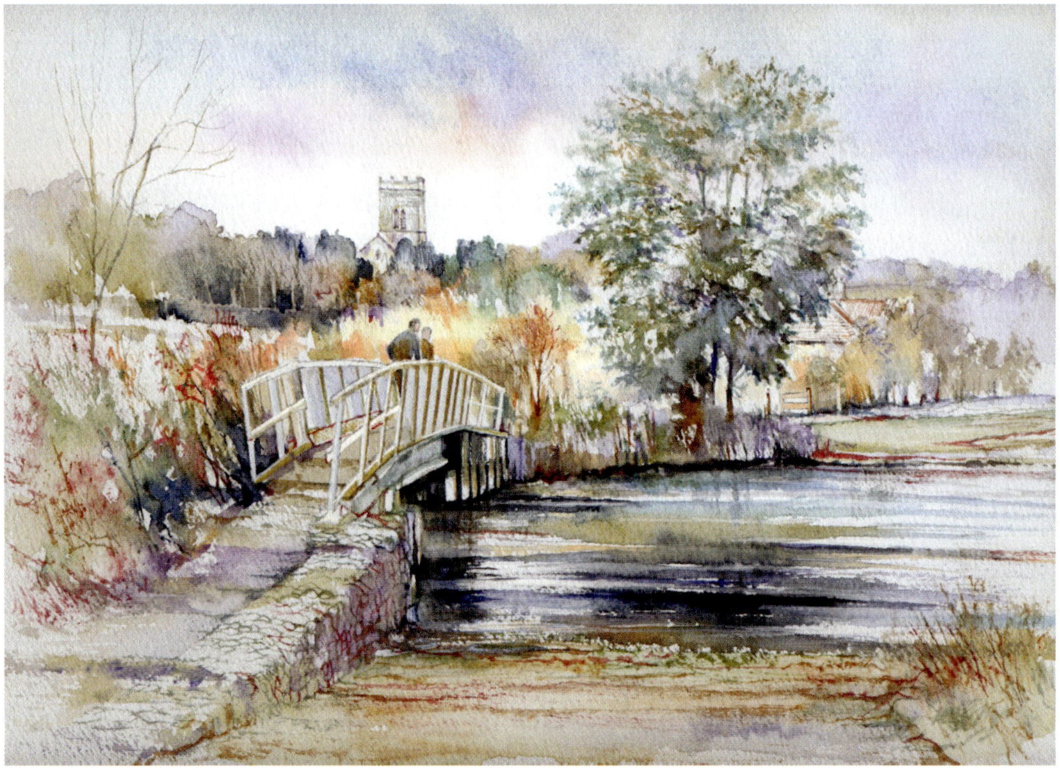

Glanford Ford

Emerging from the flint hills near Bodham, the River Glaven flows through Thornage, Hunworth, Letheringsett and Wiveton before reaching the sea beyond Cley. It is approximately fifteen kilometres long and one of its tributaries flows along Water Lane near Holt. There are three notable fords, the most picturesque being at Glanford, which I painted in early autumn. In its upper reaches the Glaven is a fast flowing chalk river, flowing over gravel rills, through valley mires, mixed woodland and twenty lakes, in comparison to Broadland rivers which tend to flow slowly across a more level flood plain.

The flow rate of the Glaven produces increased oxygen thus supporting a number of very specialised species associated with upland streams. Grey wagtail breed on the river and recently a European black bellied dipper wintered between Hunworth and Glanford. The rather unique brook lamprey, stone loach and bullhead are found in reasonable numbers here and, along with other species, support predatory otter and passage osprey. Ditch systems, grazing marsh and grassland habitats through which the river flows have been found to support twenty-six recorded species of dragonfly.

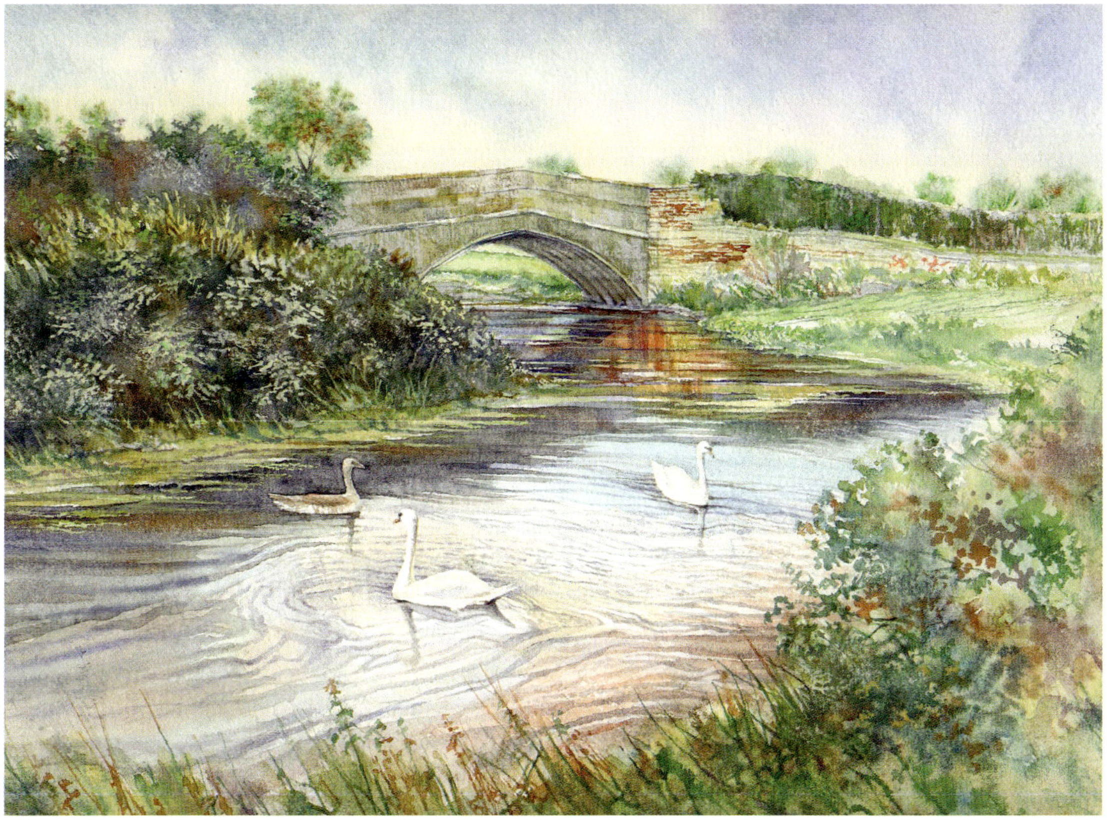

Stone Bridge, Wiveton
310mm x 220mm

As the River Glaven reaches Wiveton it flows under a time-worn stone bridge. Here the river has once again become host to sea trout that miraculously find there way through Blakeney Channel in search of fresh water and in doing so cleanse themselves of parasitic sea lice. Brown trout have also become established and there is a stable population of the indigenous white-clawed crayfish, the real gem of the Glaven. Introduced American signal crayfish exist on part of the river but are fortunately separated from their counterparts by Letheringsett Water Mill as they spread a noxious plague, which eliminates the native species. The Glaven is fortunate in having the support of The River Glaven Conservation Group who monitor the river and advise those who are responsible for its management.

It has been accepted that there is a risk from diffuse pollution and enrichment due to soil erosion and run-off, resulting in utrification of its lakes, increase in plankton and resultant species loss. To combat this, landowners are now using field margins or 'beetle banks' to act as a buffer zone between the river and arable fields. It is also accepted that a natural river will spill over on to its flood plain during times of spate thus slowing the flow, retaining water on adjacent meadows and preventing bank erosion. By the removal of banks this is being allowed to happen in some areas of the Glaven Valley.

The River Glaven is a charming watercourse. For me its 'gin-clear' water cascading through bluebell woodland is a joy to behold.

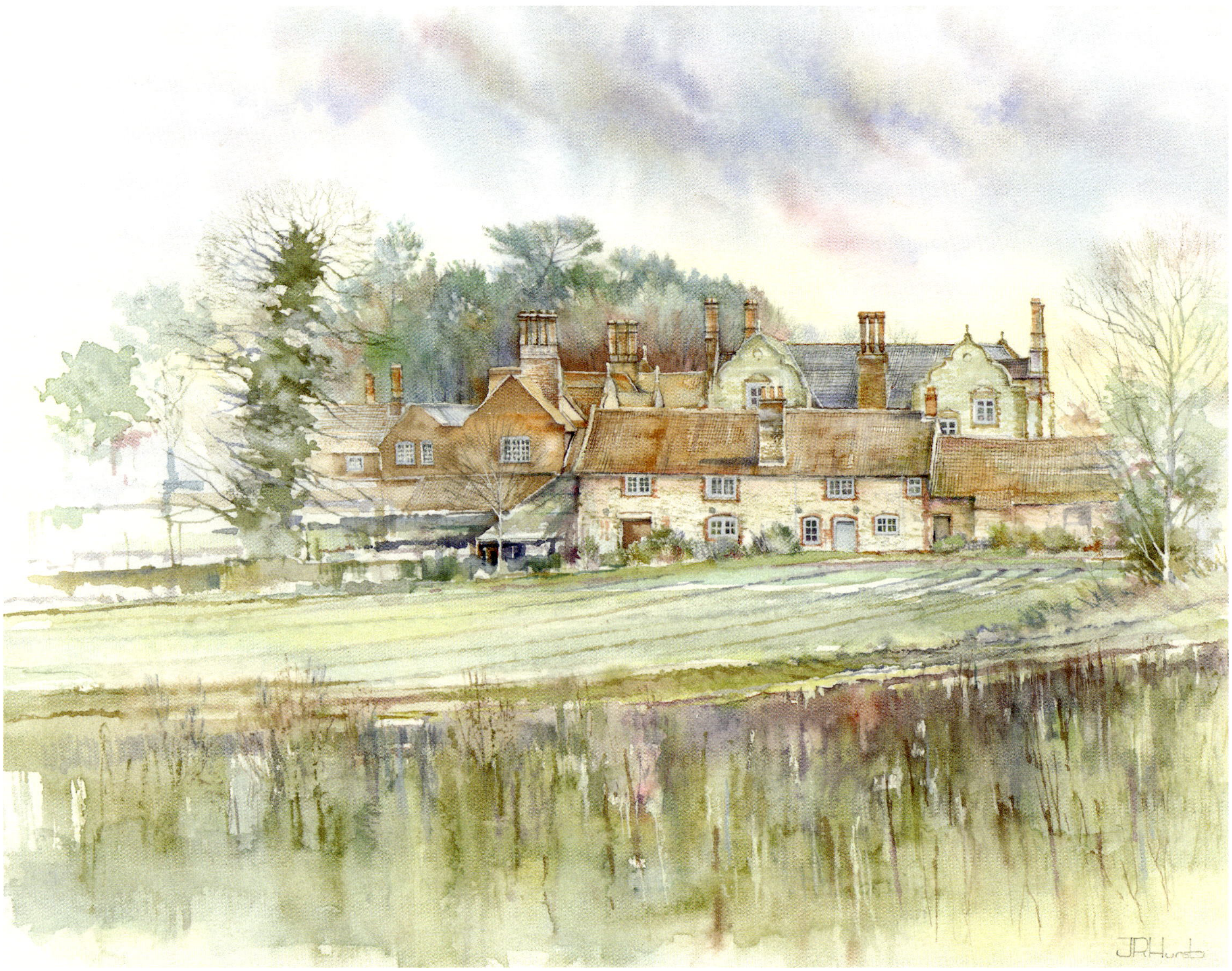

A House by the Sea

Built on monastic land by a wealthy merchant in 1650, this majestic Jacobean manor house nestles discreetly in a wooded garden by Blakeney fresh marsh. Known quite rightly as one of Norfolk's secret architectural gems, retaining its original features and untouched by the passage of time, Wiveton Hall has always held a genuine fascination for me, having been created in the heyday of Cley and Blakeney as commercial ports.

My colour studies were composed during a mellow autumnal day, accompanied by the haunting sound of curlew as they passed overhead from estuary to inland feeding grounds. In summer, this working fruit farm is alive with activity where visitors enjoy a variety of fruit, home produced asparagus, honey, eggs and pork. The brightly painted farm café has an extraordinary vibrancy about it with al fresco dining and delicious home made food being the norm. I always enjoy time spent at Wiveton Hall.

In late winter after prolonged rain, the River Glaven may flood on to the low-lying meadows by Wiveton church. In this study, low afternoon light produces shadows, whilst the flooded foreground creates a sense of perspective.

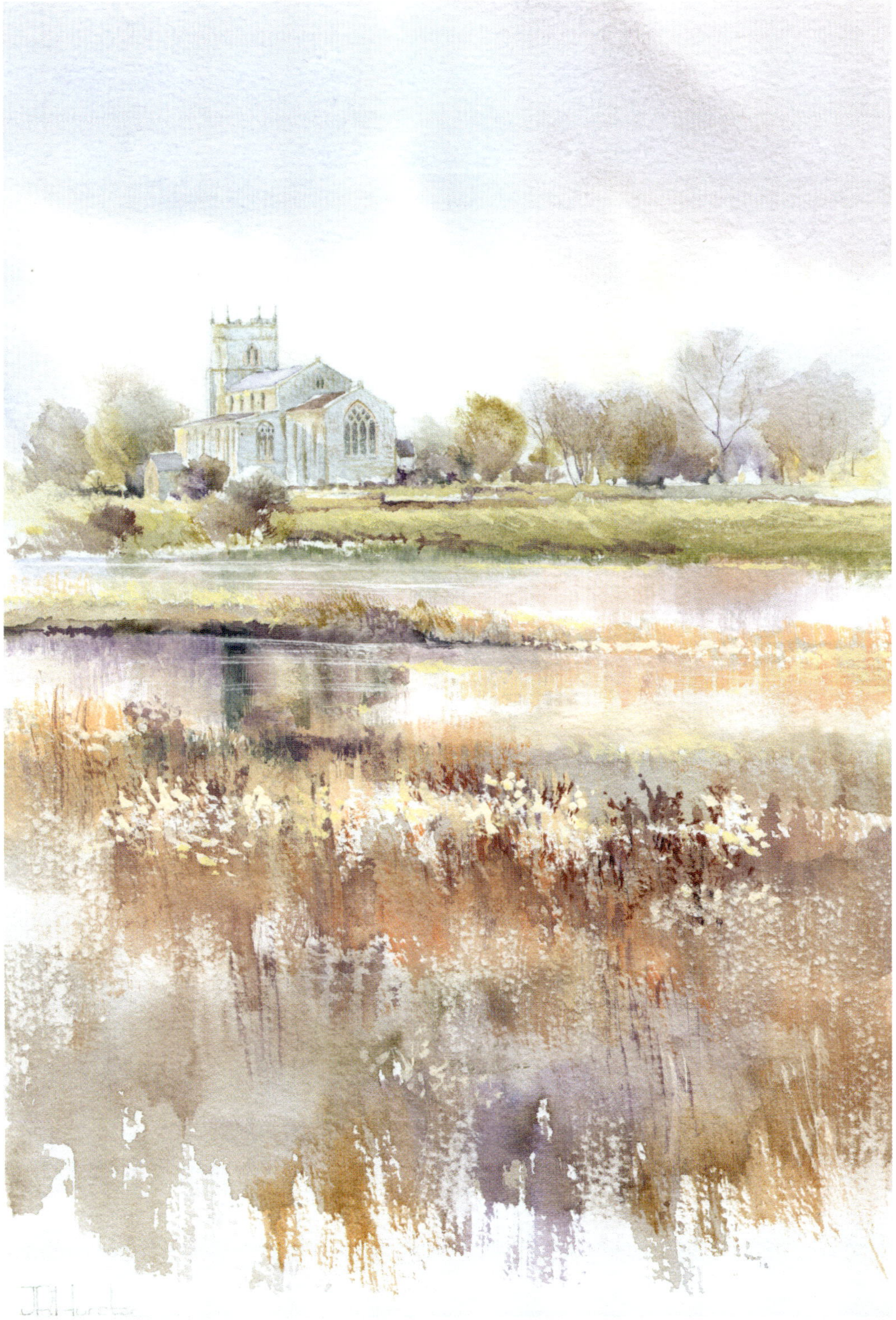

Flood by Wiveton Church
200mm x 280mm

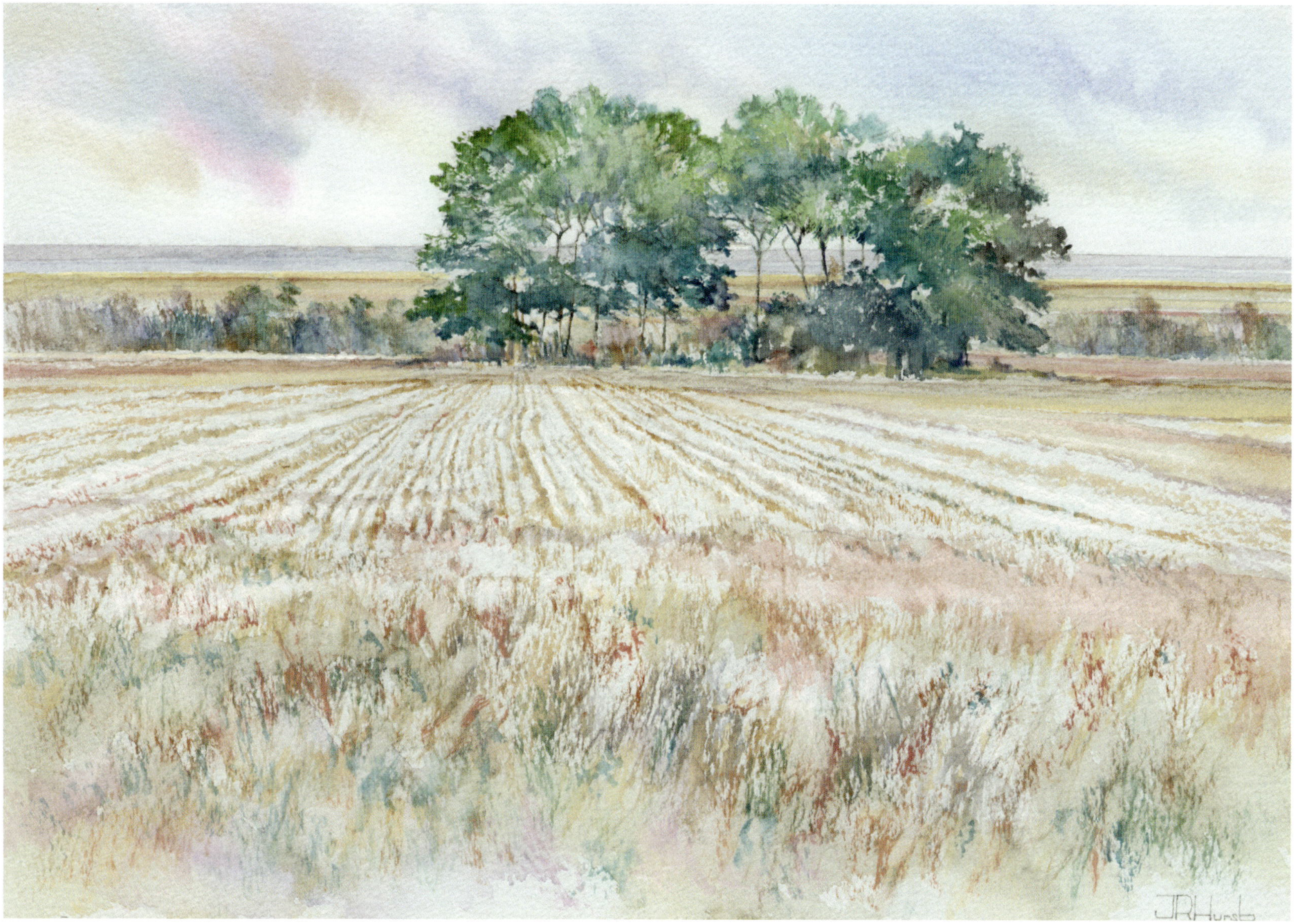

Winter Stubble by Blakeney Freshes
310mm x 220mm

A single grove of pines has survived onshore gales above Blakeney fresh marsh. I completed this study as hoar frost was thawing and rain bearing clouds indicated a change in the weather.

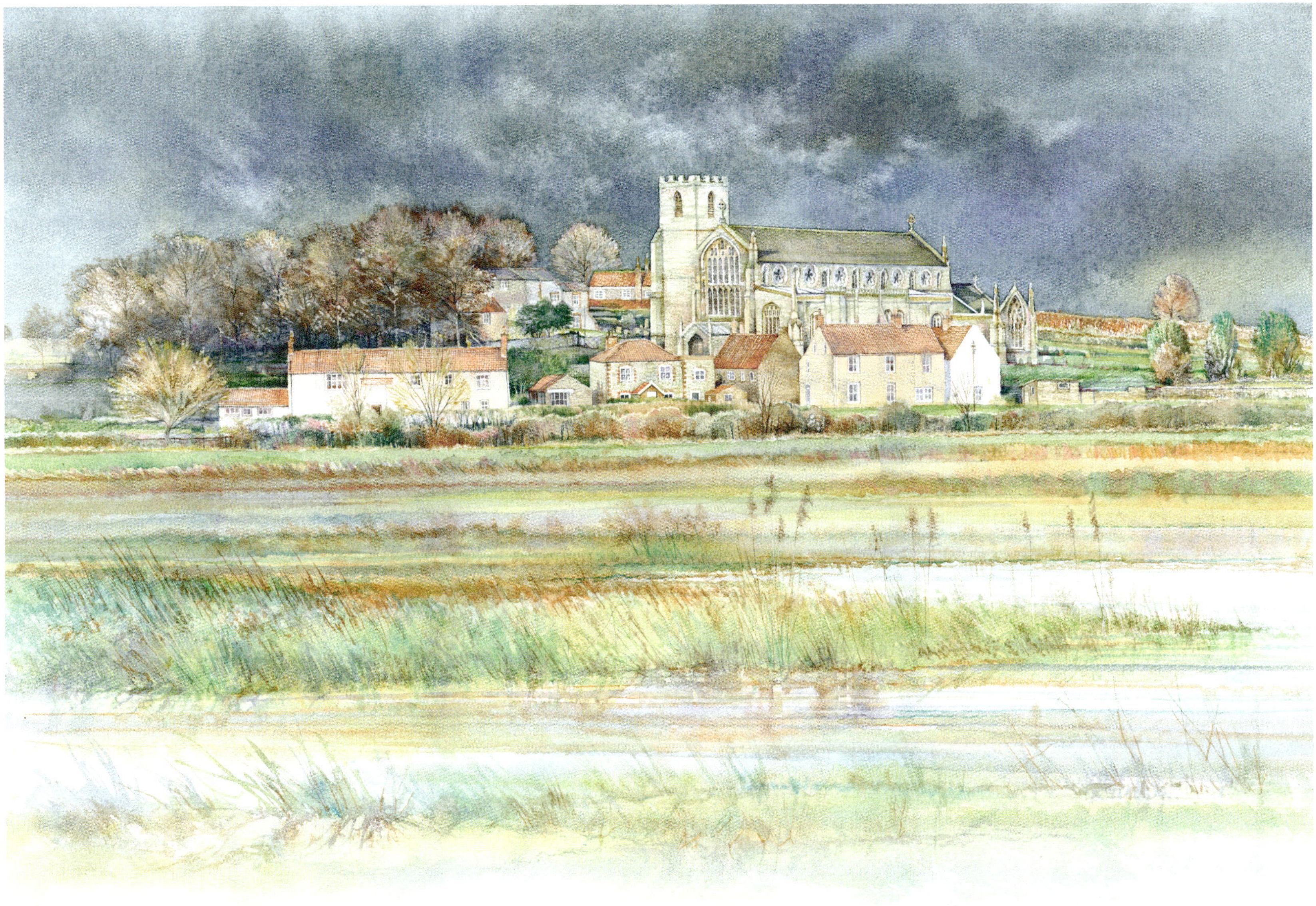

After an April Shower,
St Margaret's Church, Cley-next-the-Sea
480mm x 350mm

A heavy April storm had passed to the east revealing St Margaret's Church and the Three Swallows Inn at Cley, bathed in spring sunshine. It is here that the River Glaven sweeps across its flood plain, a beautiful valley marsh separating Cley from Wiveton, overlooked by their churches strategically placed on higher ground.

REEDS AND CREEKS

Cley-next-the-Sea

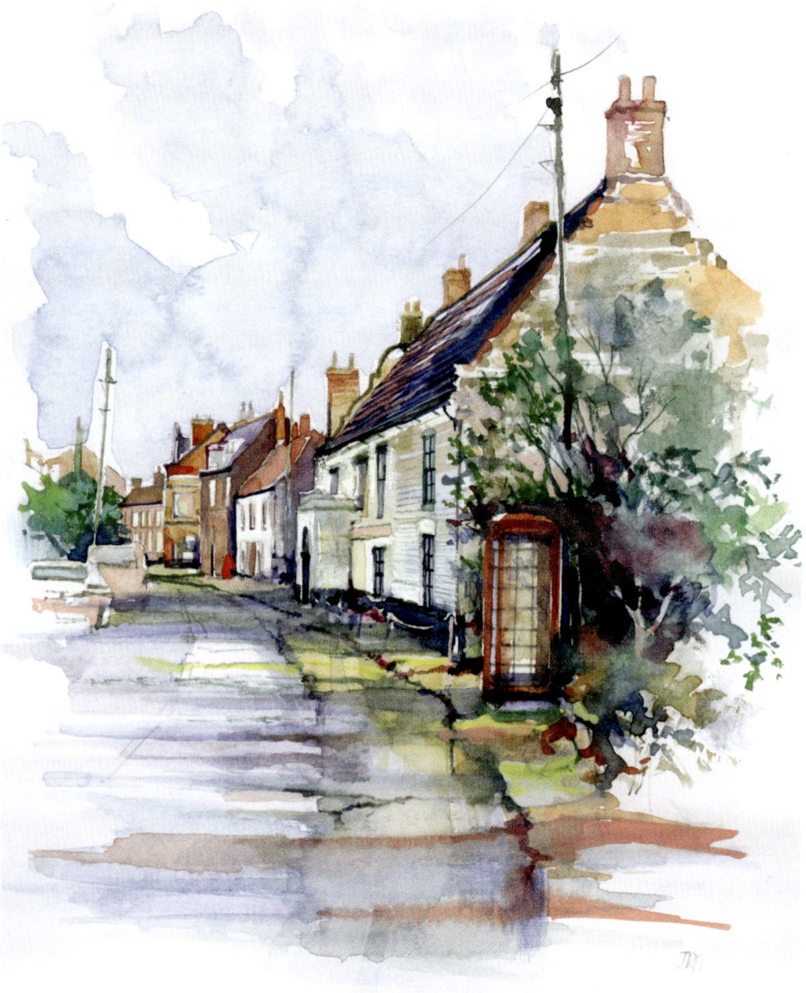

Towards the George Inn, Cley
Watercolour sketch
270mm x 210mm

It was an absolute joy to paint Mr Cooke of Cley-next-the-Sea and to record stories of the sea. Born in Salthouse in 1927, brother to Bob and George, Charlie has in his own words, "Done everything there is to be done. From crab fishing to building and working in a soup factory."

I first painted Charlie by his trusty Fordson on a cold January afternoon as he scanned the weather before retreating into his warm kitchen where a kettle is always on the boil. As I sat down, two placid retrievers, named Emma and Lucy, stirred from their slumbers and a large grey parrot also called Charlie Cooke cocked his head inquisitively from an enormous cage. Charlie remembered hearing someone at the door late one night in the January of 1953 and found on opening it, that the North Sea was there! As family members were hastened upstairs the lights failed while he desperately tried to cram everything in an old pram. Stripped to the waist in icy water he rescued belongings only to find next morning that "My boots and trousers were gone!"

The ringing of Charlie's brass bell interrupted our conversation. A lorry with 'Flaming Good Fires' painted on it in red stood outside. The coalman had arrived. Charlie continued to recall a very amusing incident where a tractor that had stood idle for two years suddenly roared back to life and overtook the one that was towing it across the marsh.
"I wish I'd had a camera!" recalled Charlie.
He also remembered the jockeys who would come wildfowling on Pope's Salthouse Broad. "They were all so small," laughed Charlie. "They had to carry their guns over their shoulders or they'd have stuck in the mud!"
"What of the changes?" I asked my host.
"Oh," replied Charlie, "Too many lines drawn around everything. If they could draw a line round my house they'd claim it!"
"And too many 'bodwatchers'," he added with a wry smile.

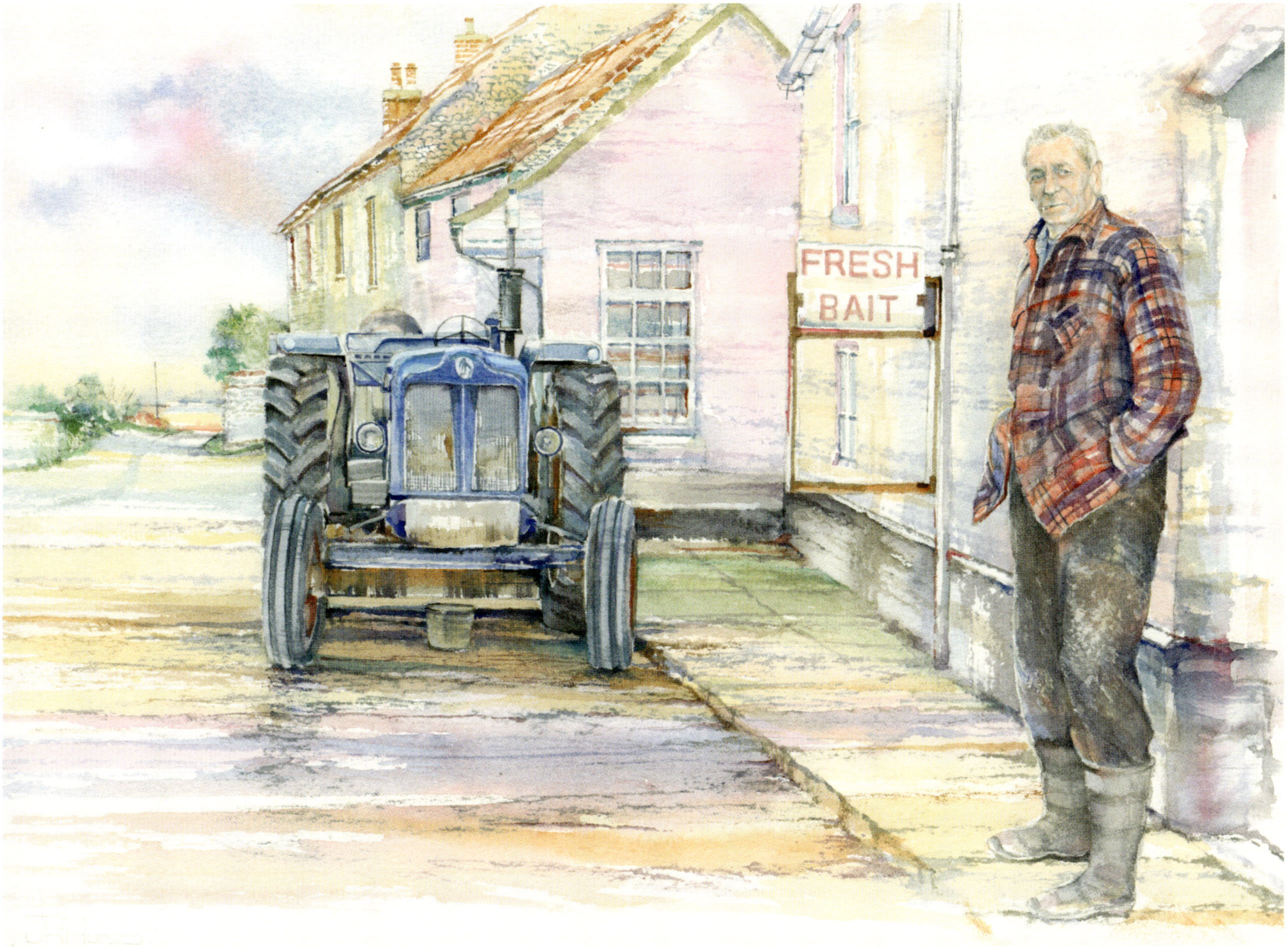

Charlie Cooke by The Old Fordson,
Cley-next-the-Sea
330mm x 240mm

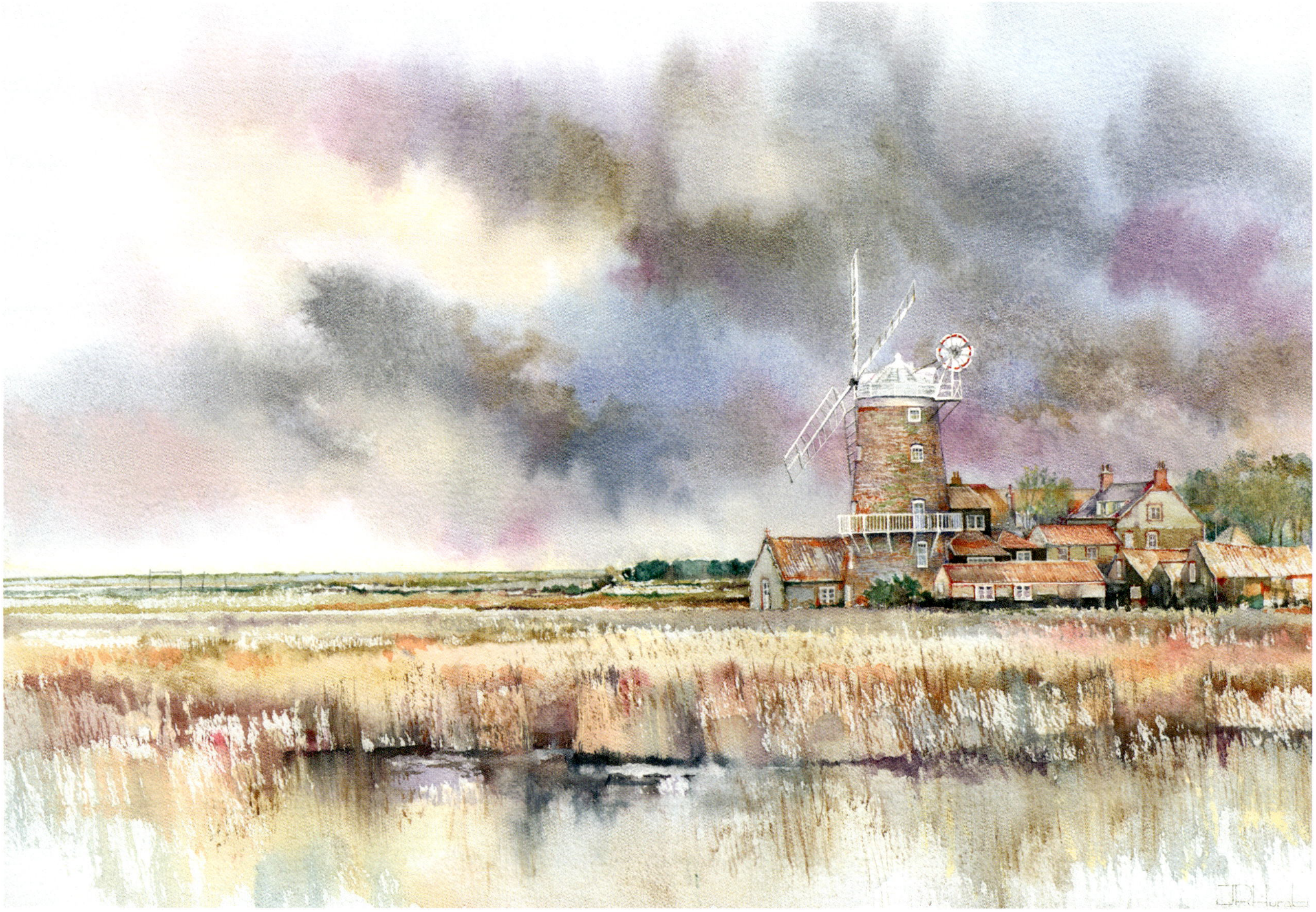

Cley Windmill Over the Reeds
410mm x 280mm

The mill at Cley-next-the-Sea must rank as one of the most famous landmarks in East Anglia, situated as it is by the River Glaven. Nestling in the reed bed it overlooks Blakeney Marshes in a village that has retained architectural characteristics of a bygone era. A location for artists, filmmakers and poets, there is little wonder that the mill, now a guesthouse, enjoys one of the highest occupancy rates in England. This painting was created from the popular north-east viewpoint in which the sails and fan are set to create a pleasing composition. Cley windmill was built around 1819 and ended its working life in 1912. By 1921 it was converted to a residence, finally becoming a guesthouse in 1983. The sails have a span of seventy feet with a topsail height of eighty-seven feet above the ground. The red-banded fan designed to present the mainsails to the wind has eight blades and is over ten feet in diameter. Five original floors now form part of the exquisite guest accommodation in addition to the adjacent stables and boathouses. I enjoy painting the character of this unique building as it becomes influenced by changing seasons and light.

I came across Billy Temple, the brother of Jim, the Morston ferryman, one cold February day by Cley mill as he gathered reeds for thatching. *Phragmites communis* or common reed grows readily across the indigenous wetlands of Norfolk and Suffolk yet needs careful management and rotational harvesting to maintain a high yield and quality product. Here the reed is gathered into a yelm, often pronounced 'yellum' a convenient weight for the thatcher, thought to derived from 'gelm' or 'gylm', the Anglo-Saxon for bundle. Once in the hands of the thatcher the reed bundle becomes a gavel, possibly a dialect form of gable, identified by the *Oxford English Dictionary* as the Old Norman French 'gavelle' or 'gavel', a heap.

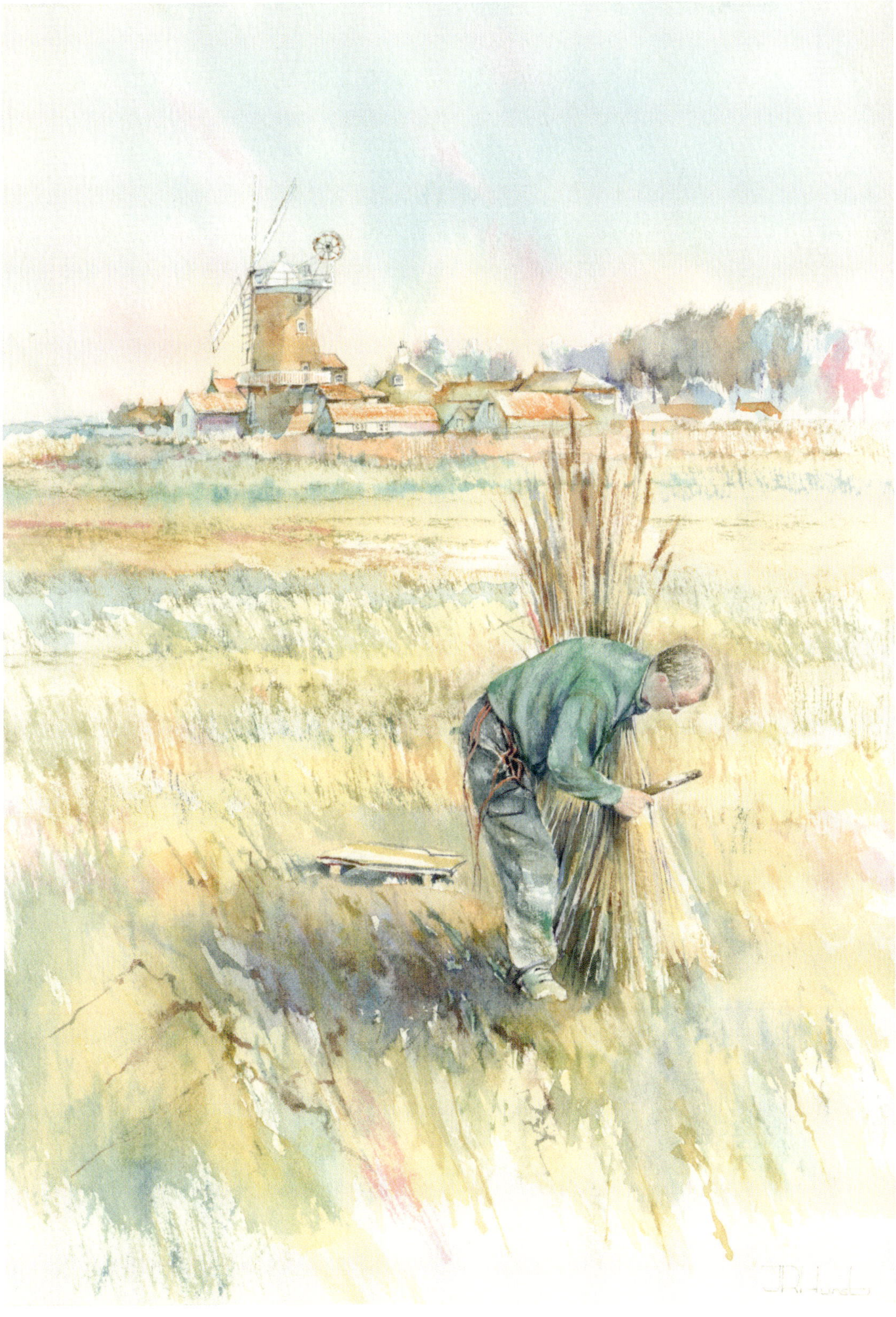

Gathering Reeds by Cley Mill

Hollyhocks pointing skywards commence flowering by the end of June. They do so in profusion in the Norfolk coastal villages where they emerge from the foot of dry walls, sheltered corners and old gardens. In Cley-next-the-Sea they have taken over the old 'lokes', the narrow footpaths leading tantalisingly from one enchanting street to another. Loke or loak is a dialect word derived from 'loca', the old English meaning enclosed place. I painted this loke during a hot July day, using two of the daring colours of summer; aureolin yellow and cadmium red. Finding respite from the heat I wandered into the indigo world of shadows, only to find the path waymarked by more intense splashes of colour created by a riot of roses and honeysuckle.

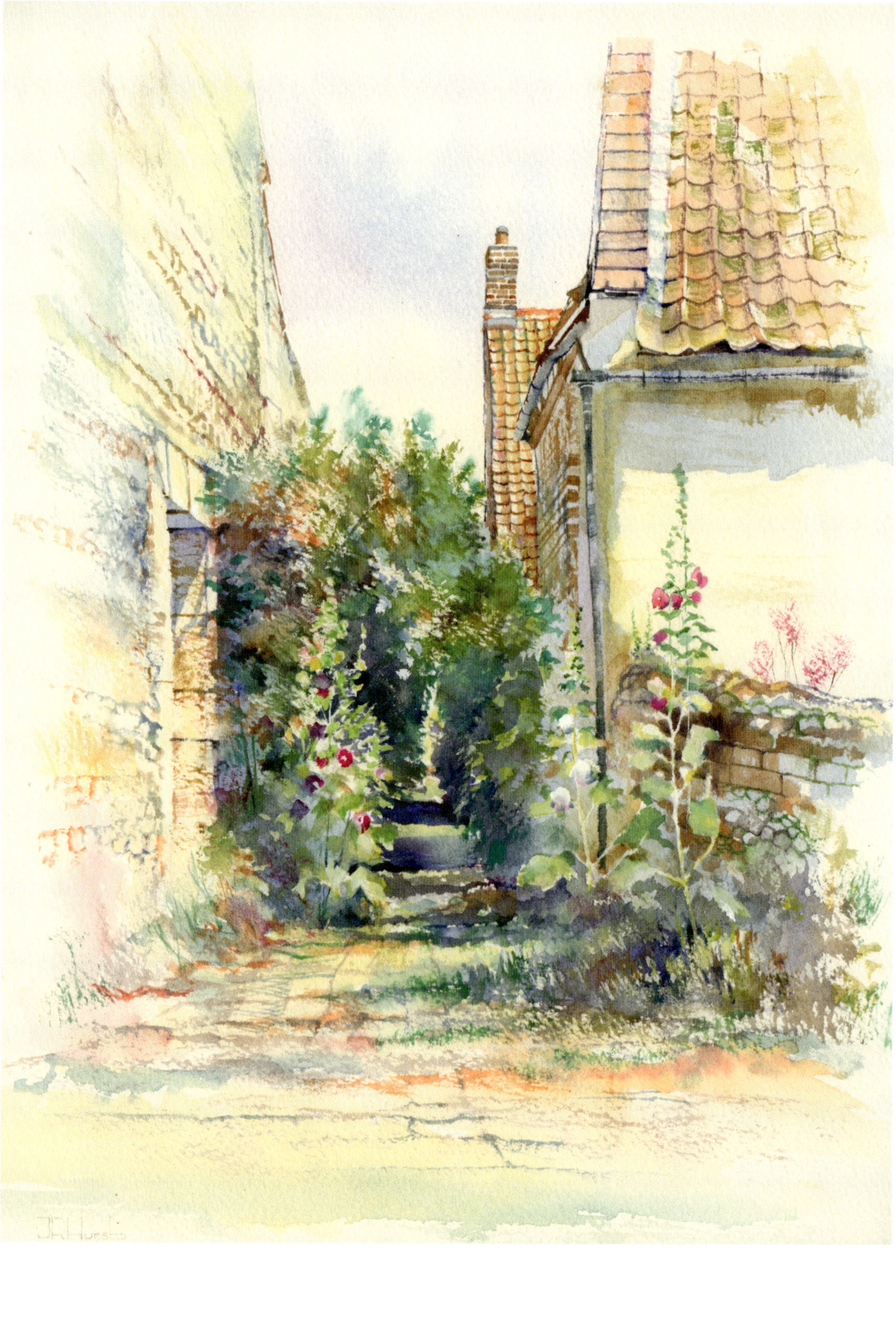

The Old Loke, Cley-next-the-Sea
260mm x 310mm

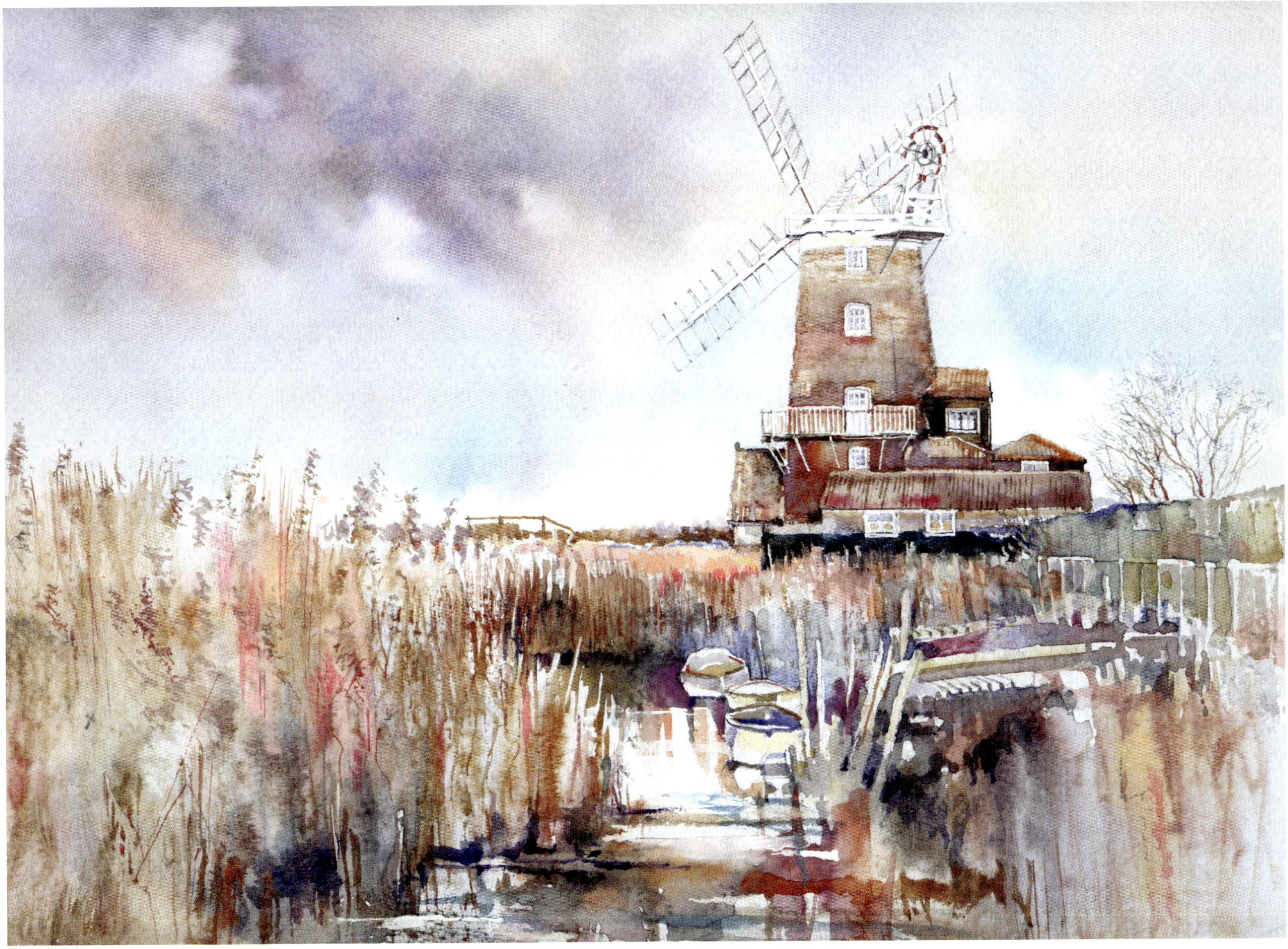

Winter Sluice, Cley Windmill
330mm x 254mm

By contrast to the heat and still air of summer, here we see the leafless tree and lifeless reeds by Cley Sluice during a cool winter morning. Refracted light created warm tints on otherwise cold seaborne clouds that sailed in on a north-easterly breeze. By using cold violets and cobalt blue in combination with warm sienna and yellow ochre, I aimed to balance the composition.

SEA AND SHINGLE

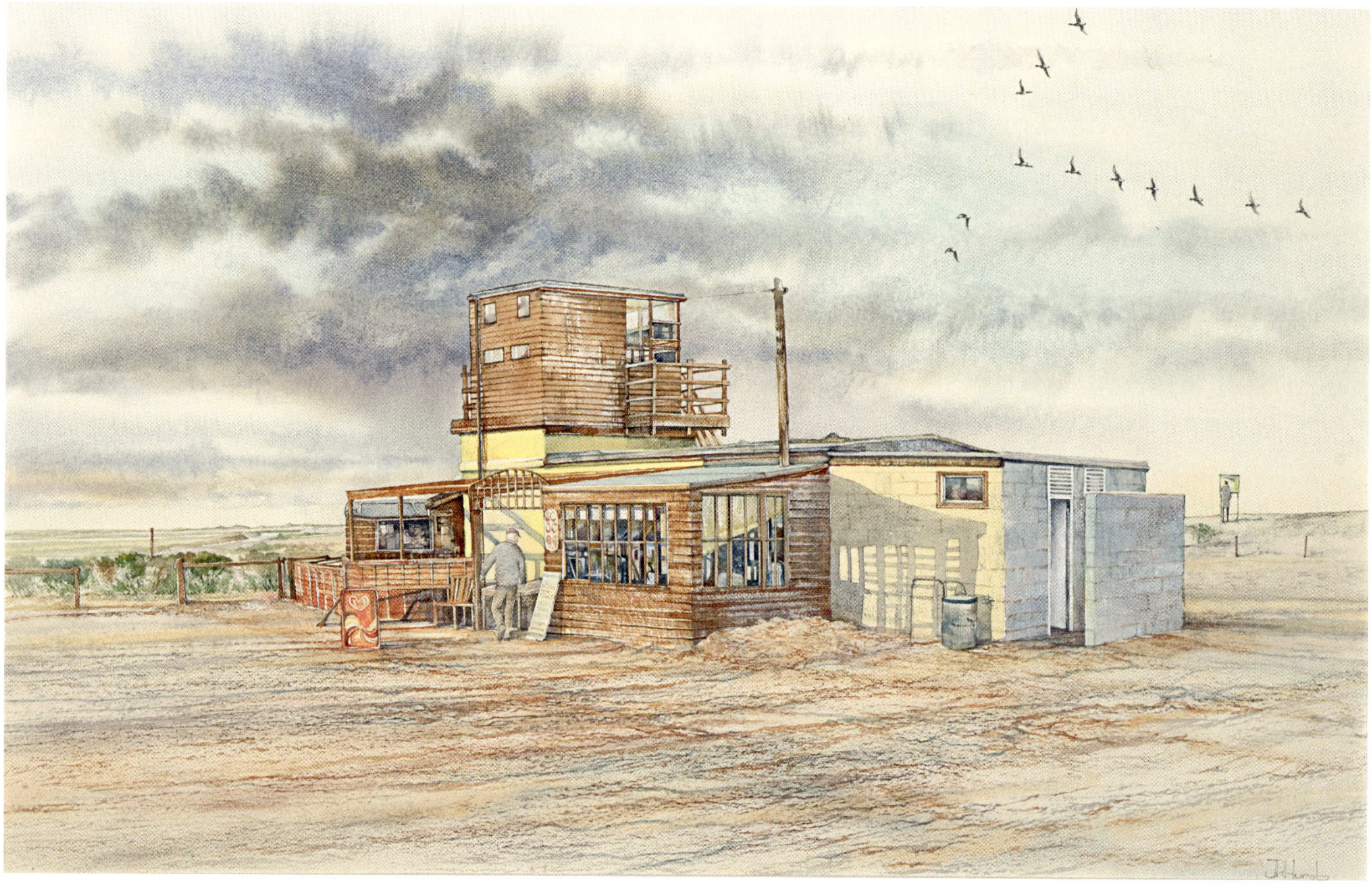

Arkwright's Café, Cley
600mm x 380mm

This iconic building was removed from Cley-next-the-Sea beach in 2008, after years of shingle encroachment and battering by storms. My memories of it go back to the early 1970s when, with fellow fledgling birders, we would find shelter and sustenance within its sparse interior. The apple pie was legendary, made all the more appetising by the pre-dawn journey from Lincolnshire and our sudden exposure to salt air. Originally a coastguard lookout station, Arkwright's became the place to find old books, ornithological records, fishing tackle, a good hot mug of tea and honest, homemade food.

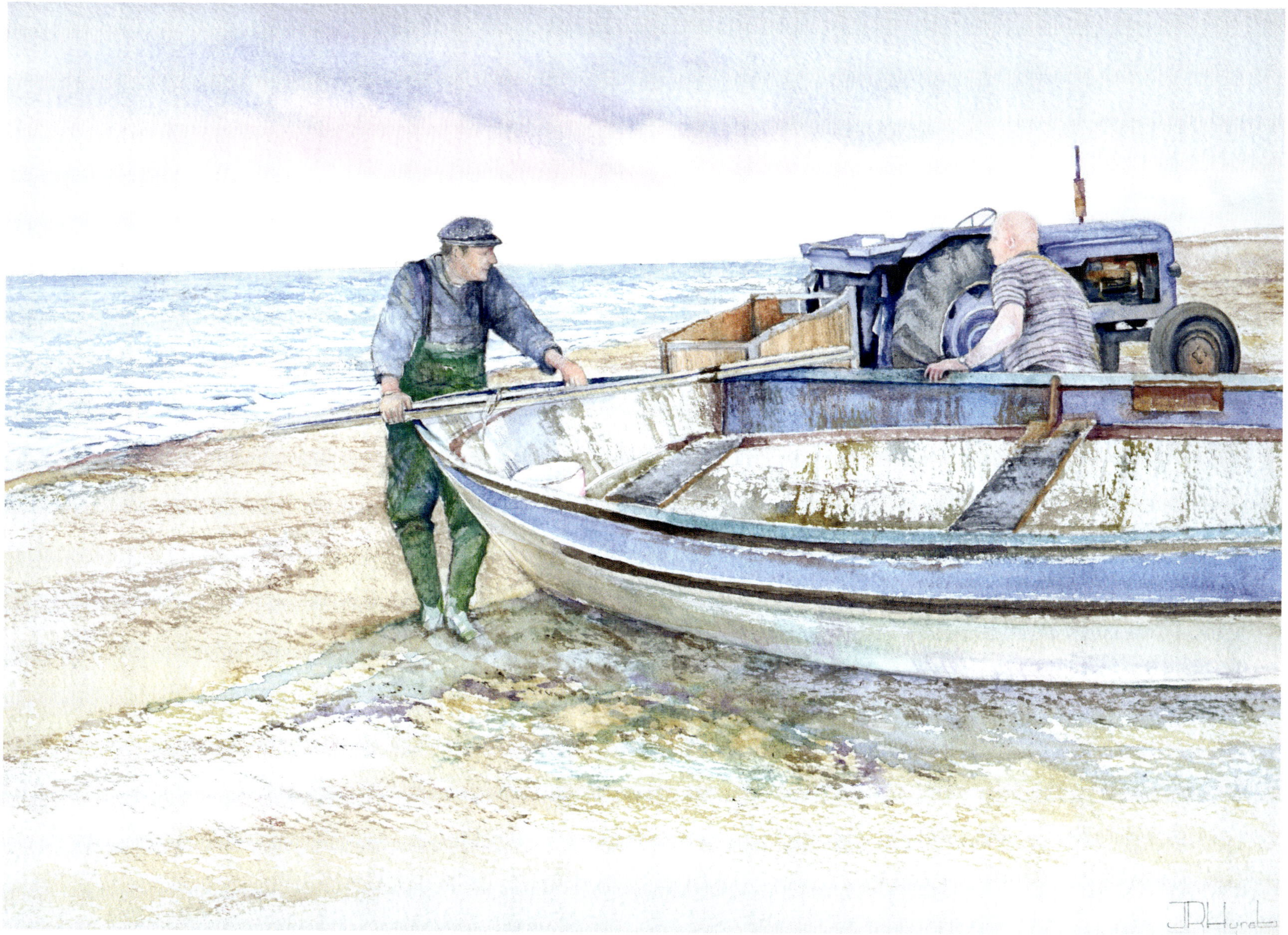

Crab Fishers Depart, Cley Beach
300mm x 220mm

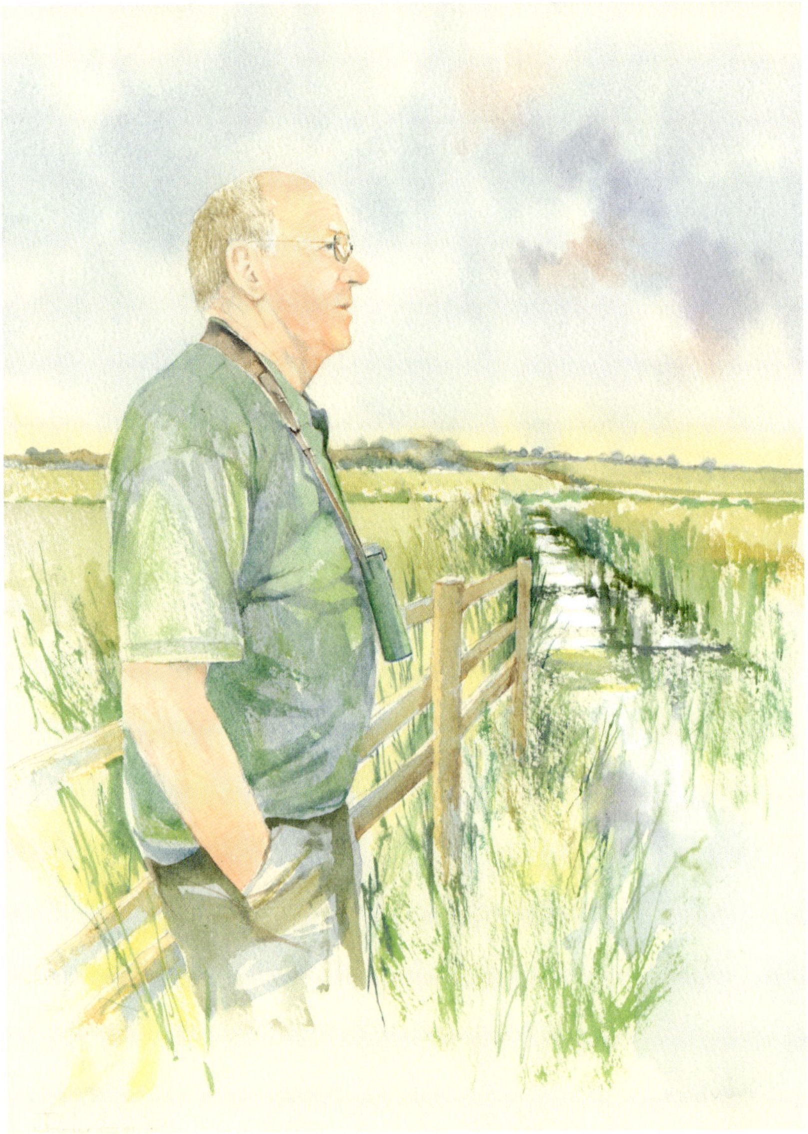

The Warden
260mm x 360mm

When considering Cley Marshes one immediately thinks of Bernard Bishop. As warden, his life's work has revolved around water management and the effect this has on dependent wildlife. In the spring returning avocets and passage waders require shallow lagoons on which to feed. The secretive bittern, called 'buttle' in the Broads, seeks reed beds standing in water, whilst black tailed godwit favour lush flooded grassland or washes. One such wash, named after Bernard's father Billy, appears to be identical to those in which godwits nest within the Great Ouse complex and Dutch Polders, yet they are reluctant to breed here at Cley.

"As a memorial to father", said Bernard, "I would like to see godwits breeding on the wash before I retire."

I encountered Bernard in 1977 in his fifth year as assistant warden. He finally 'made the grade' as warden in 1979. I remember my first May morning at Cley by the string of 'lifers' or new birds added to my life list. These included spoonbill, blue throat and red backed shrike.

"I was taught about the countryside and how to manage it by my father, who had all the time in the world for me," recalled Bernard fondly when asked about his family heritage. Enquiring about changes, Bernard's response echoed that of Clement Scott who lamented change brought about by his popular written portrayal of 'Poppyland'.

"The crowded Norfolk Coast is a victim of its own popularity, yet without our tourist visitors, with limited jobs for local people at Cley, where would we be?" When asked about the best bird recorded at Cley, Bernard replied, "That pacific swift in 1993, absolute chaos. I've never seen so many people in all of my life!"

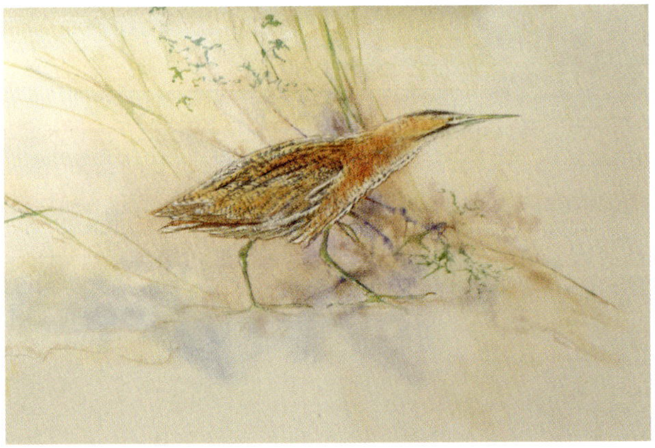

The Secretive Bittern
160mm x 130mm

The Watcher's House was built in 1936 by The Norfolk Naturalists' Trust to house the family of its second watcher, Billy Bishop, the father of Bernard, present day warden of Cley Marshes Reserve. Originally a shooting marsh and part of the Cozens-Hardy estate, a Dr Long of Norwich bought this site in 1926, and set about forming the UK's first conservation group over lunch with friends in The George Hotel, Cley. The Norfolk Wildlife Trust as we know it today was born, growing in strength to become one of the most important conservation bodies in western Europe. The Trust manages forty reserves in addition to education facilities, visitors' centres, voluntary groups, permanent staff and a membership in excess of thirty-four thousand.

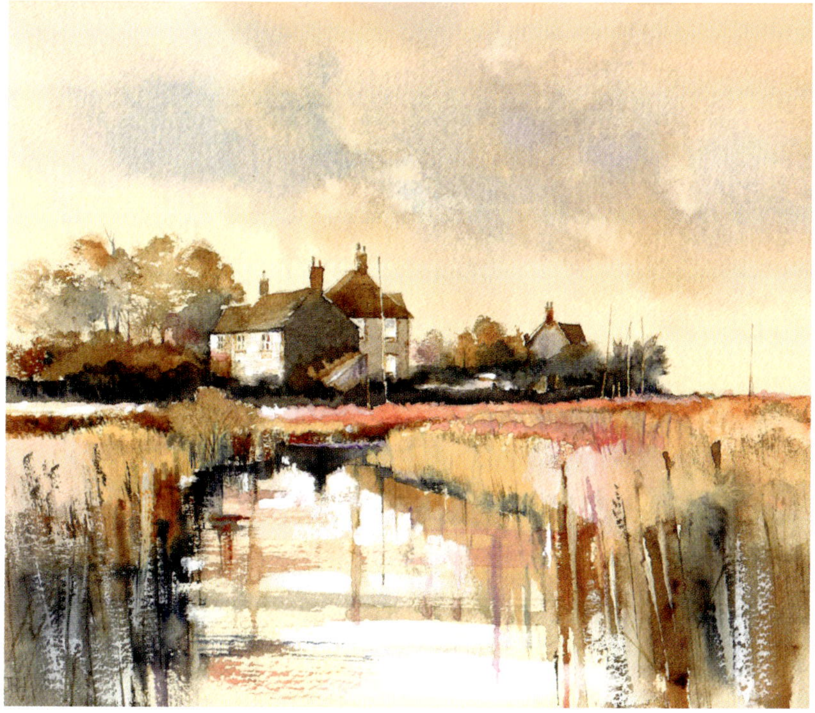

Towards The Watcher's House
Watercolour and Gouache
300mm x 270mm

The delicate ecosystem at Cley marshes includes a network of fresh water dykes fed by the crystal clear Catchwater Drain, depicted in the foreground of this painting. Filtered by underground chalk deposits this important dyke never freezes, staying at an almost constant six to seven degrees Celsius. Bernard Bishop remembers from his childhood days, a sunken barrel in the dyke from which villagers could extract fresh water. The relationship between fresh and saline water is a constant concern for The Trust at Cley and Salthouse since the shingle ridge has been left to 'naturalise', allowing the sea to overtop in extreme conditions. Bernard's own opinion is a positive one however and based upon nature's way of creating equilibrium.

"I believe the north of the reserve will become more saline but constant replenishment by fresh water will ensure that there will always be a fresh marsh in the south."

I enquired about the status of bearded reedling on the reserve and it appears that they are resident throughout the year. Many observers have seen what appears to be sporadic migration of this charming reed dweller, seeing airborne flocks of birds spiralling out of sight in the autumn. Some ornithologists believe that many actually return to their dedicated reed bed after this aerial excursion, whilst some birds reach southerly wintering sites.

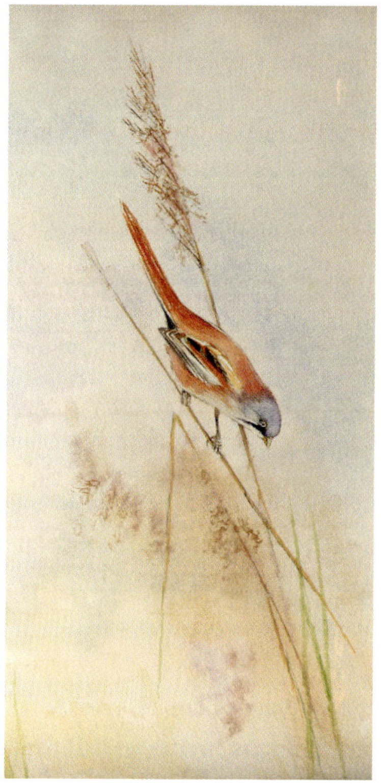

Bearded Tit
40mm x 90mm

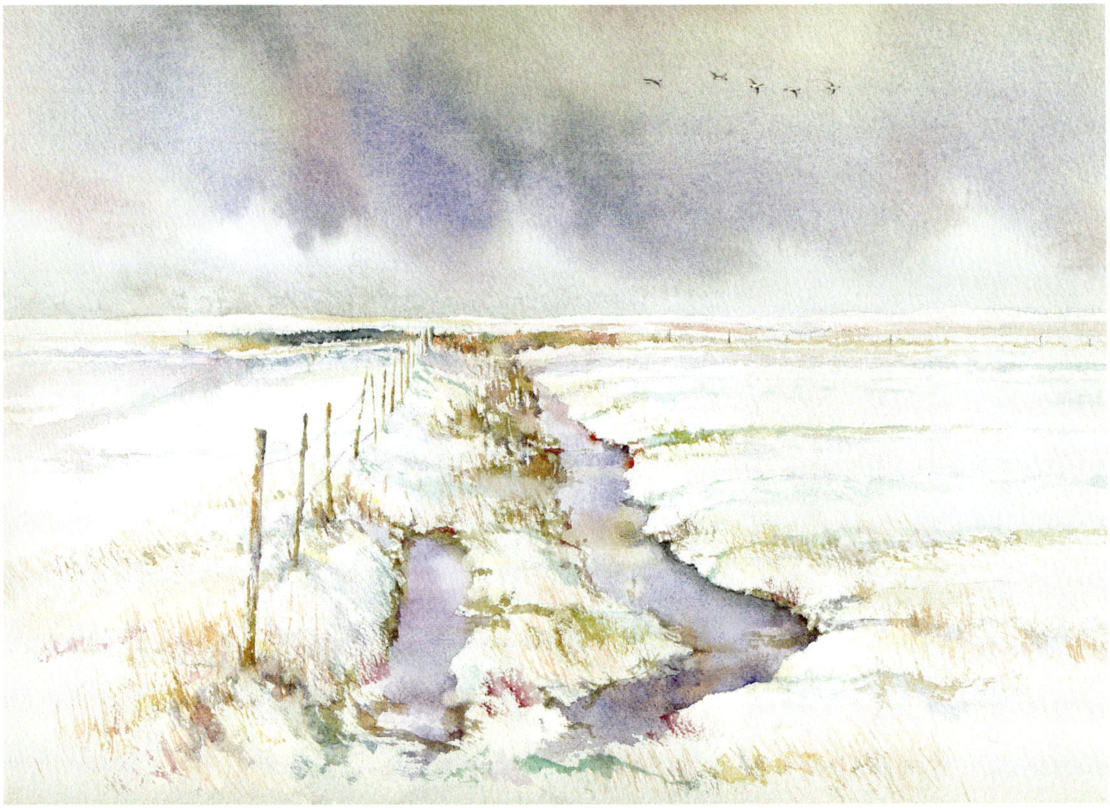

Snow or even frost in Salthouse is unusual due to its close proximity to the sea. Winter temperature differences between the coastal zone and upper heathland area can be as much as three degrees. This painting was composed shortly after a blizzard accompanied by a bitterly cold northern airflow coming directly off the sea. As freshwater pools rapidly iced over they reflected the snow-laden clouds as deep indigo. 'Wheeoo' calls of widgeon carried on the wind as they sought open water.

Blizzard, Salthouse
280mm x 180mm

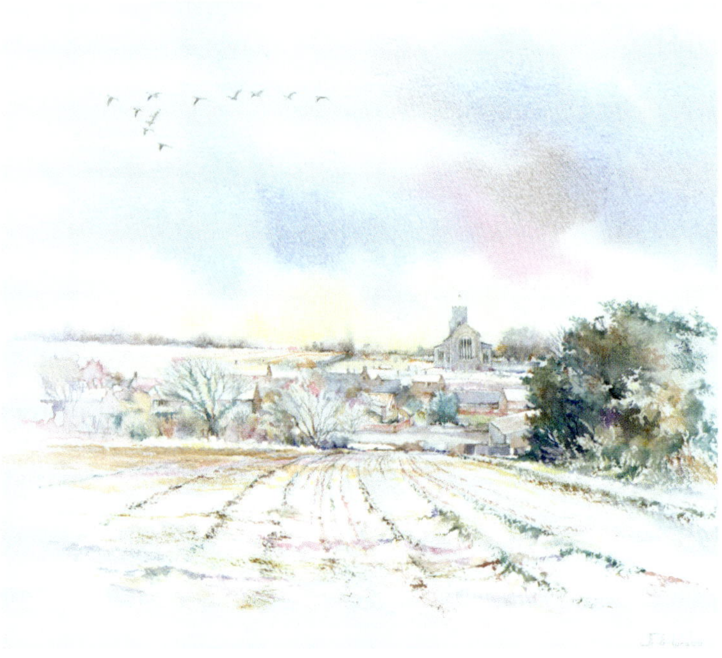

Salthouse in the Snow
310mm x 290mm

In recent years, an old four bore wildfowling gun found its way into the care of Brent Pope, a wildfowler who was named after the now numerous 'seven bob' coastal goose. I met Mr Pope during a February blizzard when he agreed to have his portrait drawn with gun in hand on his private marsh. A raw easterly wind with horizontal sleet made the encounter most memorable, as did the stories as they began to unfold.

On the 11th January 1938, a boy was born in the Manor Hotel, Blakeney who received his name by the most unlikely of circumstances. Some weeks earlier a local doctor had prepared to examine the pregnant mother and reached into his pocket for a stethoscope. As he did so a lifeless partridge dropped on to the bed.

"This child will be born with a beak, not a nose!" was the mother's shocked response, hence the naming of Brent.

Edward Roy Pope acquired the marshes formerly known as Salthouse Broad in 1927 as a commercial duck shoot. The Broad had been dissected by The New Cut, a drainage channel linking Salthouse and Cley marshes with Blakeney harbour, resulting in numerous pools and splashes, the ideal habitat for wildfowl. Edward planted *phragmites*, gathered from the Norfolk Broads and established several flight ponds. During the 1940s numerous eels were netted on the site, being kept in 'eel coffins' before being shipped alive to London markets. There are now forty acres of reed beds on the marsh, creating an undisturbed habitat in which marsh harrier, bearded tit, avocet and bittern regularly breed. Whatever one's view is of field sports, the conservation of scarce species can and does go 'hand in hand' with the annual harvest of duck, which takes place on this SSSI and RAMSAR site.

For seventy years a succession of marsh keepers have wardened the marsh. Characters like Little Bill Holman, Hopper Holman, Billy Bishop, Bob Cooke, Jo Reed, Jeffery Crow and Paddy Archer have provided sport for HRH The Duke of Edinburgh, Prince Charles and many other well known countrymen who have chosen to experience the majestic dawn and dusk flights of wildfowl in this unique place.

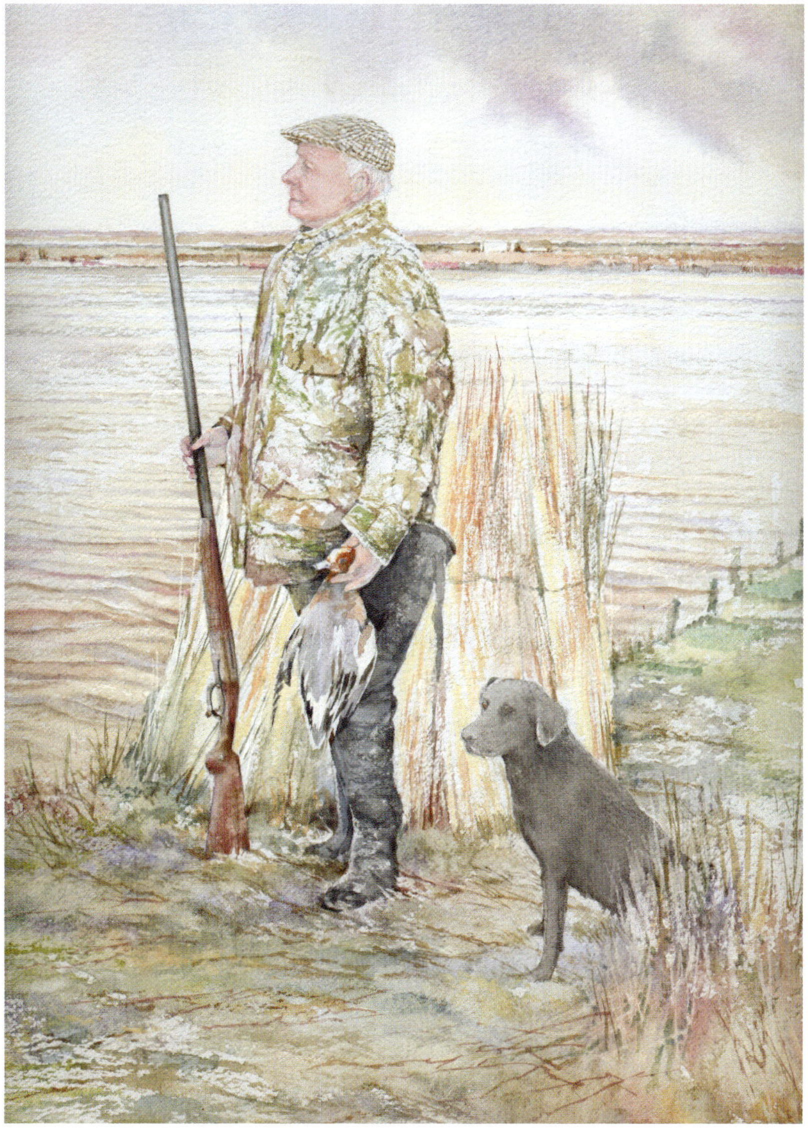

Flight Time Memories: The Wildfowler
280mm x 310mm

Following the sea bank north from Blakeney village and glancing back over the duck pond The Manor Hotel is the most prominent building in view. It has had a variety of uses including a doctor's surgery and a gentleman's club where airmen from the nearby Langham Field would spend their precious wartime evenings. Brent Pope recalled one such evening when a near disaster occurred. The visitors in the bar, on smelling smoke clambered to the top floor rooms where one of the doors was jammed closed. On eventually breaking in they were astonished to find an unexploded parachute bomb hanging where it had landed. Three year old Brent was rudely awakened from the room below and evacuated to a friendly neighbour who produced a diversionary liqueur chocolate.

"I can still see the green shiny wrapper on that chocolate as if it were today," recalled Brent, even though it was almost seventy years ago.

Another frightening experience took place in Blakeney harbour when young Brent was taken on an excursion by flat-bottomed mussel boat. On returning they became the target of a Messerschmitt Me109. A hail of bullets passed straight through the boat missing the occupants. Unfortunately at the time, the Ack Ack duty officer by the harbour was apparently chatting to girls, allowing the enemy to roar back out to sea without one shot of retaliation being fired. A grim accident that did occur in Blakeney involved an old punt gunner who found himself with an unfired shell jammed in the breach of his punt gun. Using a rowlock he tried to prize the shell free, which caused it to explode, severing his arm and pitting his face with blue powder.

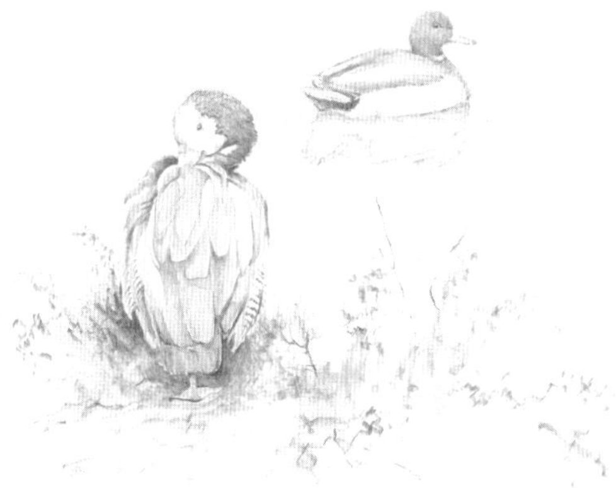

Ducks, Pencil Study
200mm x 170mm

Another inimitable character, born at Blakeney in March 1934 is Colin Cobon, 'Cobo', who has been chief duck breeder and feeder at the Blakeney waterfowl collection since its founding in 1977. Created by The Blakeney and District Wildfowlers' Association as a Queen's Silver Jubilee Year celebration, the collection is acknowledged as a fine example of conservation work, in addition to providing an excellent focal point and educational facility for visitors.

There are now in excess of fifty species in the collection, including the once endangered Asian Teal, originating from The Philippines, which by 1957 had dwindled to fourteen individuals in the world.

Five freshwater springs flow into the original 'hoss pond', an area where horses from nearby Manor Farm would be led to drink. Colin and his friends would skate on the old pond, always avoiding the area of thin ice where the springs emerge and where in the depths of winter, steam can still be seen to rise.

Final preparations for the grand Jubilee Day opening were hectic, having involved the rather delicate removal of all manner of live armaments ranging from 303 rifle clips to hand grenades which had been dumped in the old pond by the departing military!

As Colin recalled, "We worked like stink to get it finished on time!"

This included the safe release of the first four residents; pairs of wigeon and barnacle geese, the latter which came from Bob Cooke at Salthouse. When remembering 7th June 1977, Colin's face fell.

"It blew all day from the east, poured with rain and not one visitor looked over the bank to admire our efforts!"

Needless to say, with the constant dedication of Mr Cobon and his fellow club members, the wildfowl collection at Blakeney has since given a great deal of joy to visitors. It always makes me laugh to see 'Dirk' Dewson dressed in his duck suit prior to the grand summer duck race, and to enjoy charity events in The Harbour Room or by the pond when funds are raised for the wildfowl collection. Like most wildfowlers, Cobo is a knowledgeable and passionate conservationist, having also cared for the nearby fresh marshes at Wiveton Hall for over 30 years.

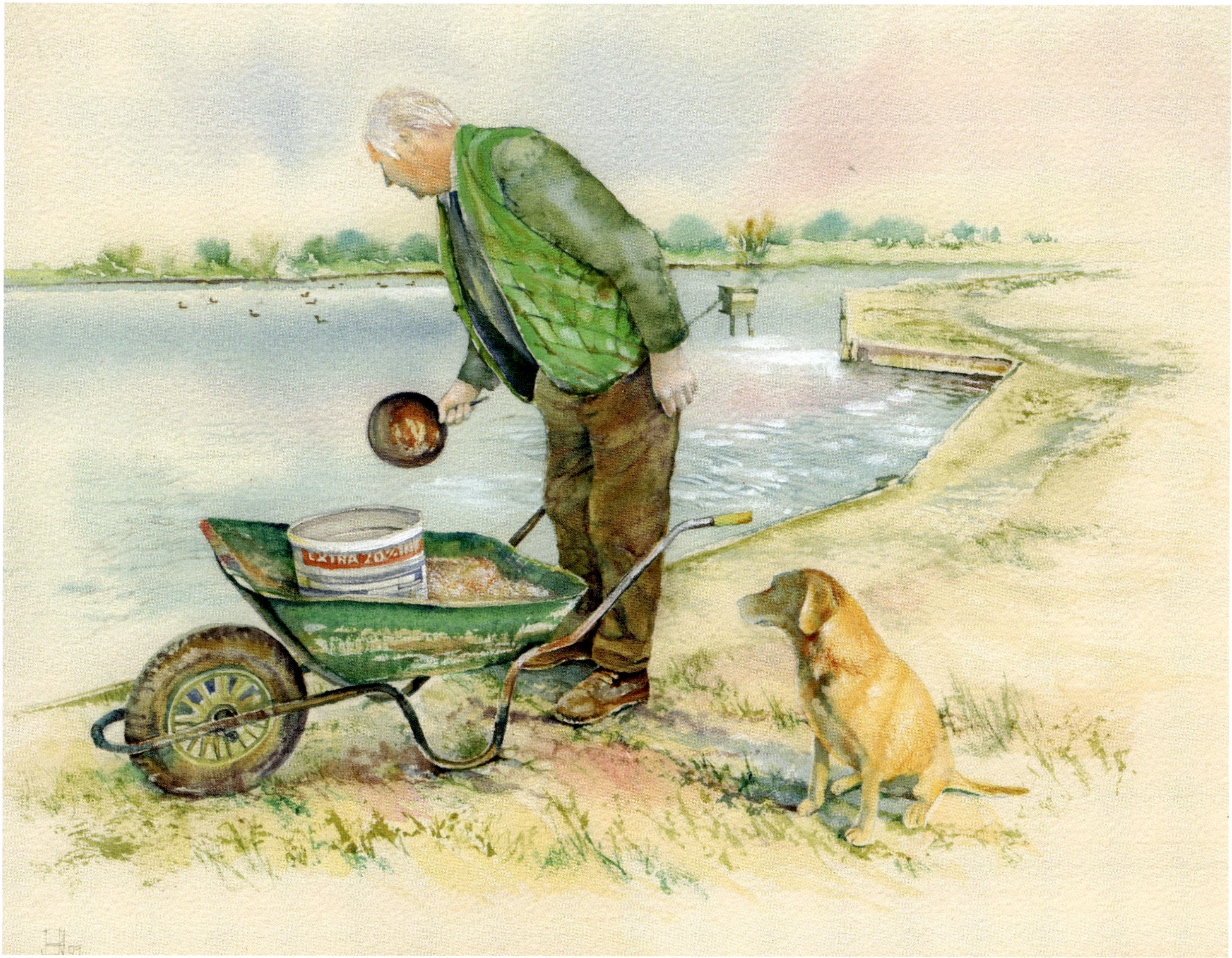

Cobo: The Keeper of Ducks

BETWEEN SEA AND SKY

Salthouse

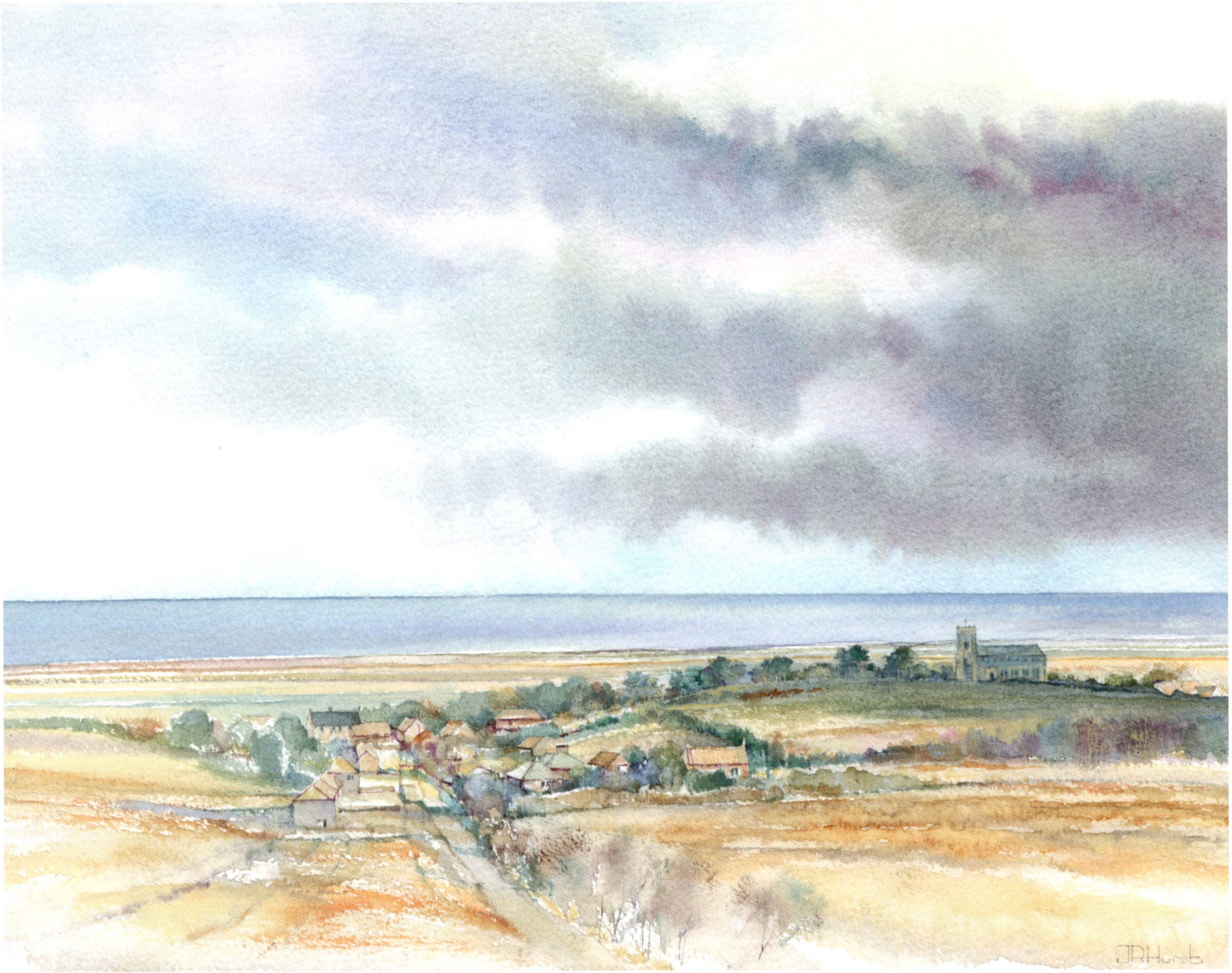

Big Sky, Salthouse
300mm x 270mm

I was led along a maze of paths through newly emerging bracken fronds to a secret heathland location to find the almost mythical May lily. The colony is thriving and was in full flower during mid May. *Maianthemum bifolium* or false lily of the valley is a native of Western Europe, east to Siberia, China and Japan. The white star-shaped flowers are formed on a stem that rarely grows taller than twenty centimetres. This painting was completed with some discomfort as from under the leaf litter a nest full of angry ants erupted in activity.

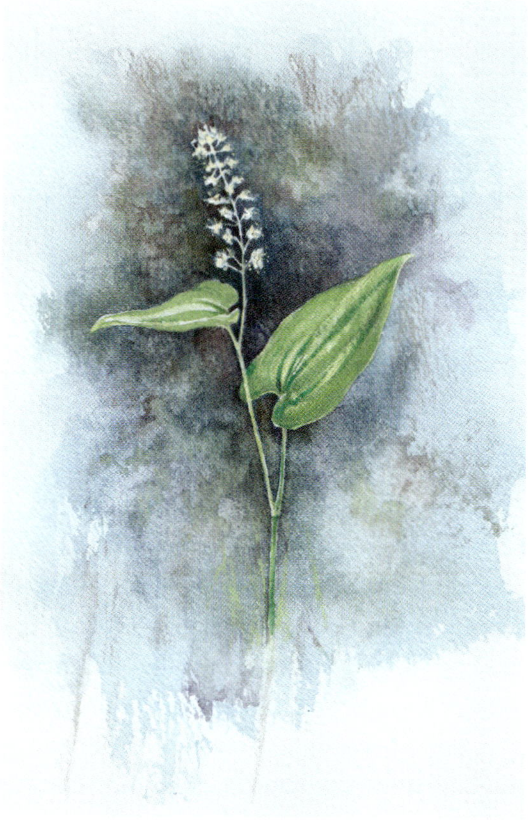

In The Shadows, May Lily
120mm x 170mm

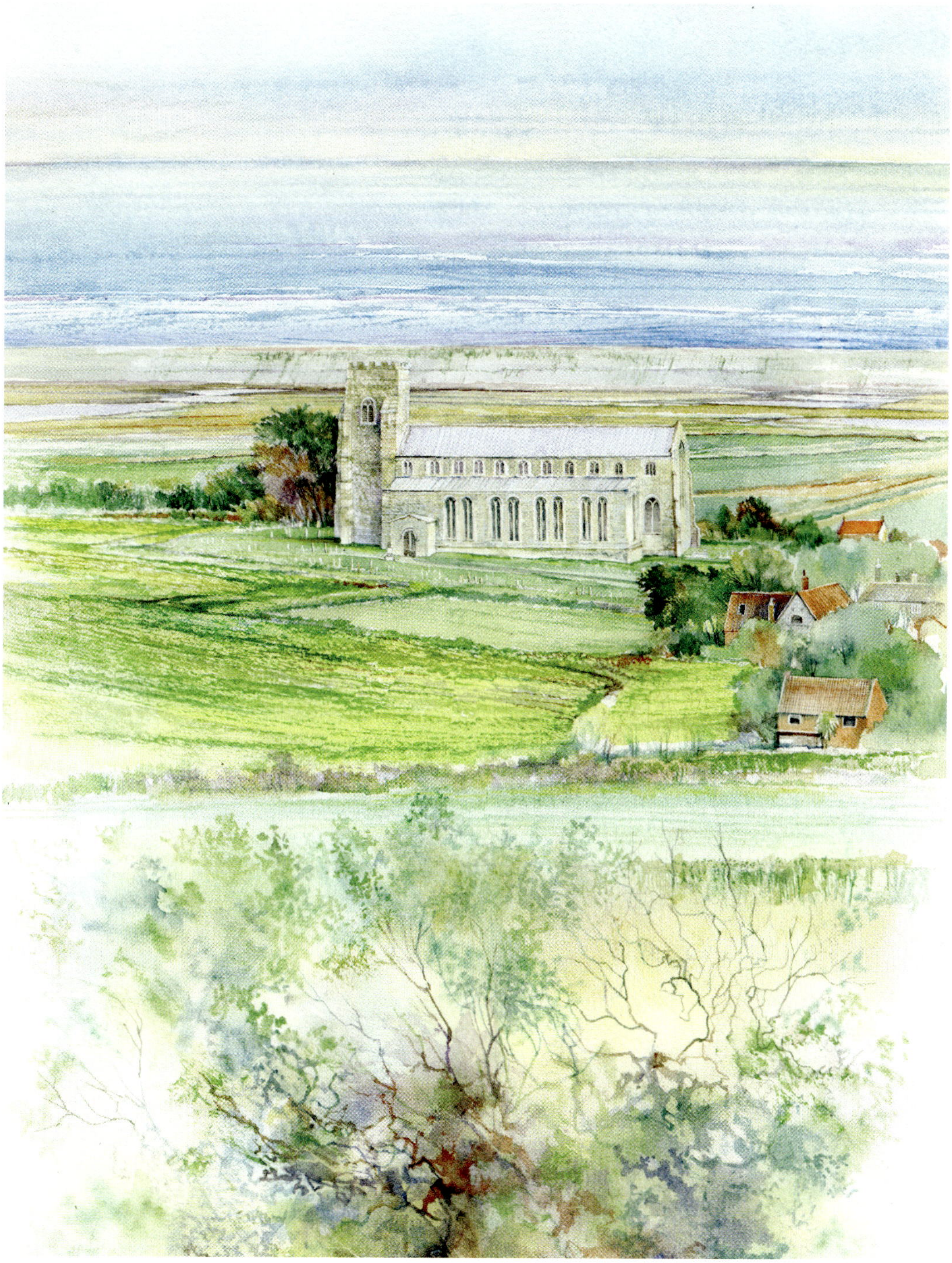

A View from the Heath, Salthouse
310mm x 500mm

Cattle, which graze on Cley and Salthouse marshes in summer, play a very important role in the management of the freshwater habitat. They crop the lush sward and create invertebrate-rich feeding conditions for waders as their dung is incorporated into the soil. Andrew Gray is the farmer responsible for grazing the marshes between the shingle ridge and coast road north of Salthouse in a designated Area of Outstanding Natural Beauty. This brings the added responsibility of High Level Stewardship as dictated by Natural England in which grants are awarded to land-owners and tenants who farm with consideration for the environment. In this case the grazing marshes and ditches support a regionally important breeding population of lapwing, redshank and avocet with many other wetland species using the area as a migration staging post.

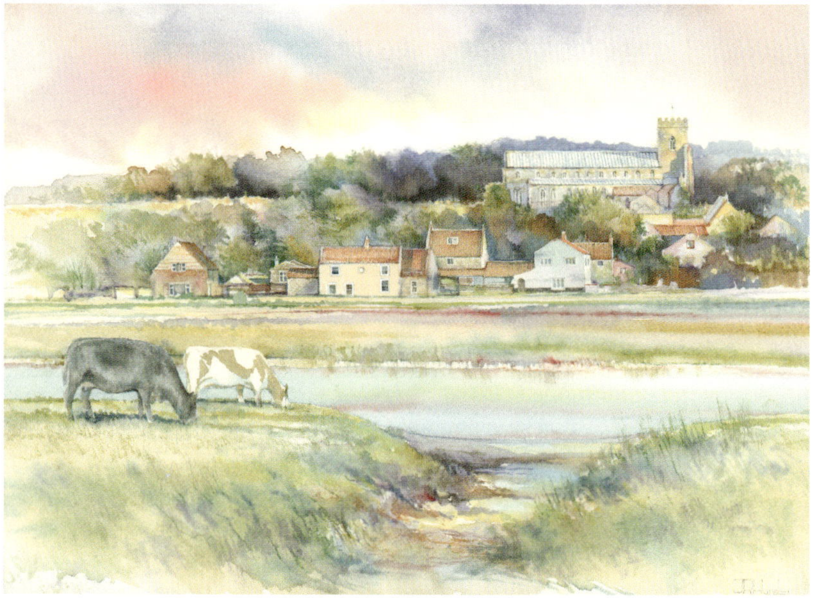

Salthouse, Grazing Cattle
300mm x 250mm

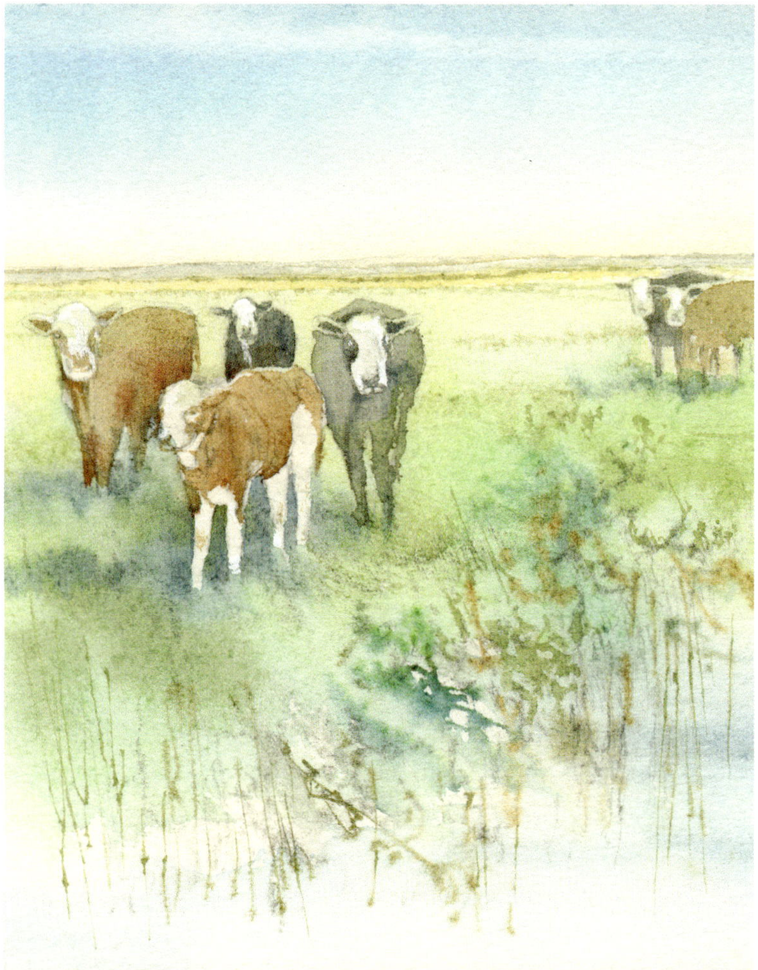

Beasts by the Crick
160mm x 130mm

Andrew currently grazes two bulls and seventy-five Simmental hybrid cows with attendant calves, all of which move from their sheltered winter quarters to the marsh in May. Originally from Switzerland, the Simmental is an outstanding suckler cow and noted for its ability to milk calves to weaning off grass. It is a wonderful occasion at this time of year for when liberated on to pasture, both young and old seem to leap and frolic with joy.

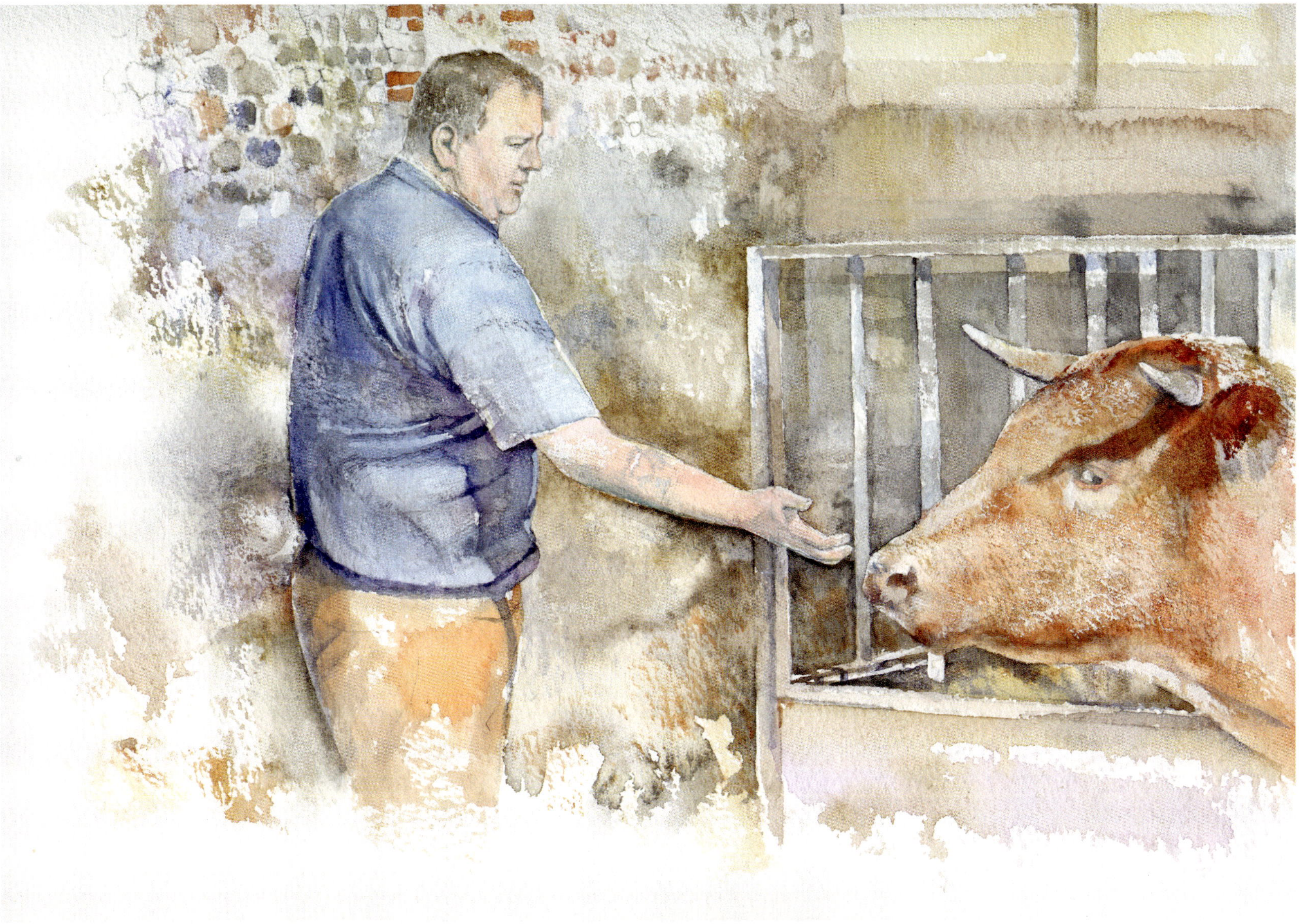

Andrew Gray
300mm x 220mm

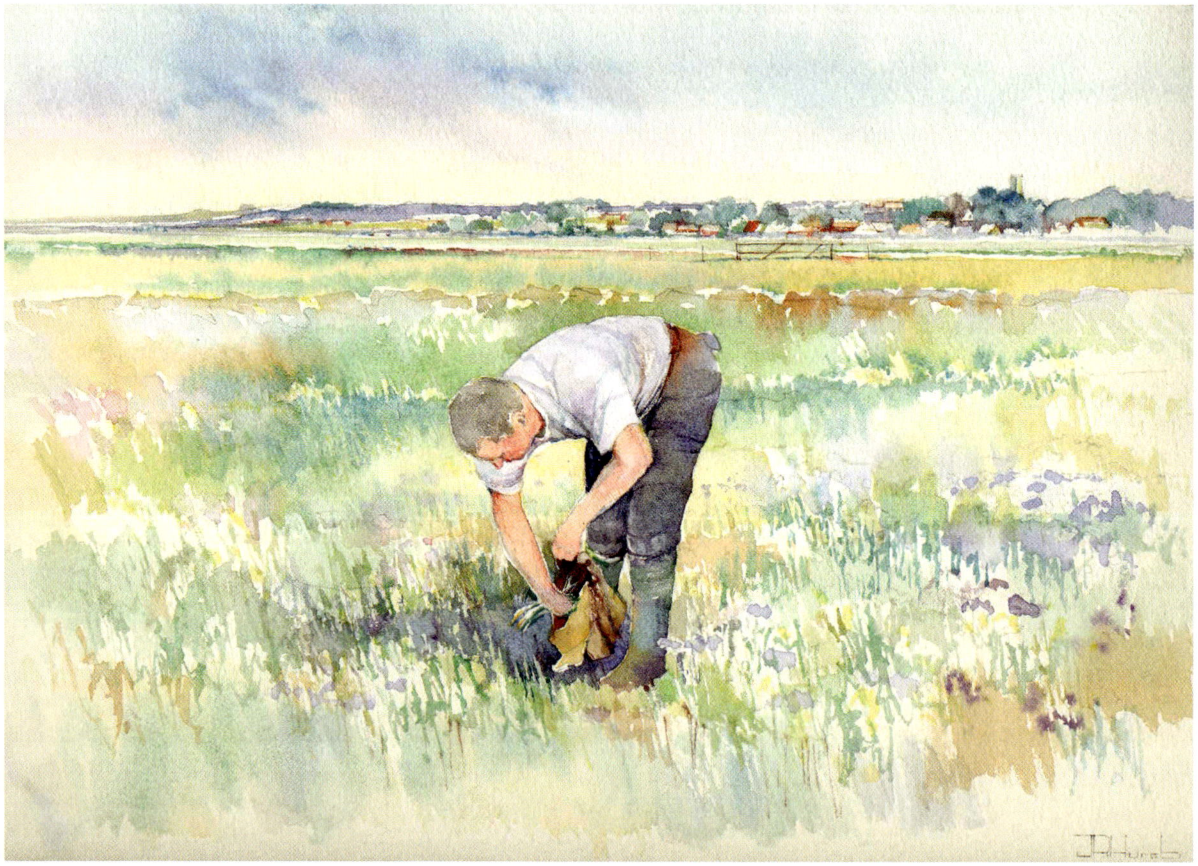

The Samphire Harvest
300mm x 220mm

Samphire is gathered annually on the Salthouse marshes by my friend Clifford, in much the same way as his family has done for several generations. In order to complete my colour studies he kindly took me out in his Land Rover one hot evening in June, and after negotiating our way across the marsh I found myself helping him to fill his gaping sack with this unusual saline succulent. Made famous by numerous TV chefs for its culinary properties, samphire or glasswort, a member of the *salicornia* family, was primarily known as a plant for industrial use. The common name, glasswort came into use during the sixteenth century when it was found that the ashes of the plant have high soda content, namely sodium carbonate. This is an important ingredient in glass and soap making, its use reaching England by immigrant Venetian glassmakers, famed for their 'cristallo' or very clear glass that uses soda ash as a flux. Prior to this time it was said that the plant "Hath no name in English." Lightly steamed for a few minutes and served with vinegar or a slice of lemon, this 'sea vegetable' is a wonderful seasonal dish. Samphire is an annual and as such requires seeding plants to sustain growth. Due to its popularity and commercial value, some local people are of the opinion that regulation may have to be introduced in the future to preserve stocks and minimise disturbance to the fragile Norfolk saltings.

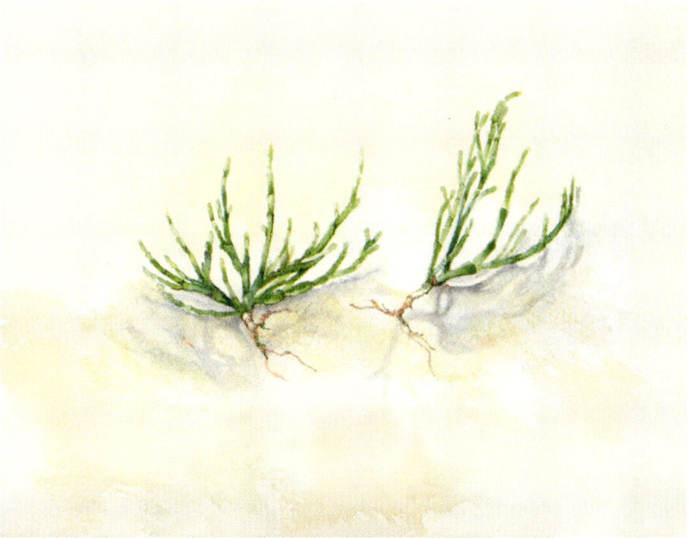

Marsh Samphire
Sketchbook Study
290mm x 190mm

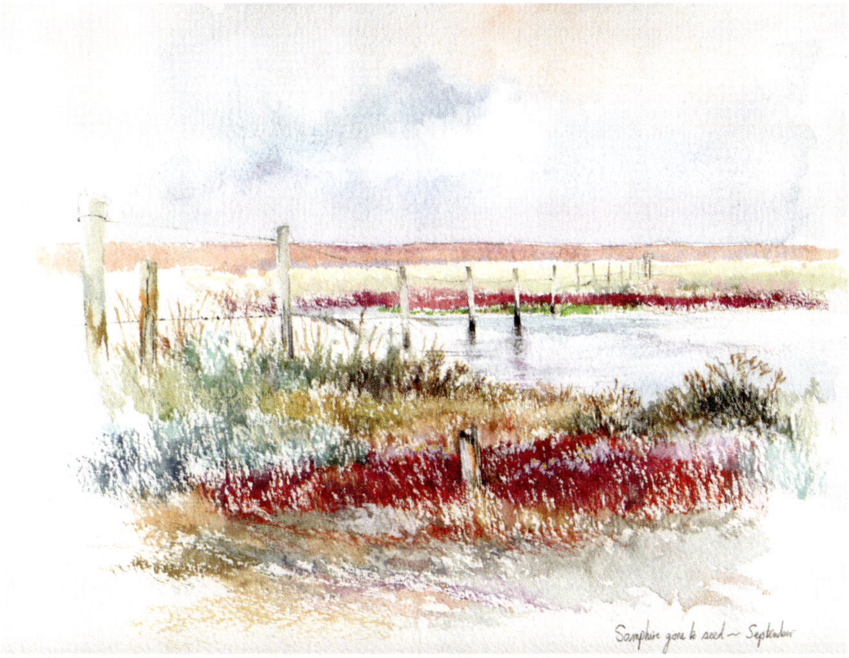

Seeding Samphire
Sketchbook Study
300mm x 230mm

HOUSES, GARDENS, SHEDS AND GAME

As a painter of architectural subjects, I enjoy dragging a semi dry brush over coarse paper in order to create the eroded surfaces of brick, stone and wood. When these surfaces are combined with shadow and the clutter of everyday objects found inside rural buildings, the effect can be stimulating. Not only is the artist able to work with light, shade and form, there is also an opportunity to record social history. By considering the contents of these interiors we are able to interpret local human lifestyles and economic activity.

I have observed the worn stairs of a windmill interior and imagined the countless journeys aloft taken by millers over the years. There was a cellar in my parents' home, complete with red brick gantry on which stood the meat safe and anything that needed chilling during the summer months. The steps leading down to this cool, whitewashed larder were worn at the same angle as my father's shoes, a testimony to the way in which we almost become shaped by the environment in which we live.

I was looking for an old crab fisherman and stumbled upon a museum that had evolved quite naturally. This could be a scene from Staithes or Newlyn a century ago. There were willow baskets stacked on oak planks, marker buoys leaning at precarious angles and a heap of crab pots filtering afternoon light which cascaded through a broken window pane. Rusty iron anchors hung from the rafters like meat hooks in an old butcher's shop. Everything looked homemade; reminding one of the reliance by the community upon each village craftsman. Looking around, I could see the evidence of other visitors. As in so many interiors, the delicate mud castle built by a swallow balanced on a nail in the wall caught my attention, as did the wren's secret parlour hidden snugly in an old sack. I have seen the nest of this mouse-like bird built in an old coat, cartwheel and once, quite bizarrely in a human skull!

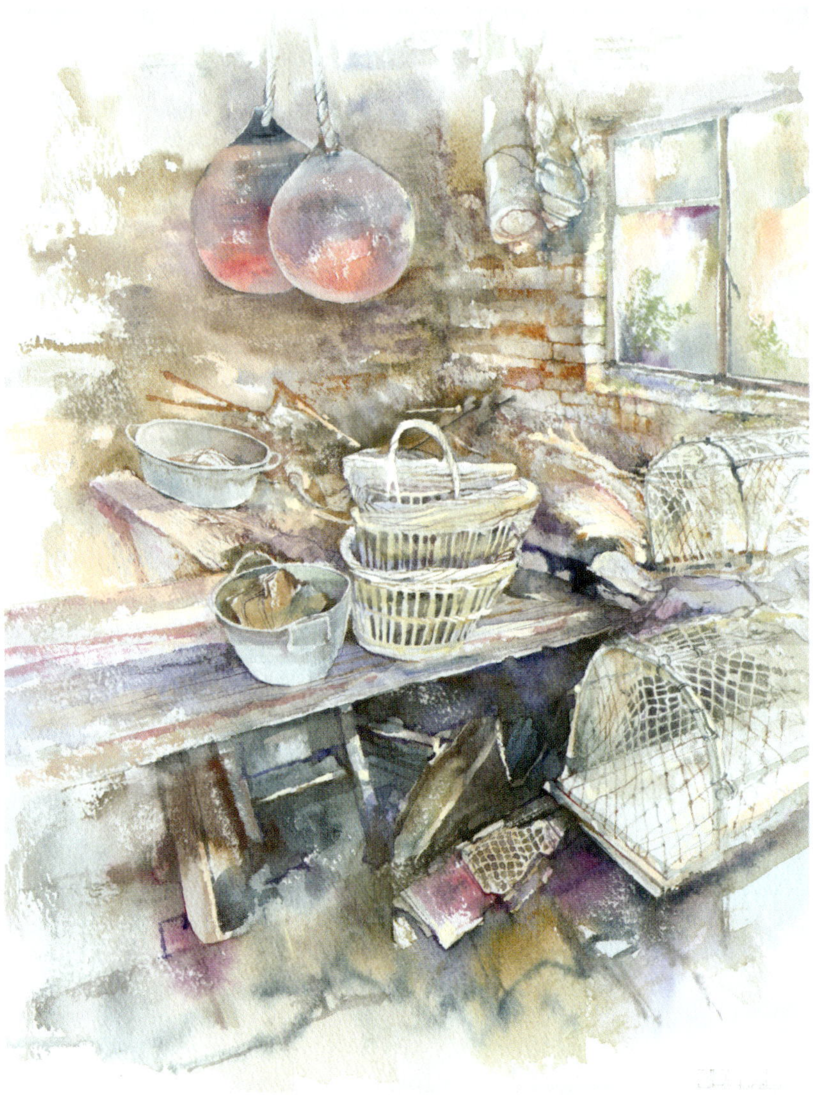

Old Crab Shed, Salthouse
320mm x 400mm

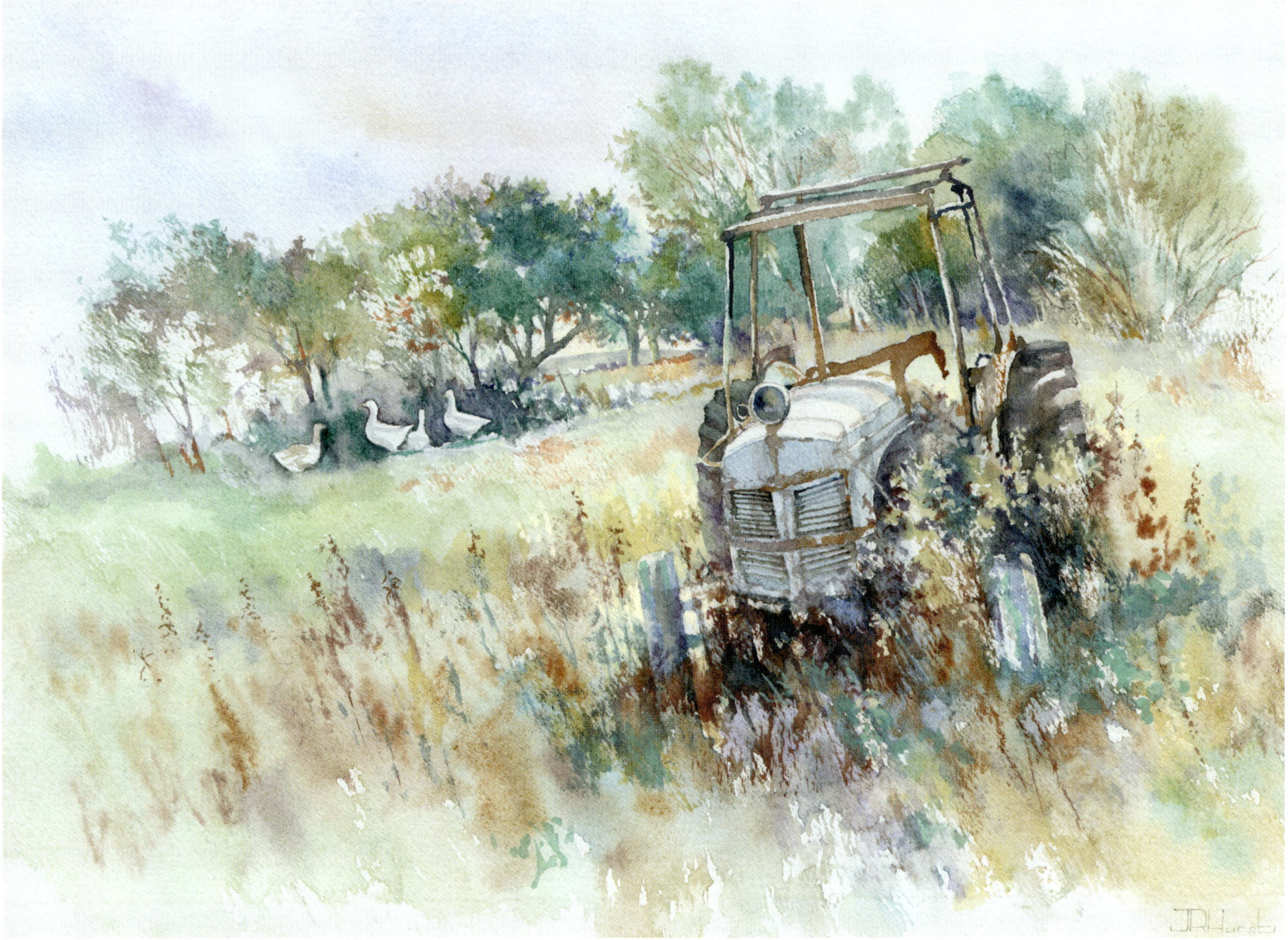

Fergie's Rest

My father owned a grey Ferguson tractor, using it for all manner of operations from basic cultivating to pulling out tree stumps. I found this one in an old Norfolk orchard and was captivated by nature's attempt at reclaiming the space where it lay. Nettles and brambles wove their way through rusting metal as they struggled towards the low afternoon light. How did this treasure finally end its days? Did it slowly fall apart or just abruptly stop in its tracks?

Mr Fox lives in a Norfolk flint cottage and like me, is an incomer from over the border, originating from the fens near Spalding. He retired to the Norfolk coast with his wife Lorna in 1978, inheriting their flint cottage from the Hancock family. It had been passed down through several generations. Tom had farmed approximately four hundred acres in the fens prior to retirement yet started from humble beginnings. His life changed in 1937 when as a nineteen year old he overheard his father talking to a farmhand about the thrill of horse racing. Taking his life savings of three pounds he cycled the ten miles to Wisbech, placed one pound each way on 'Chulmleigh' and ten shillings each way on 'Fair Copy'. At twenty-five to one and seven to two respectively these fine horses galloped to victory with first and second places in the St Ledger Stakes. The young Tom took his princely winnings of forty pounds and paid the rent on ten acres of overgrown orchard near his home. He grew mustard for Coleman's of Norwich and eventually bought the land.

"That's the only help I had," said Tom, "I'm self made."

This charming house is typical of so many cottages built in Norfolk coastal villages, being of flint, brick and pantile, with adjacent cottage garden that seems to be an integral part of the immediate landscape. Riotous hollyhocks, ceanothus, rose of Sharon, weigela and mahonia complement the deep yellows of heathland gorse and blue roadside scabious. The rear garden produces all things edible and the windowsills are lined with self-grown geraniums. Mr Fox is proud of his achievement in the field and garden, all with a little help from 'Chulmleigh'!

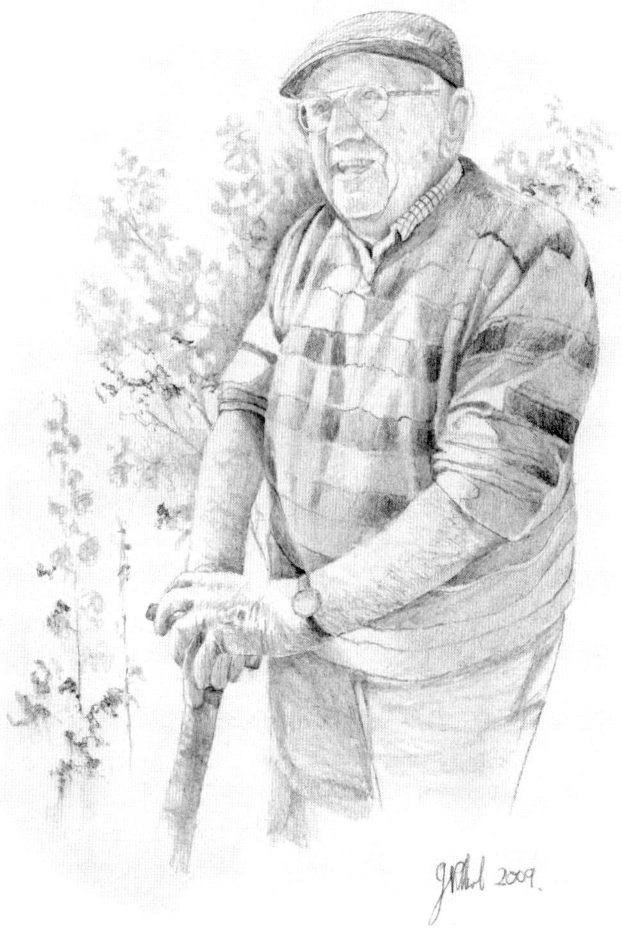

Mr Tom Fox
Pencil Study

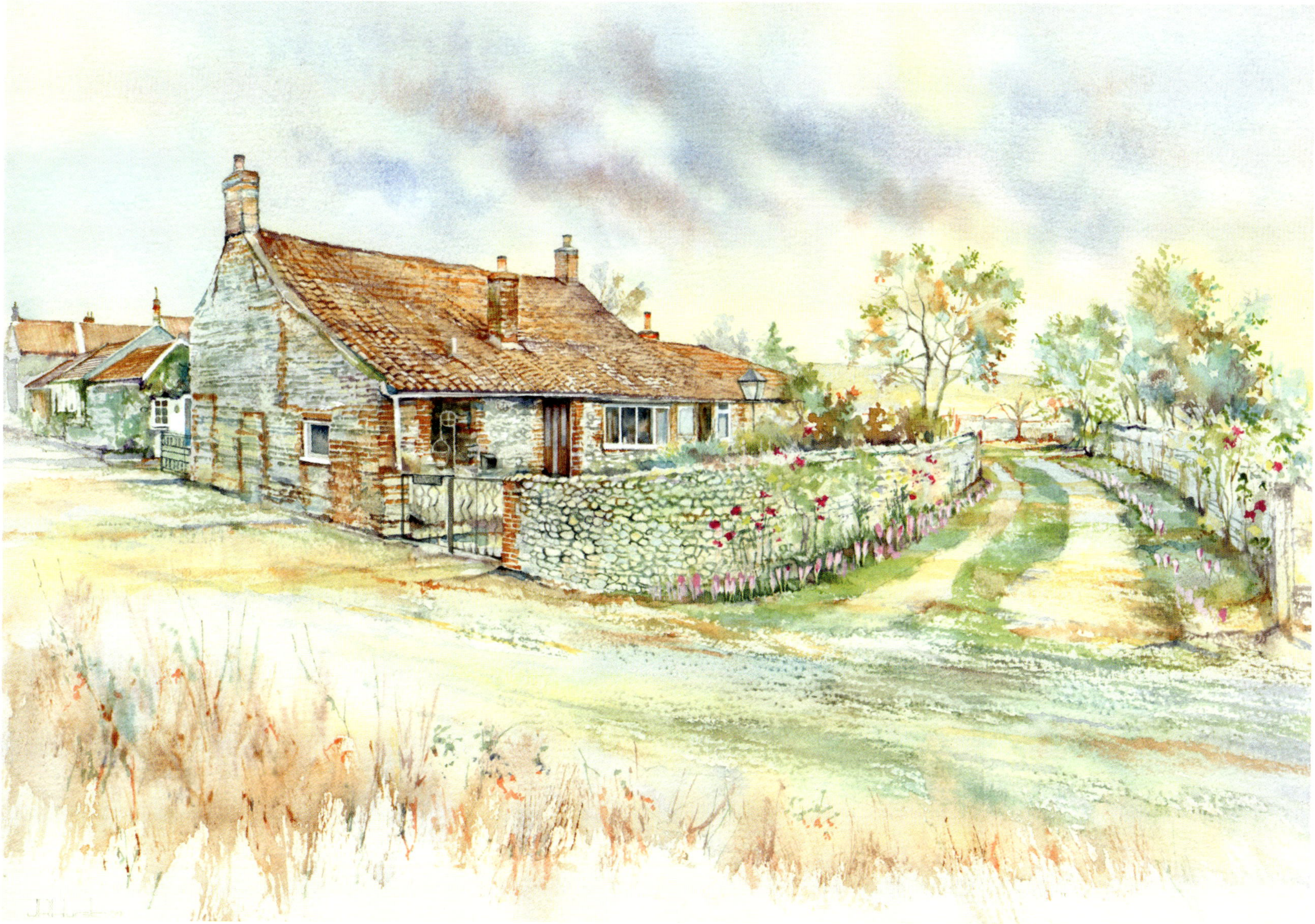

Tom Fox's House
400mm x 230mm

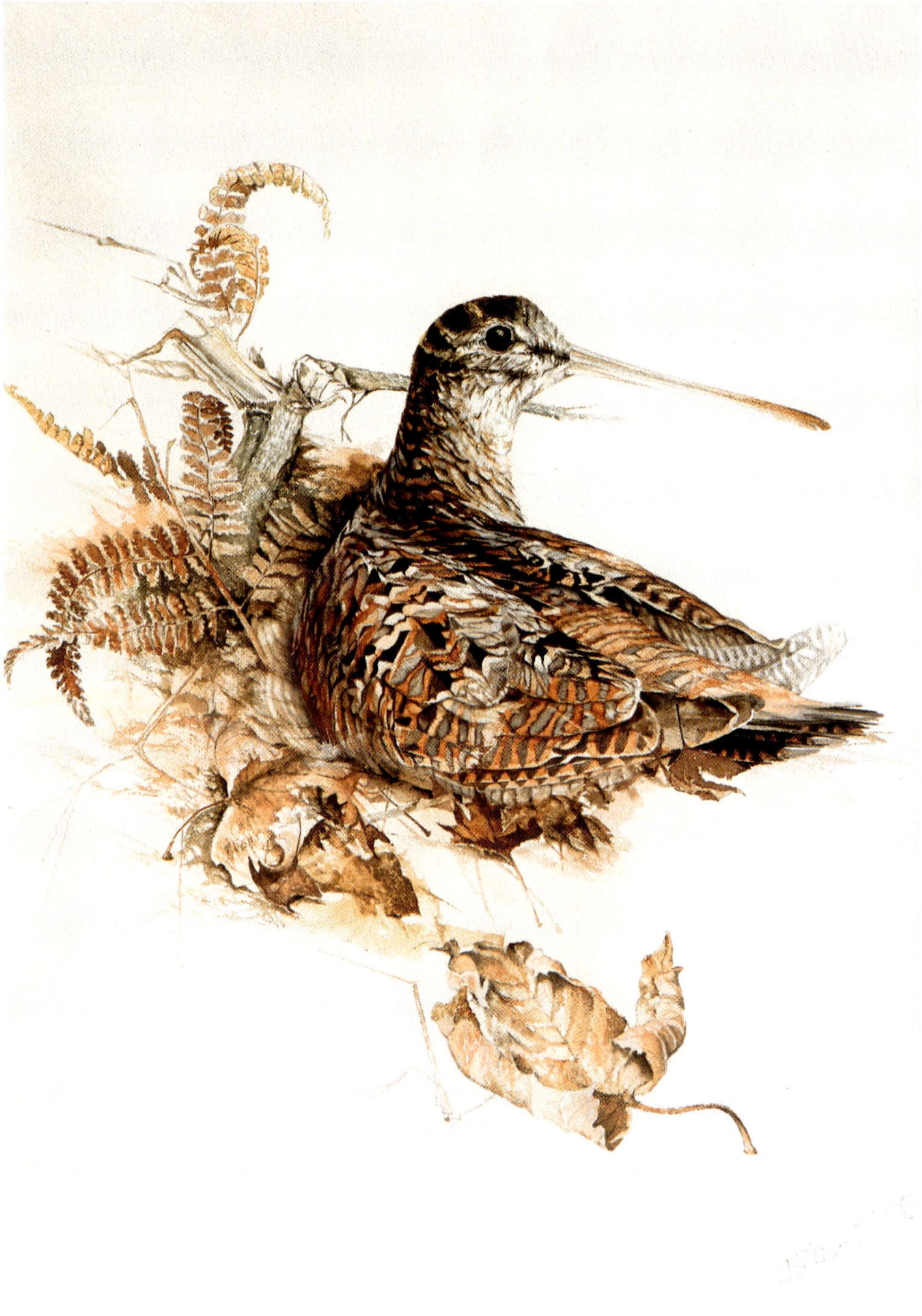

Woodcock Plumage Study, 1972
240mm x 320mm

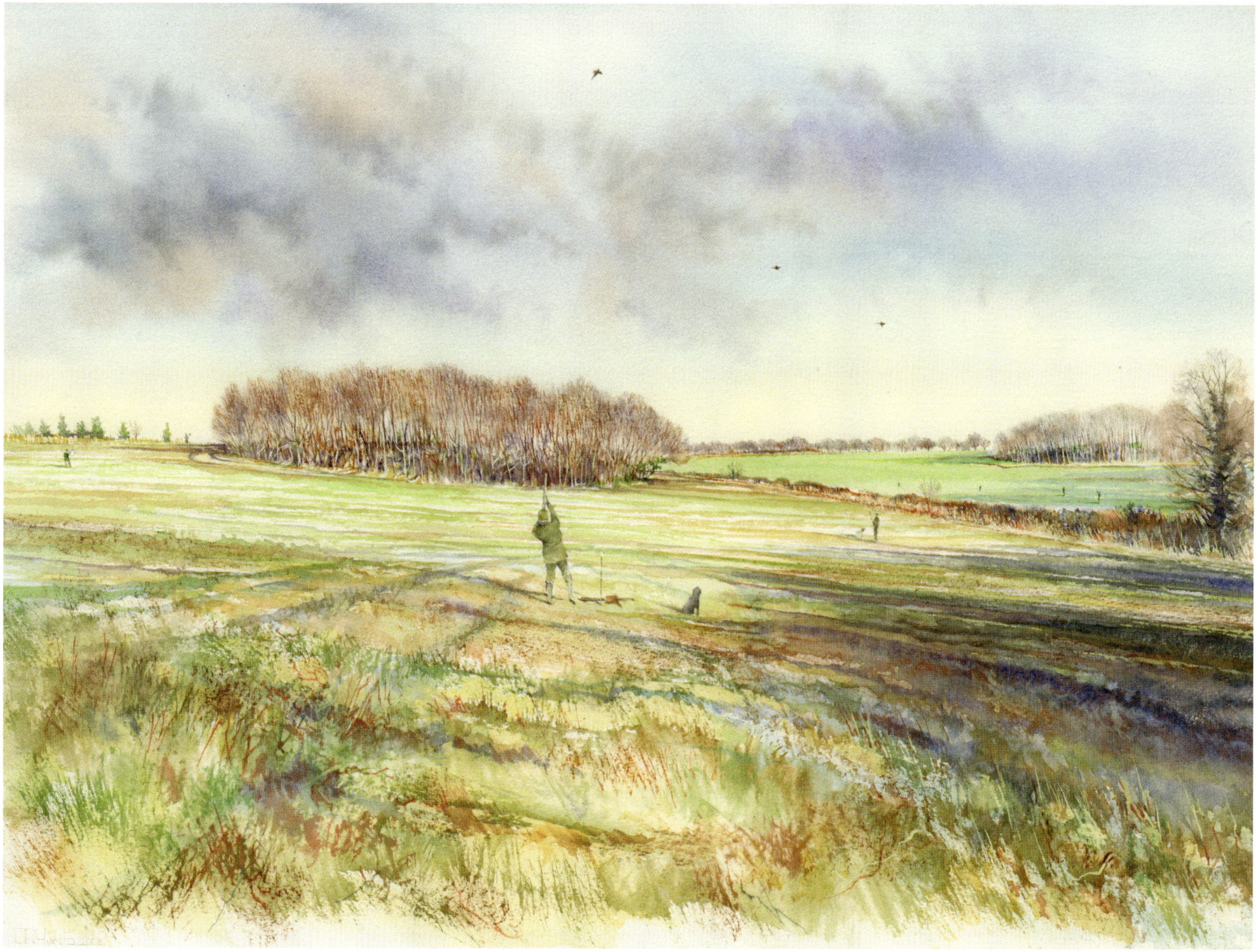

High Pheasants
570mm x 430mm

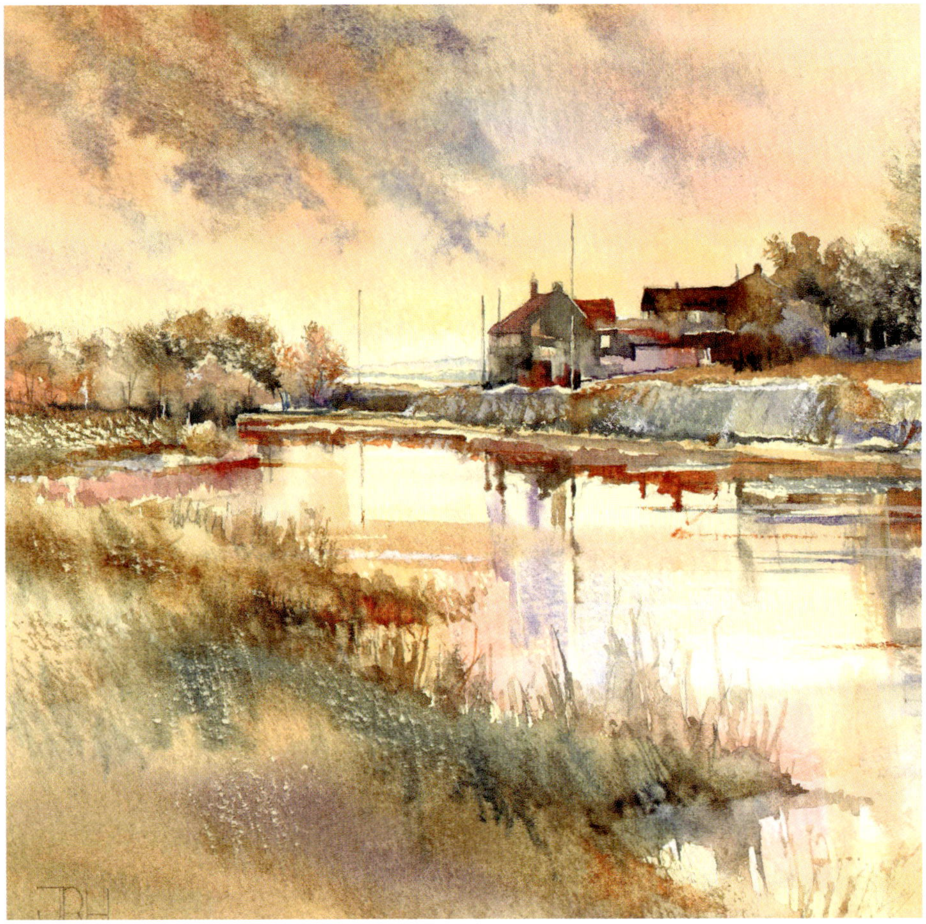

Evening Draws Near, Salthouse
Watercolour and Gouache
200mm x 200mm

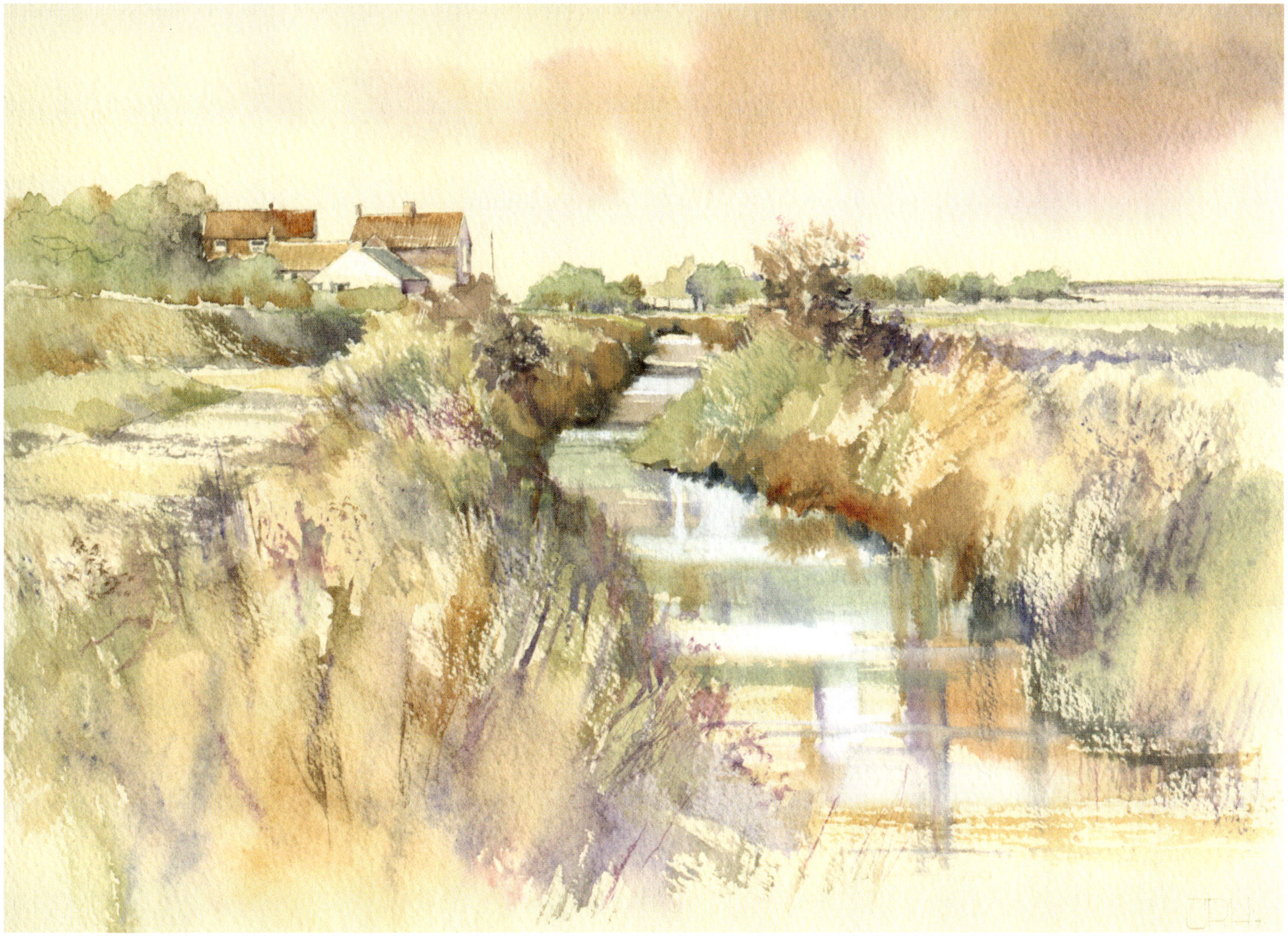

Meadow Lane
Watercolour and Gouache
340mm x 250mm

Walking east from Friday's Barn at the end of Beach Road, Salthouse you will find a lane that forks to the left away from the A149 coast road as it winds its way to Kelling. Known as Meadow Lane and running alongside the Catchwater Drain, this rutted track separates two distinct environments united only by simple bridges. Inland there are rolling fields of marl and flint deposited by the last Ice Age, whilst on the seaward side, known as The Skirts, East Marsh or Salthouse Common are the grazing marshes, not yet engulfed by a sea of encroaching shingle. By the lane it is possible to find an ancient flint wall encrusted with a mosaic of vivid yellow lichens. This is believed to be the old Salthouse quay, a remnant of the time when seagoing vessels could navigate what is now a barely discernible channel of silt. Meadow Lane eventually meets Kelling water meadows and here, sheltered from easterlies by Muckleborough Hill and constantly replenished by water from Kelling Beck, a shallow basin of fresh water known locally as The Quag has formed. Emerging insects in spring and the shallow pool margins entice newly arrived migrant birds to feed and rest here. Scarcer species such as little gull, spotted crake and black tern have all been observed recently on this quiet backwater.

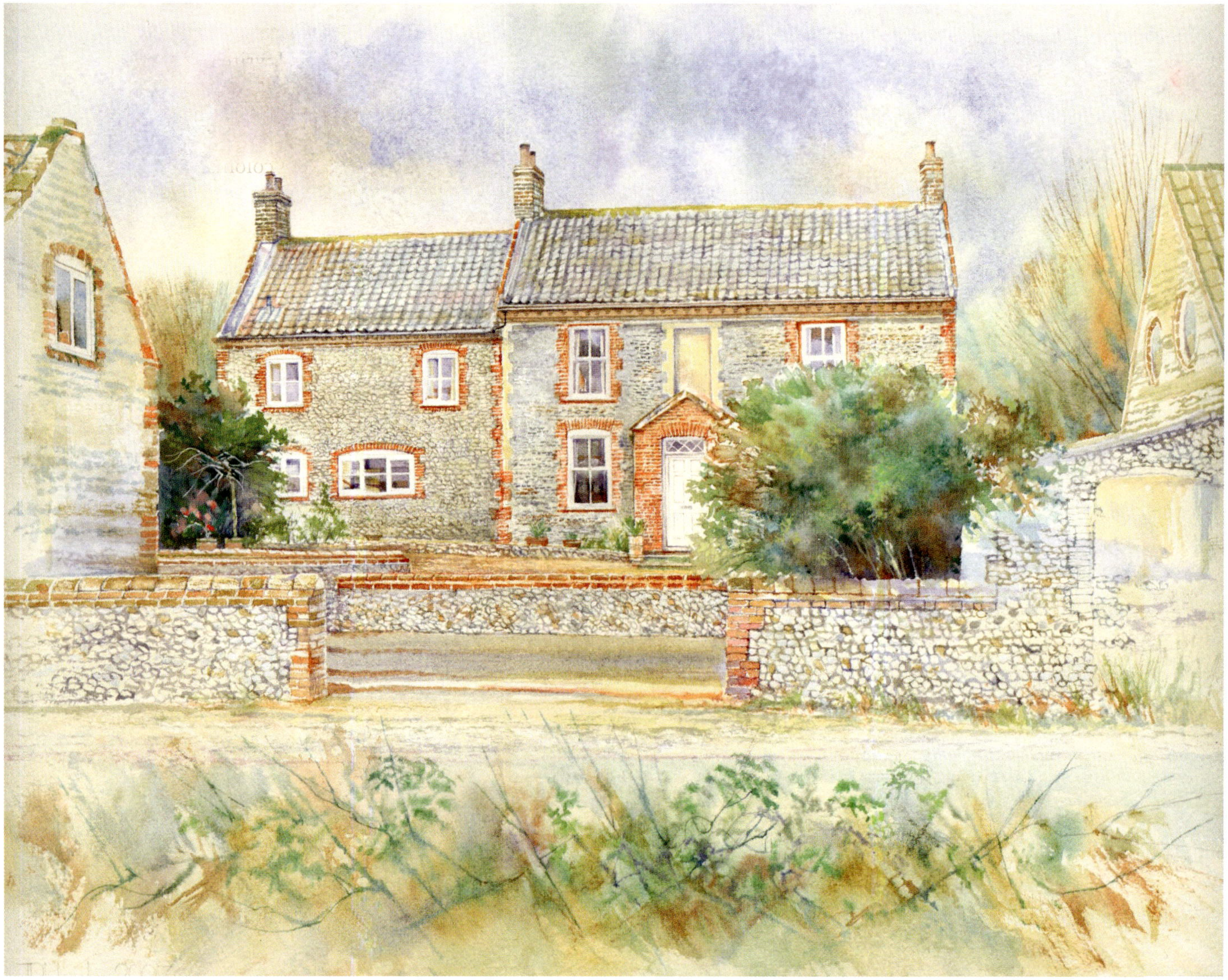

A Norfolk Farmhouse
370mm x 290mm

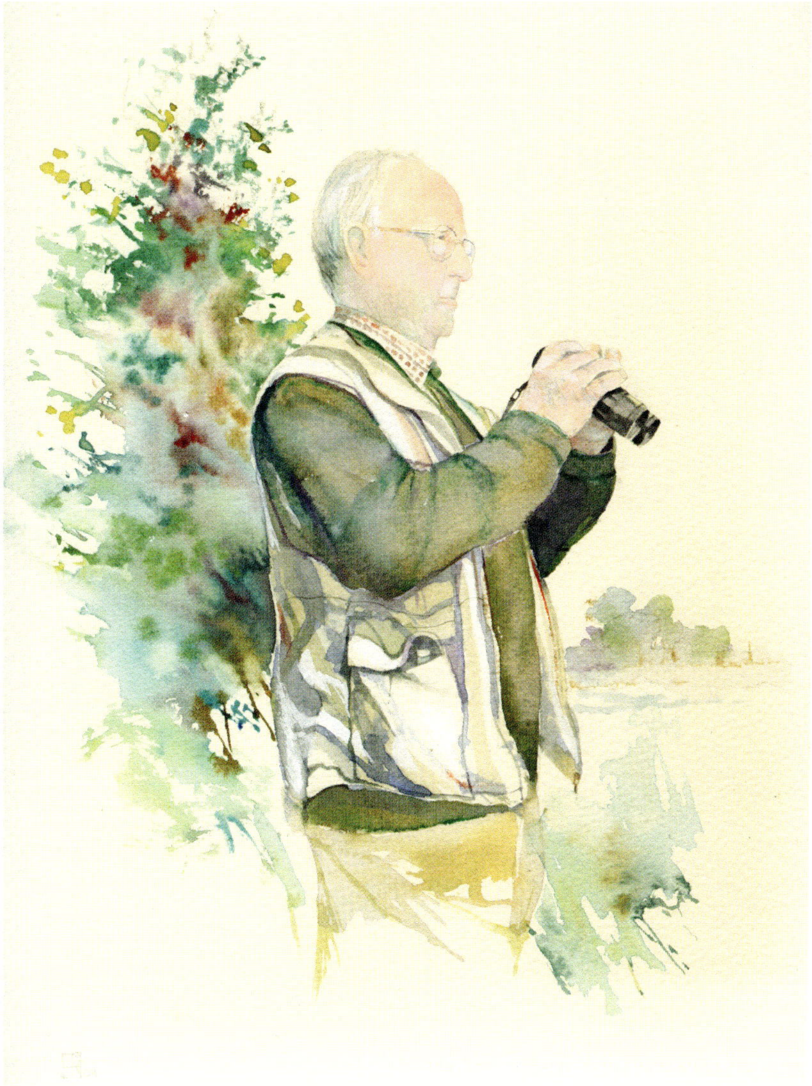

It is highly likely that you will encounter John Wagstaff on Kelling Heath or by 'The Quag', for as I write he spends countless hours at both sites whilst watching wildlife. I first met this quietly spoken naturalist one day in early spring when trying unsuccessfully to locate one of the few Dartford warblers that are slowly colonising these eastern heaths. In his unofficial capacity as 'fountain of knowledge', John knew of a territory and I was soon observing a male warbler as it dashed across the gorse beds. My host pointed out an intriguing relationship between Dartford warbler and the resident stonechats that seem to cohabit one area without conflict. Apparently, the latter has a habit of exposed perching and acts as an early warning system for the more skulking, easily predated warbler. Basking adders, crossbills in the pines and woodlark on sandy heath were all on John's agenda that spring day; not that I managed to see any of them!

John Wagstaff
215mm x 295mm

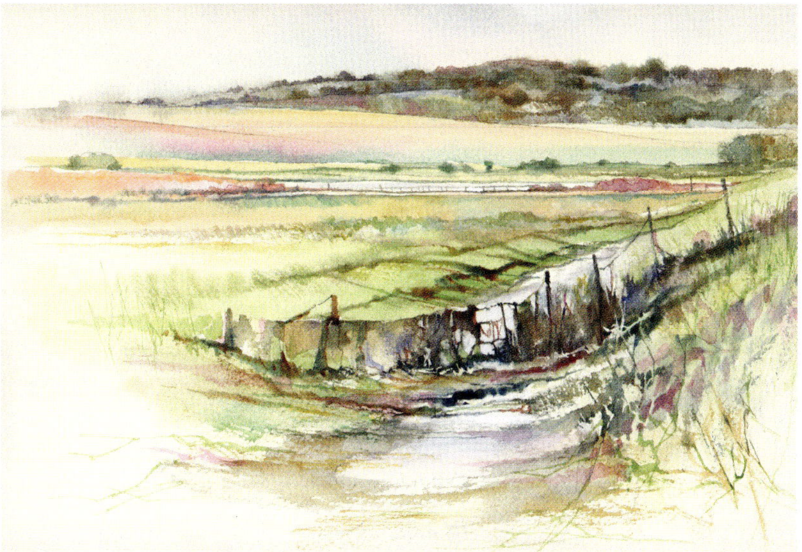

After the Flood at Kelling Quags
340mm x 250mm

KELLING
A Year on the Estate

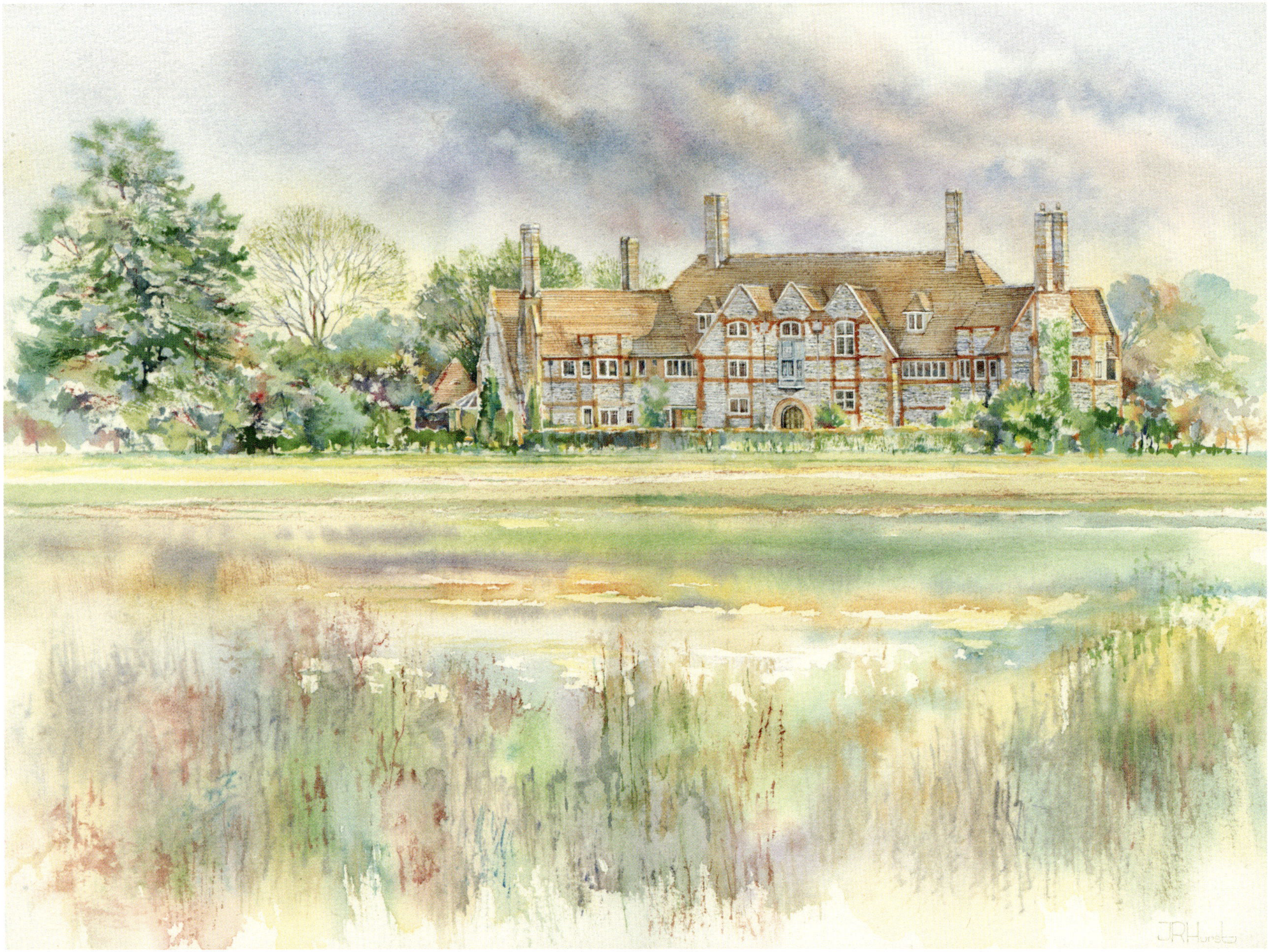

Kelling Hall

Our journey takes us to the beautiful estate at Kelling, overlooking the sea and dissected by a glacial valley, the centrepiece of which is the hall. It was the first commission for the architect Sir Edward Maufe for Sir Henry Deterding, one of the founders of the Royal Dutch Petroleum Company. Completed in 1913 the elegant symmetry of Kelling Hall like nearby Voewood, is architecturally known as a 'butterfly house'. I painted this watercolour from the west, choosing morning light to emphasise the Arts and Crafts chimneys, gables and beautifully proportioned brickwork. My patron, Mrs Shirley Deterding lived here with her husband Jimmy until spring 2009.

AUTHOR'S NOTE: *The following estate studies are all watercolour sketchbook extracts. 260mm x 200mm.*

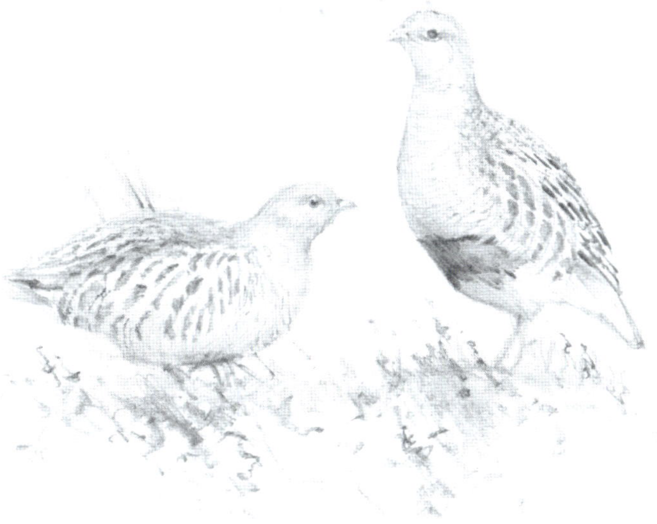

Grey Partridge
Pencil Study
100mm x 80mm

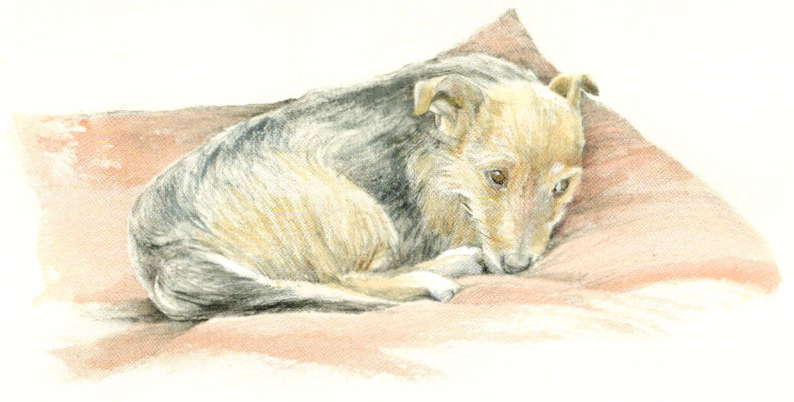

Teasel, Keeping One Eye on Me

My visits to Kelling Hall were always met by a distant clamour as Teasel, a scamp of a terrier, barked her way to the door. Only after being introduced to her on several occasions would she return to her bed and even then would keep a constant eye on me. I once made the mistake of asking my host, "So, she's a house dog then?"

"No!" retorted Mr Deterding. "She retrieves, she brings partridges you know."

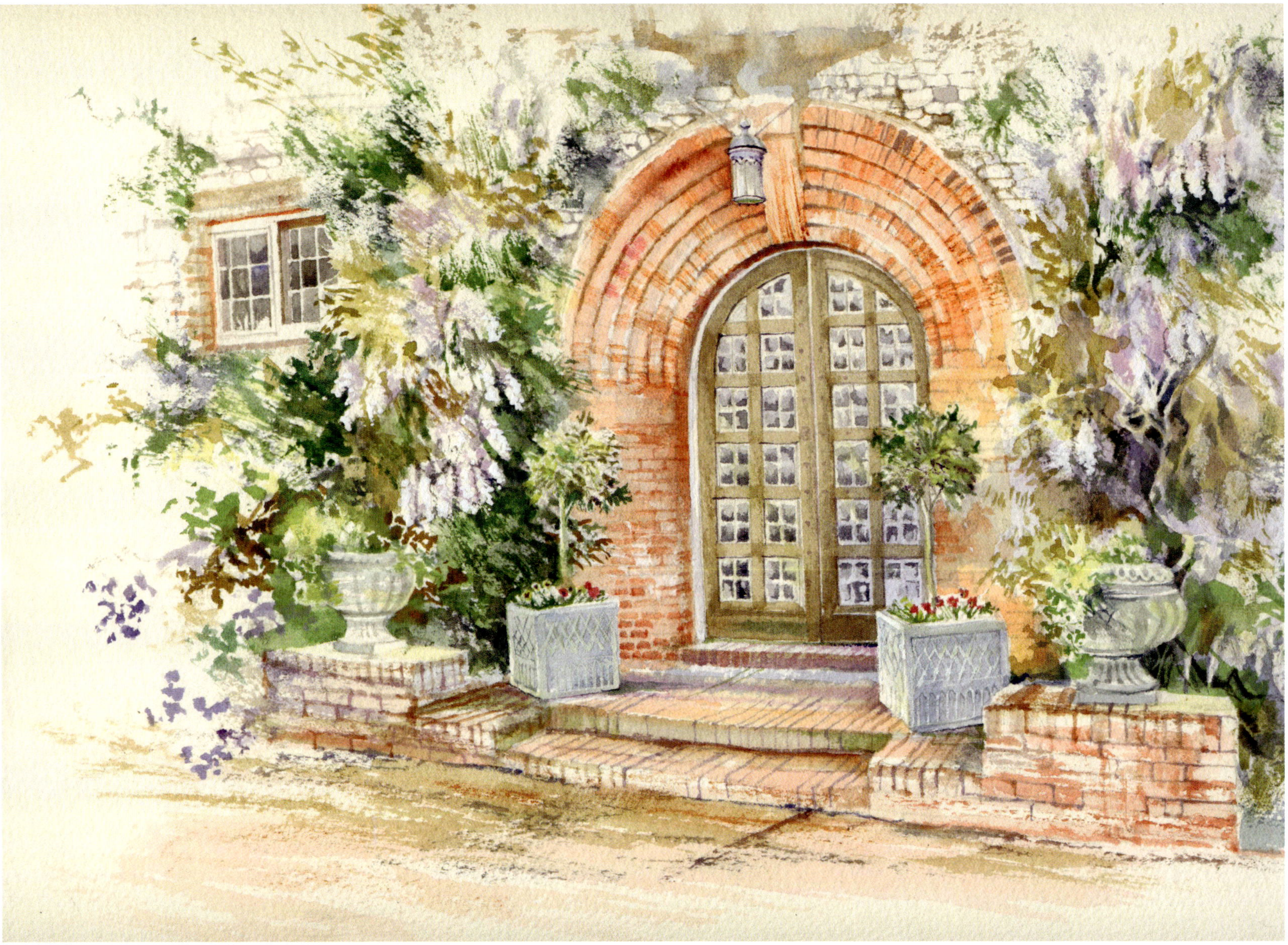

Wisteria and Pansies

I will always remember the grand entrance to Kelling Hall by the cascade of wisteria in spring, the overhanging oriel window, almost medieval in style, and a side door, known as a trunk door through which the luggage of house guests would be transported. It was painted the brightest yellow and the sun always seemed to shine upon it.

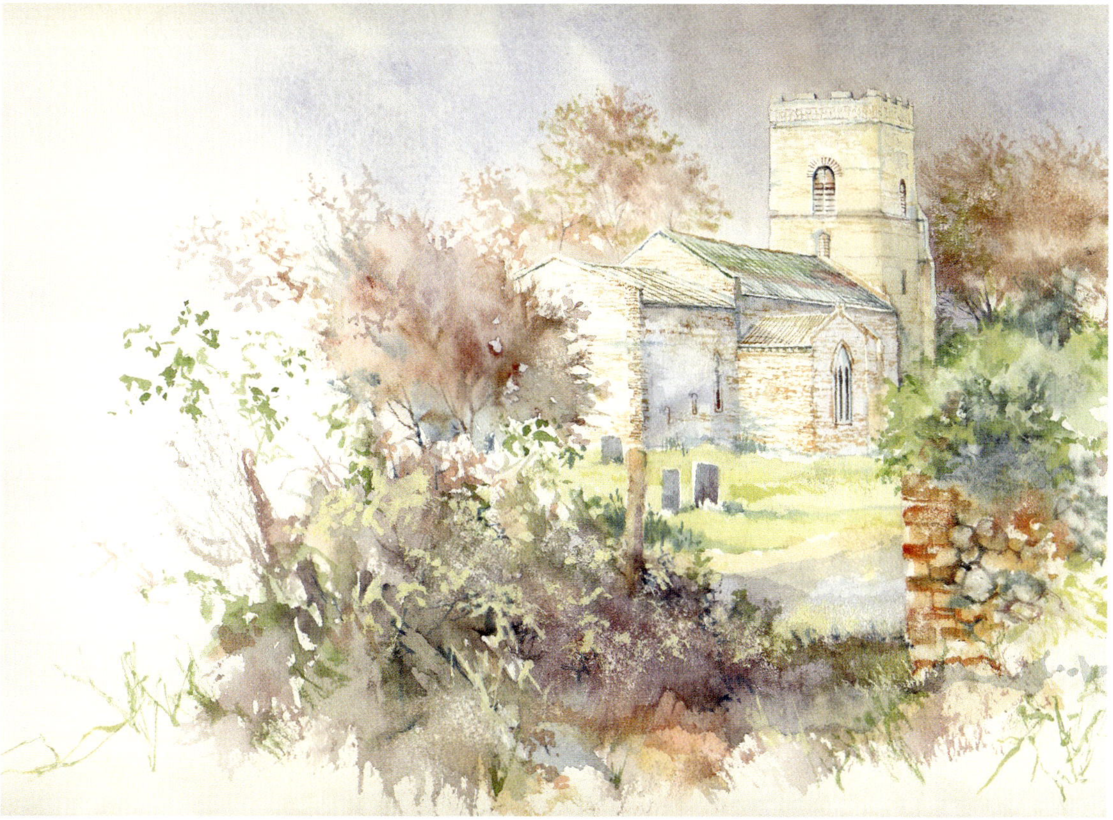

The Church Gate

The church of St Mary, Kelling stands by the original hall drive with a convenient access gate for the residents. It is from here that I chose my viewpoint in order to create a link between the estate and church. An intriguing story relates to the regular appearance in this area of a young lady who seemed to be weeping, dressed in brown and carrying a bundle. When the hall drive was resurfaced, the skeletal remains of a mother and infant were found, yet after they were re-interred in consecrated ground, no further sightings have occurred.

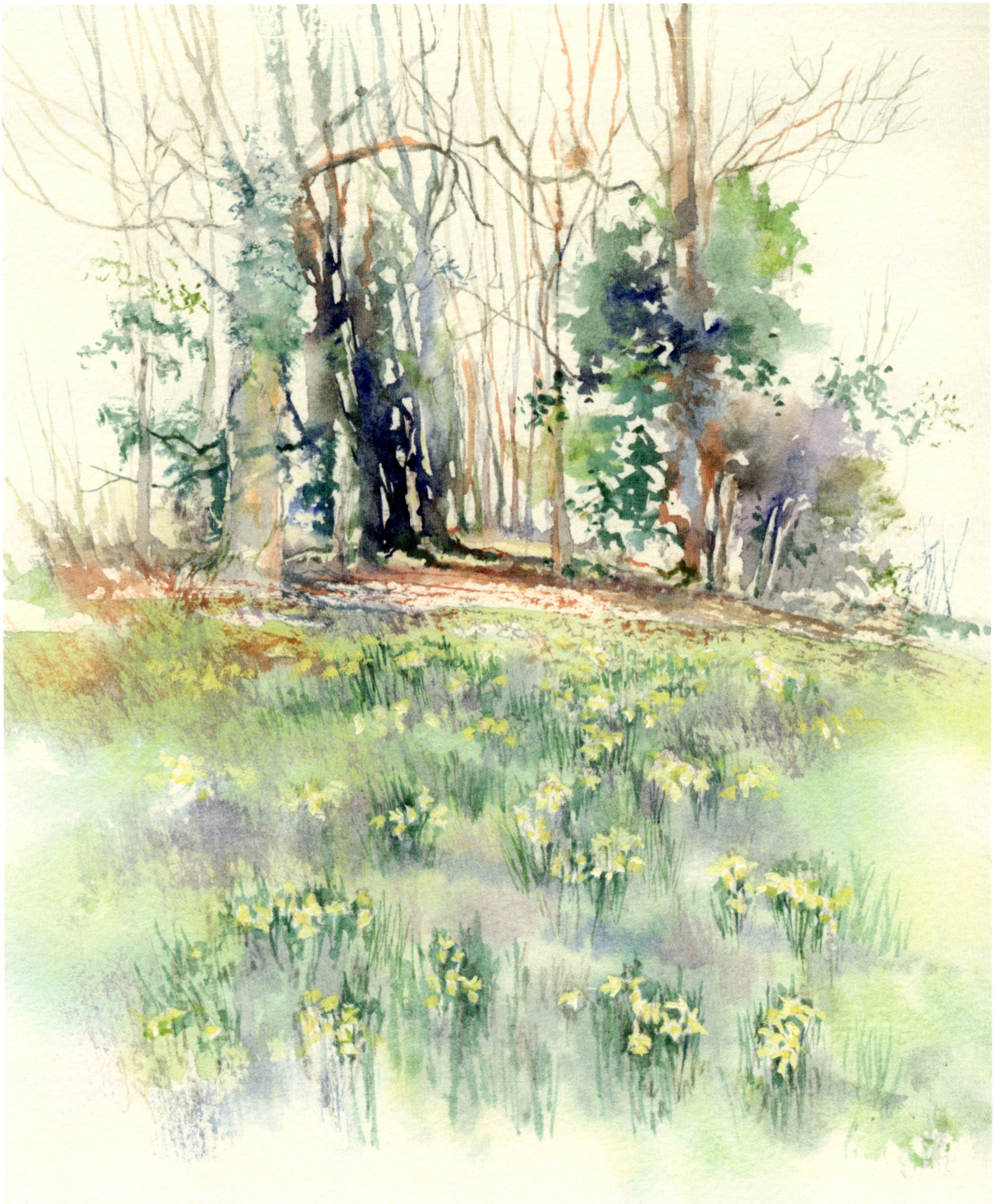

Spring Shadows

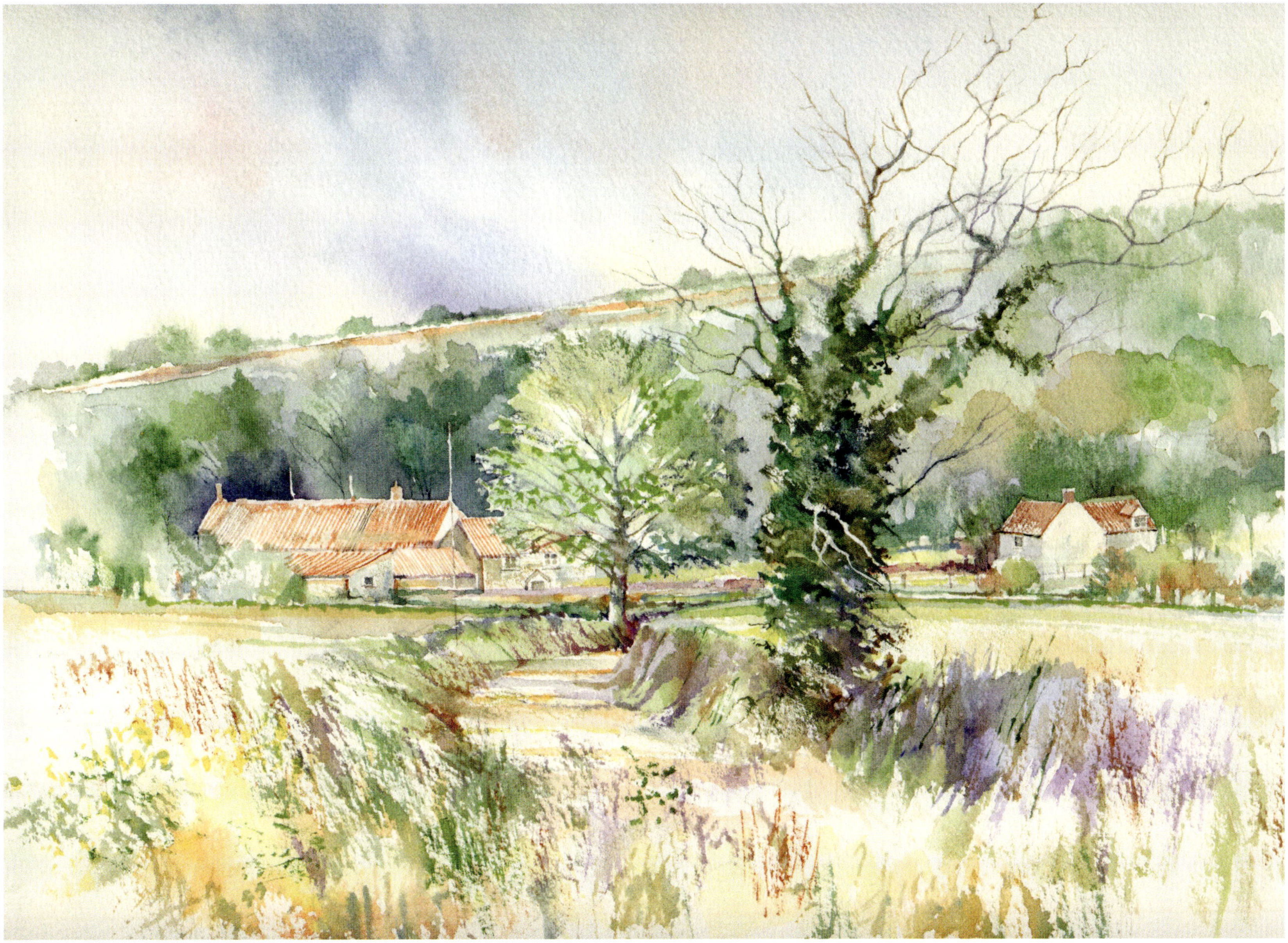

Oilseed Rape Towards Kelling

I don't mind the acid yellow of oil seed rape; after all it doesn't last long. My memories of this location sketch looking down the valley to Kelling village were enhanced by the sudden appearance of a honey buzzard being mobbed by crows. This scarce migratory raptor that once bred at Kelling, is alas now restricted in the county to the area around Swanton Novers and Sennowe Park, Guist.

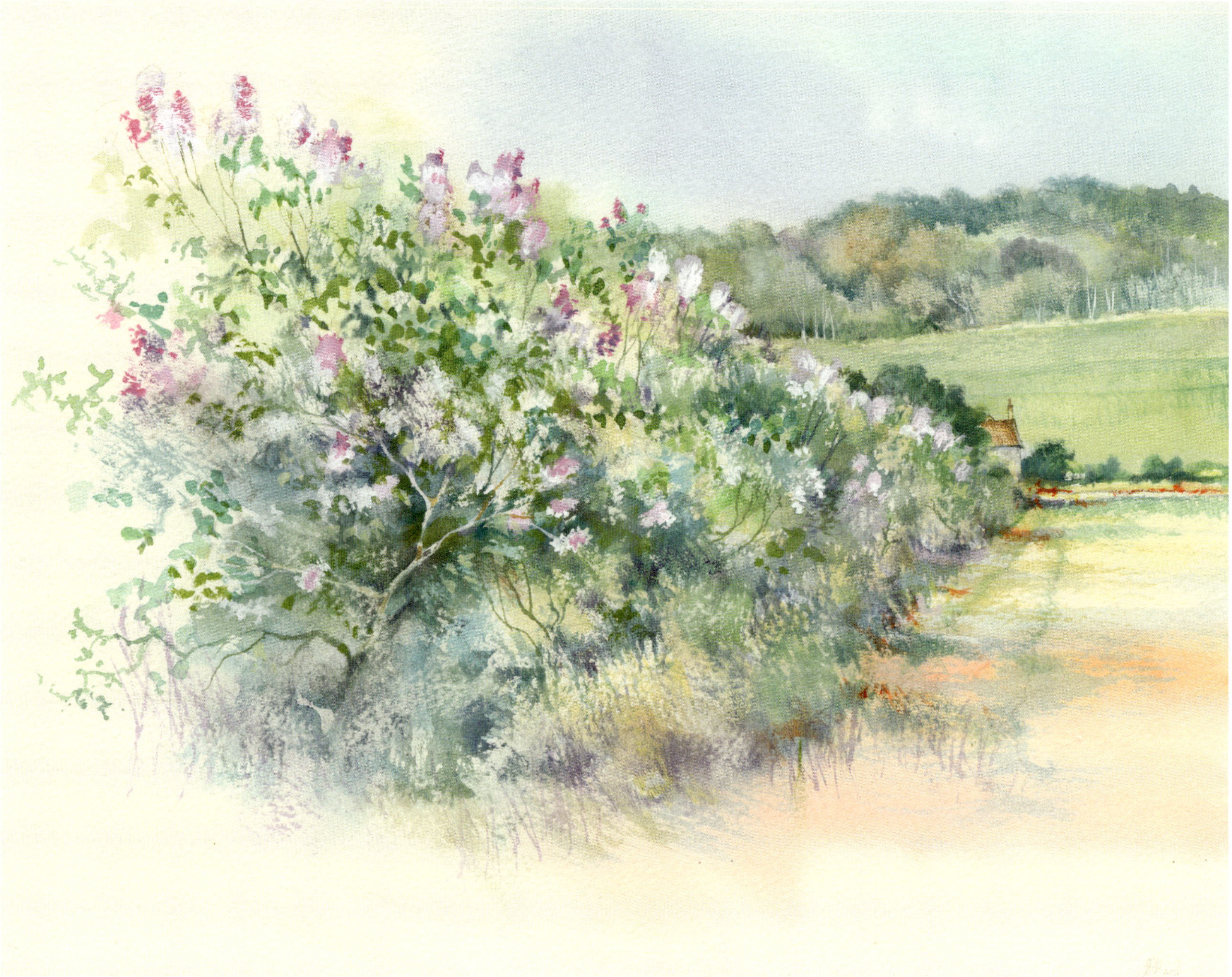

Lilac Hedge

Kelling post mill was built in 1820 by Edward Nurse and is described as 'set over a roundhouse with a balcony porch'. Little remains of the site where in April 1934 the unfortunate George Gidney, employed by the estate to reclaim bricks from the derelict mill, was crushed to death by a falling buttress. It is fitting perhaps, that this tragic site is marked by a beautiful lilac hedge which flowers in profusion each spring.

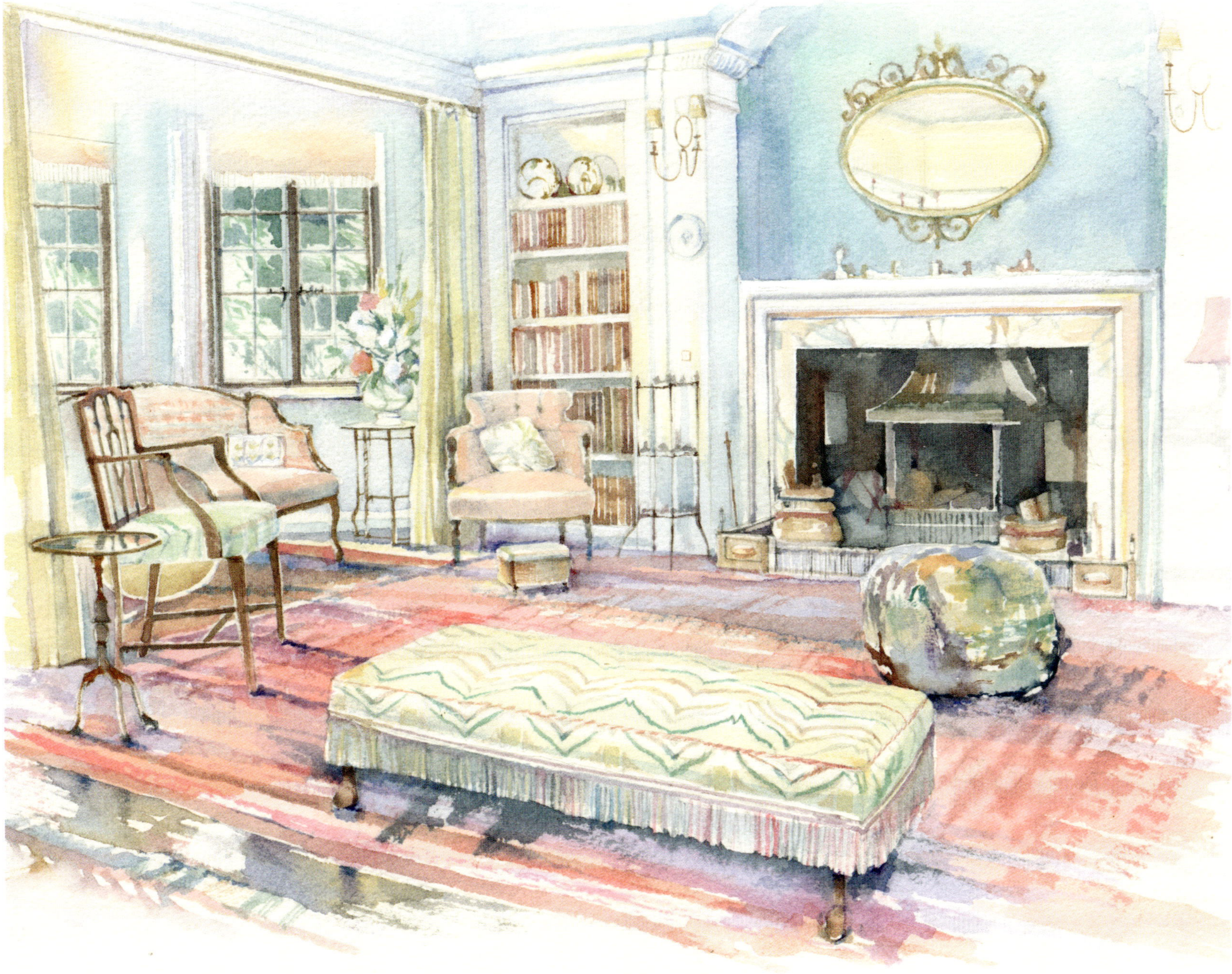

Drawing Room Interior

In order to optimise on the available light, I spent time in the drawing room at Kelling Hall during the early afternoons. As well as a record of the furnishings I hoped to capture the wonderful sense of calm that seemed constant within this space.

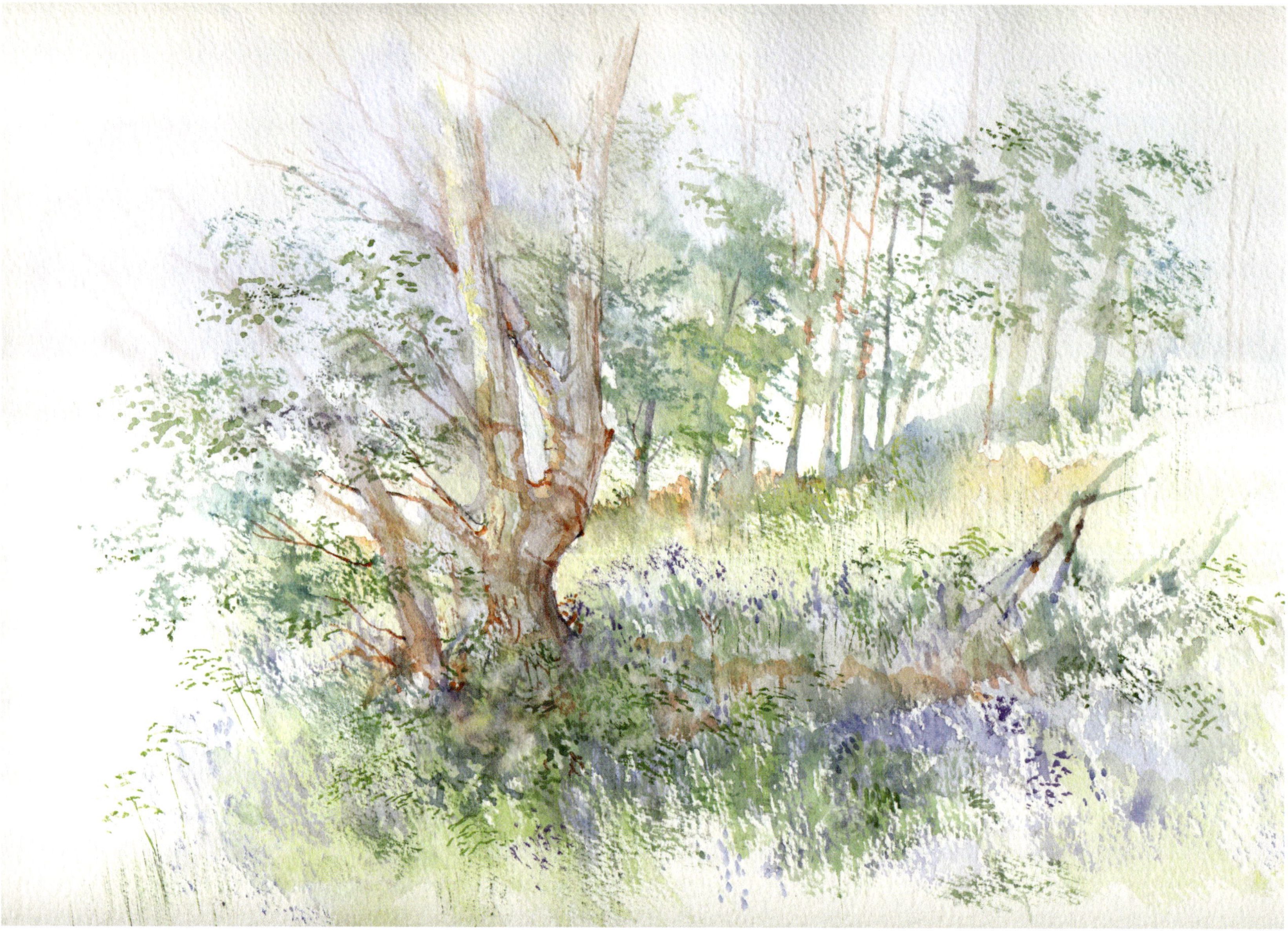

Evening Bluebells

On the 6th May I found a carpet of bluebells in woodland overlooking a field called Bloggs. Using cobalt and cerulean blue with a strong yellow called aureolin, my aim was to capture the intense colour created by evening light.

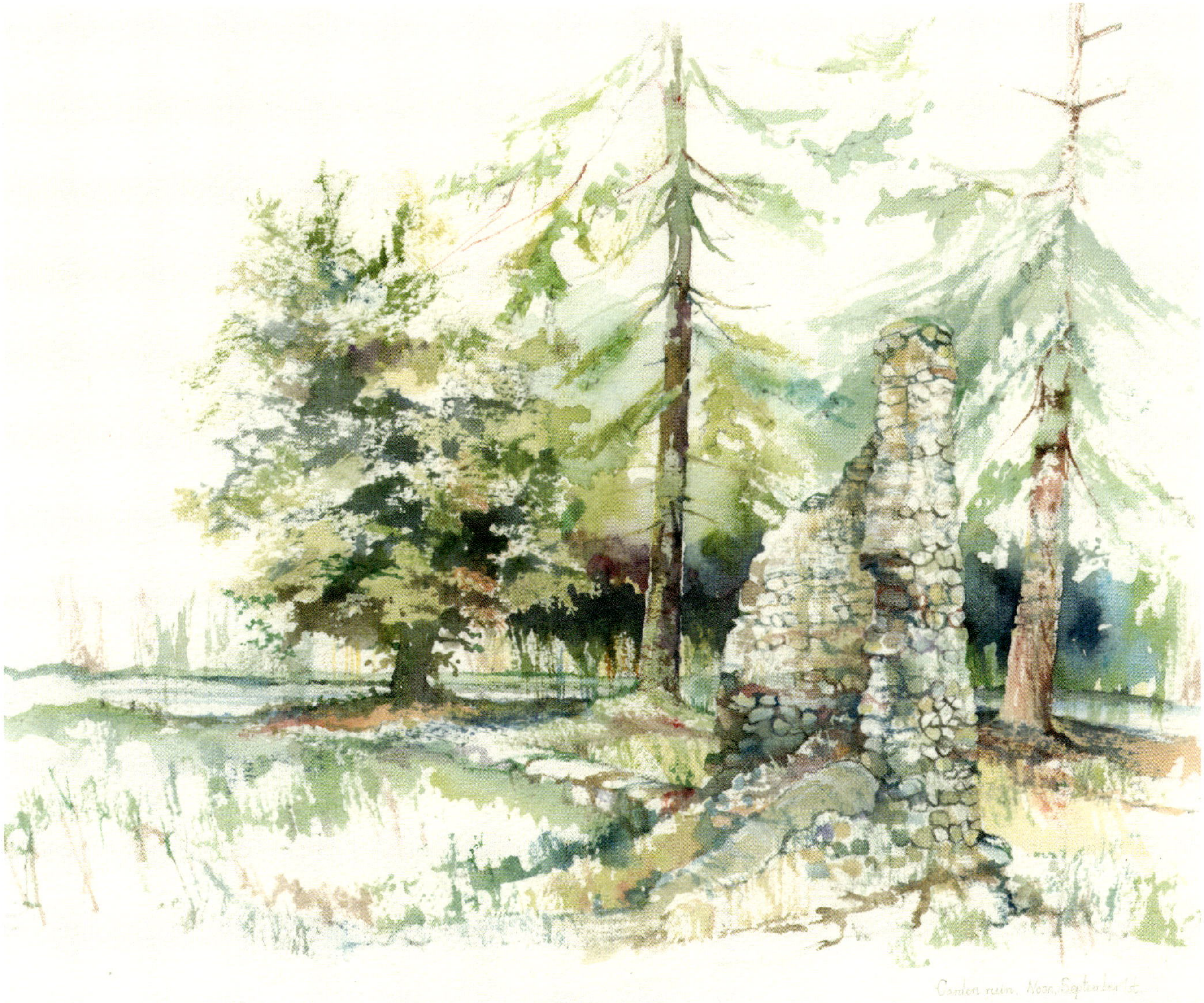

Garden Ruin

There is a ruin in the garden at Kelling Hall, yet few if anyone seems to know of its origins. Surrounded by a moat, all that remains is a pillar, which appears to be the corner of a building.

William Deterding, grandson of Sir Henry remembers that the adjacent pheasant drive was once called the 'manor drive' indicating that perhaps the remains are those of an ancient manor house. It is also believed that the site is very close to a Roman causeway linking coastal settlements with those inland. Shirley Deterding once told me, "It's a rather haunted place."

These gardens are laid out to present the admirer with a variety of sensual pleasures and despite her youthful looks; the fountain statue is a lady of considerable years! The water gardens, accessed by bridges are an extension of the moated ruin and reflect glorious arboreal autumn tints while in spring one is assailed by the scent of unusual azaleas. Leaving the garden by an uphill slope one passes enormous topiary structures, which act as the guardians of a hidden world.

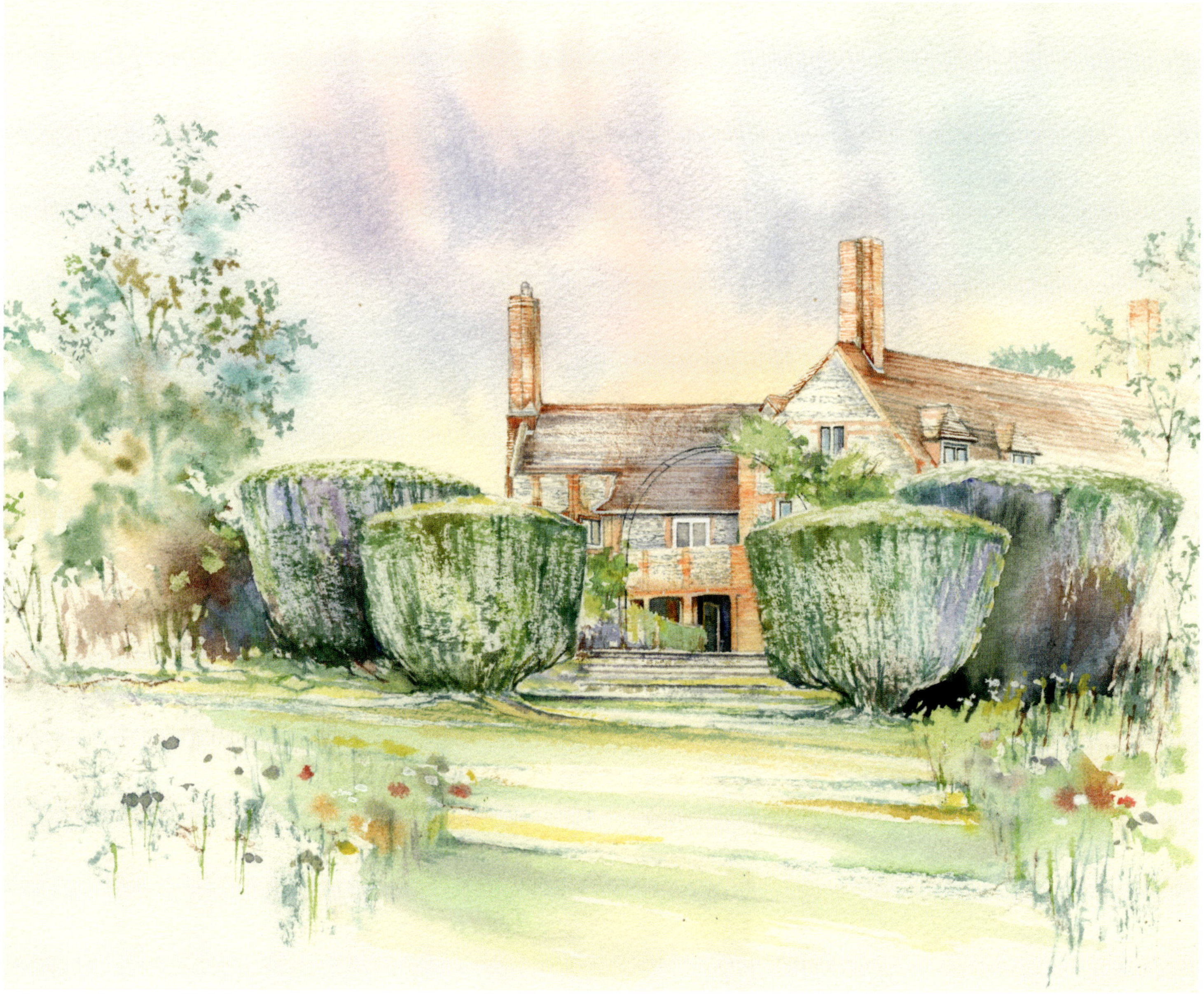

Garden Topiary

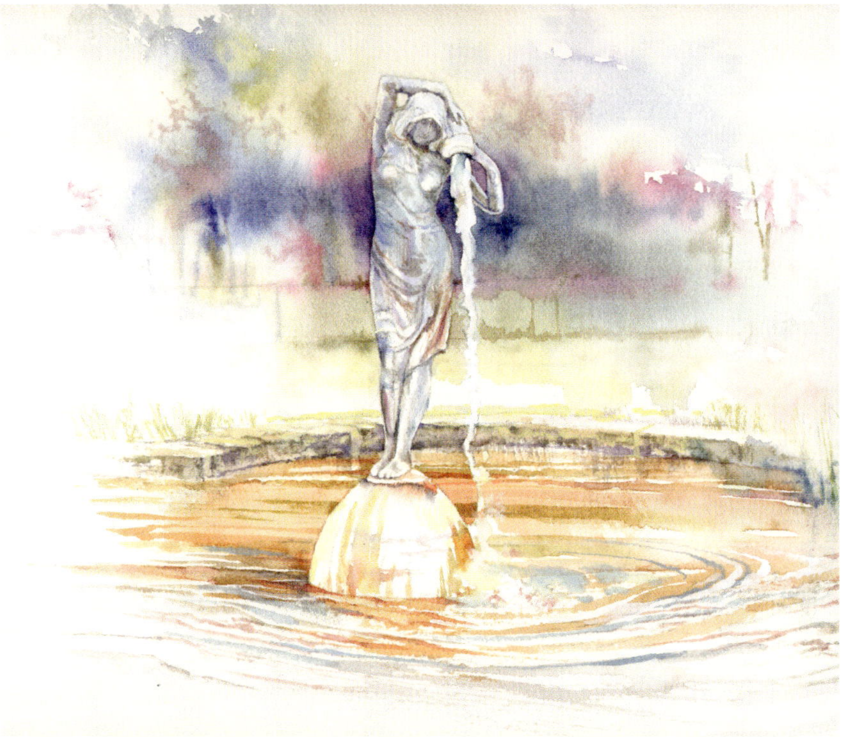

Fountain Statue

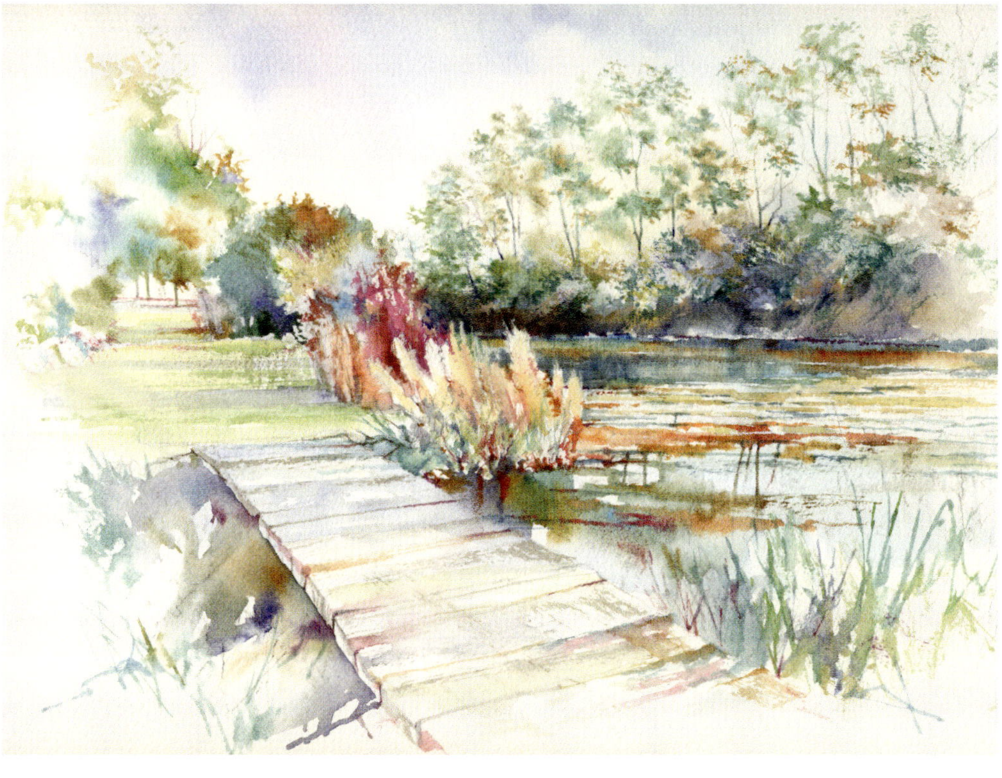

Water Gardens

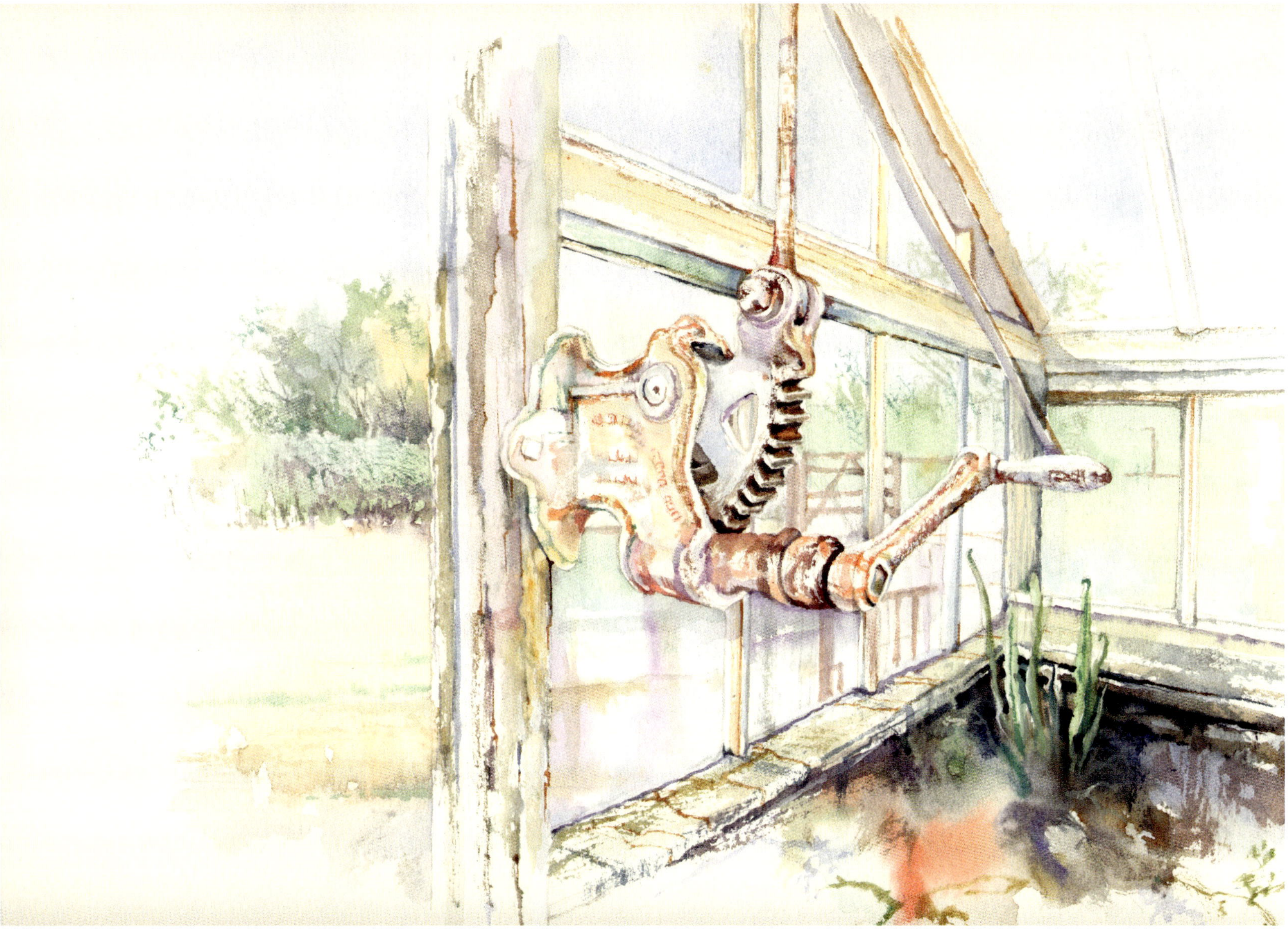

Greenhouse Ventilation Handle

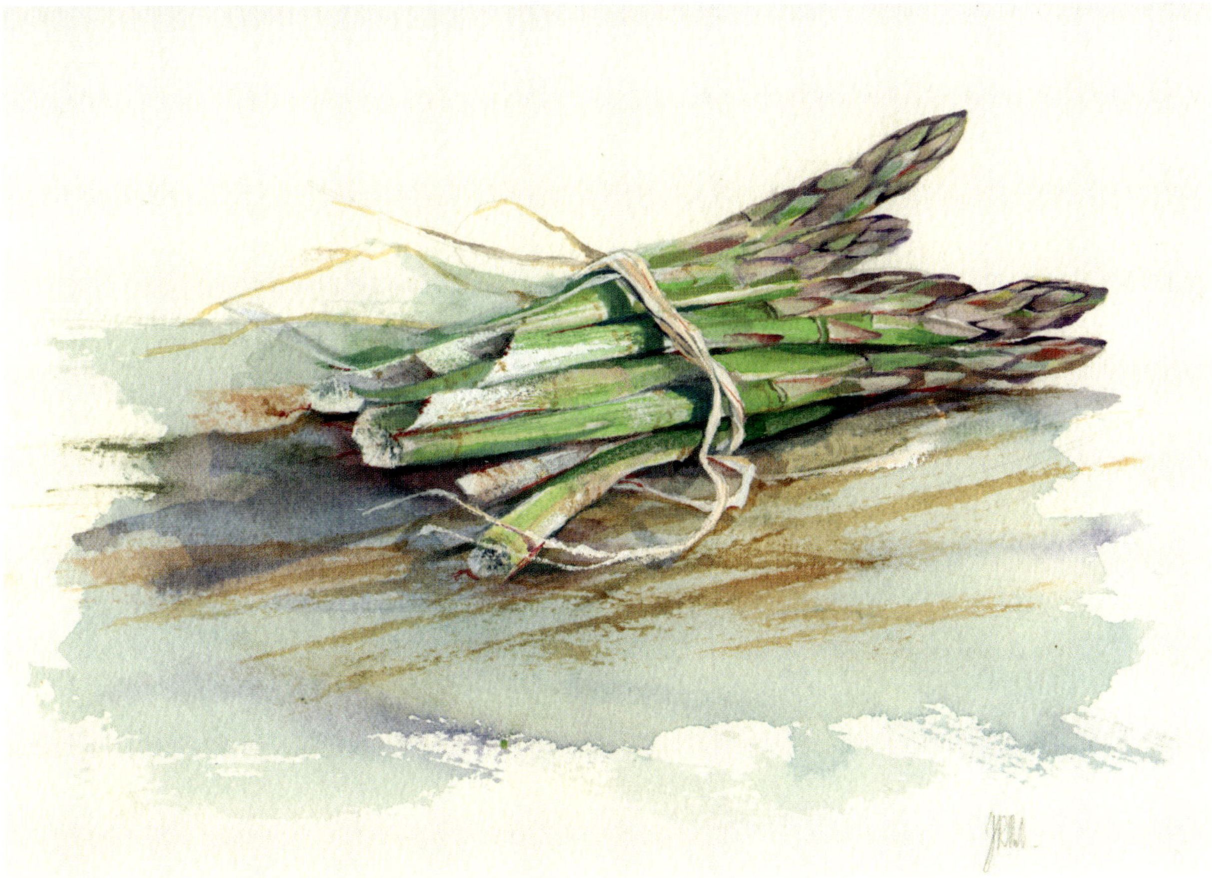

Fresh Asparagus

Within the walled garden at Kelling Hall there stands the typical range of hothouses including an area for growing pineapples and other exotics favoured by the owners of many great houses during the Victorian era. I chose to paint the handle of the ventilation system in what had become a rather fragile greenhouse, and include a study of freshly-cut asparagus, which along with early strawberries are Norfolk specialities.

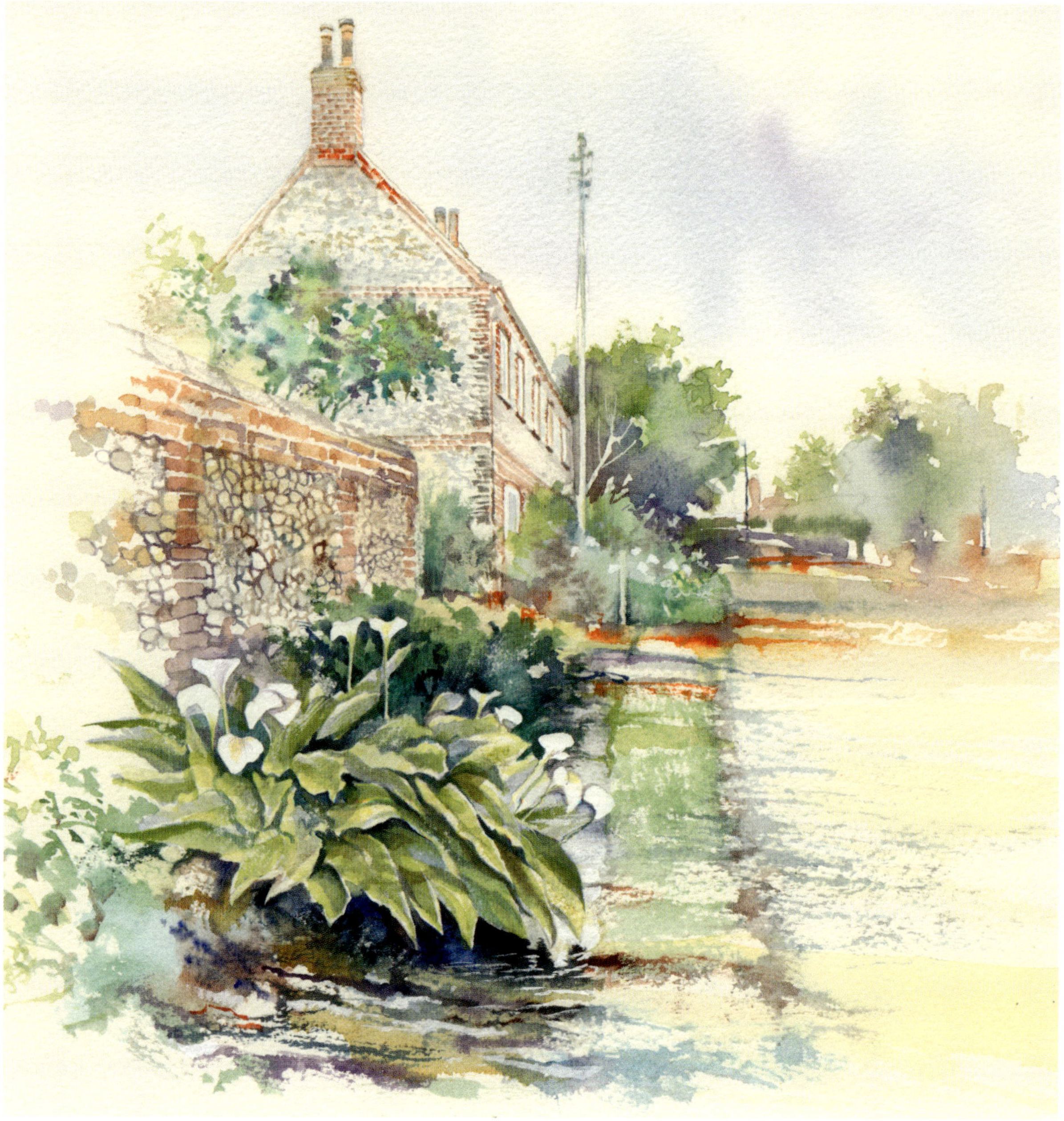

Arum Lilies

From its source as a glacial spring, Kelling Beck flows through the water gardens of the hall from where it follows the valley to form a charming roadside rivulet. Its flow, even during the driest summers cannot be stemmed, thus creating a perfect environment for the arum lilies that bloom in early summer, and for elvers that make their annual journey along its course. The beck continues north through marsh meadow to The Quag, a fresh water pool of great importance to wildlife.

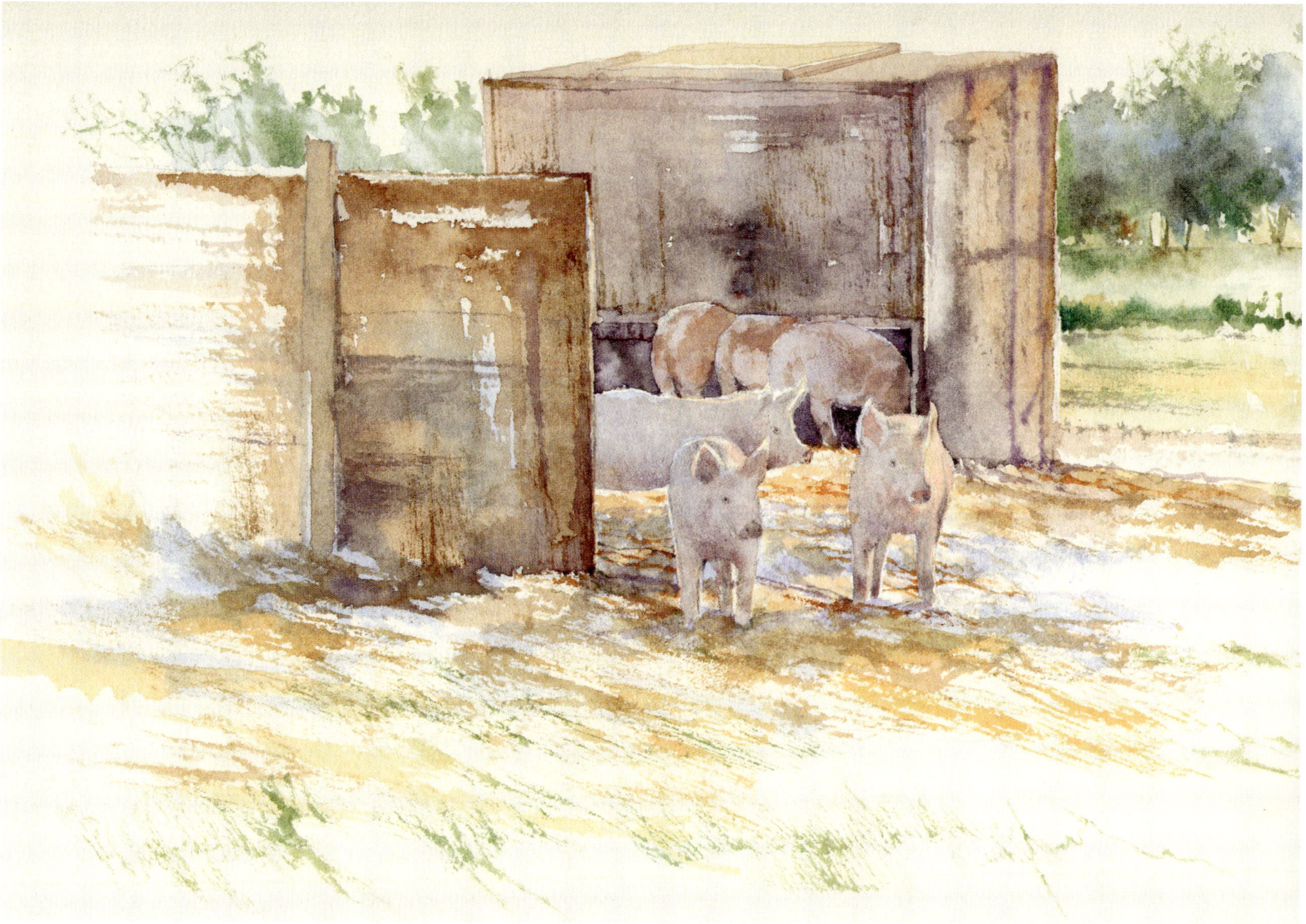

Three Little Pigs

Whilst wandering the fields at Kelling in search of subject matter, I came across three sunlit little pigs and could not resist adding them to the 'wildlife' in this collection!

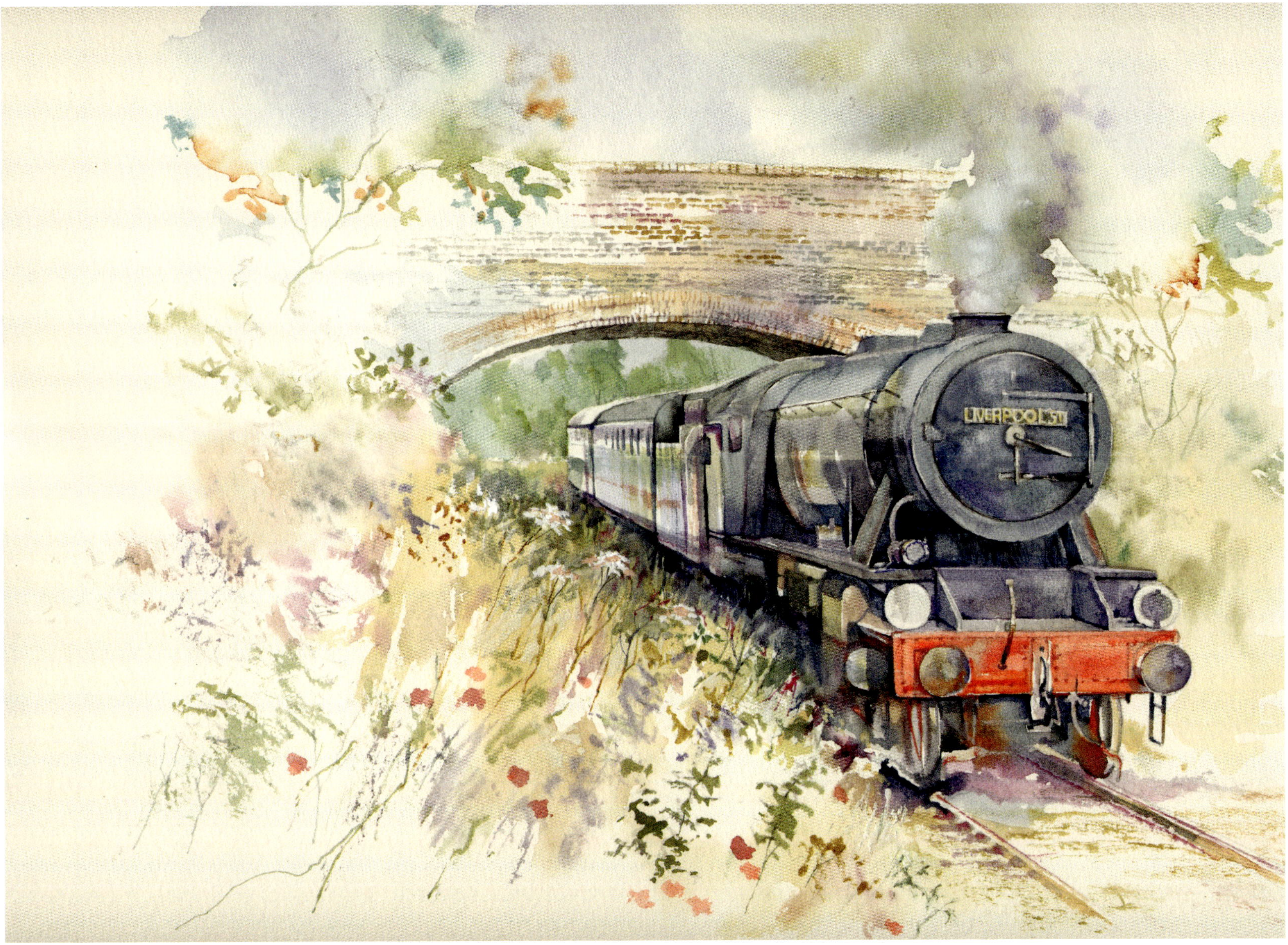

Full Steam Under Bridge Road

Poppyline, the local steam railway runs from Sheringham to Holt via Weybourne, cutting across the south-eastern boundary of Kelling estate by the aptly named railway field. In this study we see 'Liverpool Street' in full steam passing below Bridge Road just prior to its arrival at Holt station.

Vast woodlands stretch across the glacial ridge from Salthouse Heath to Cromer and it is therefore no surprise that there is a colossal population of resident woodpigeons in the area. With crop protection of paramount importance, landowners go to great lengths to operate bird scarers and in some cases pigeon shooters, to limit damage or move flocks to less vulnerable areas. In this June sketch the Kelling estate head keeper is shooting over laid barley. Notable bags at this time of the year have included one pigeon per minute for seven hours, achieved by William Garfit the well known artist, conservationist and passionate pigeon shot.

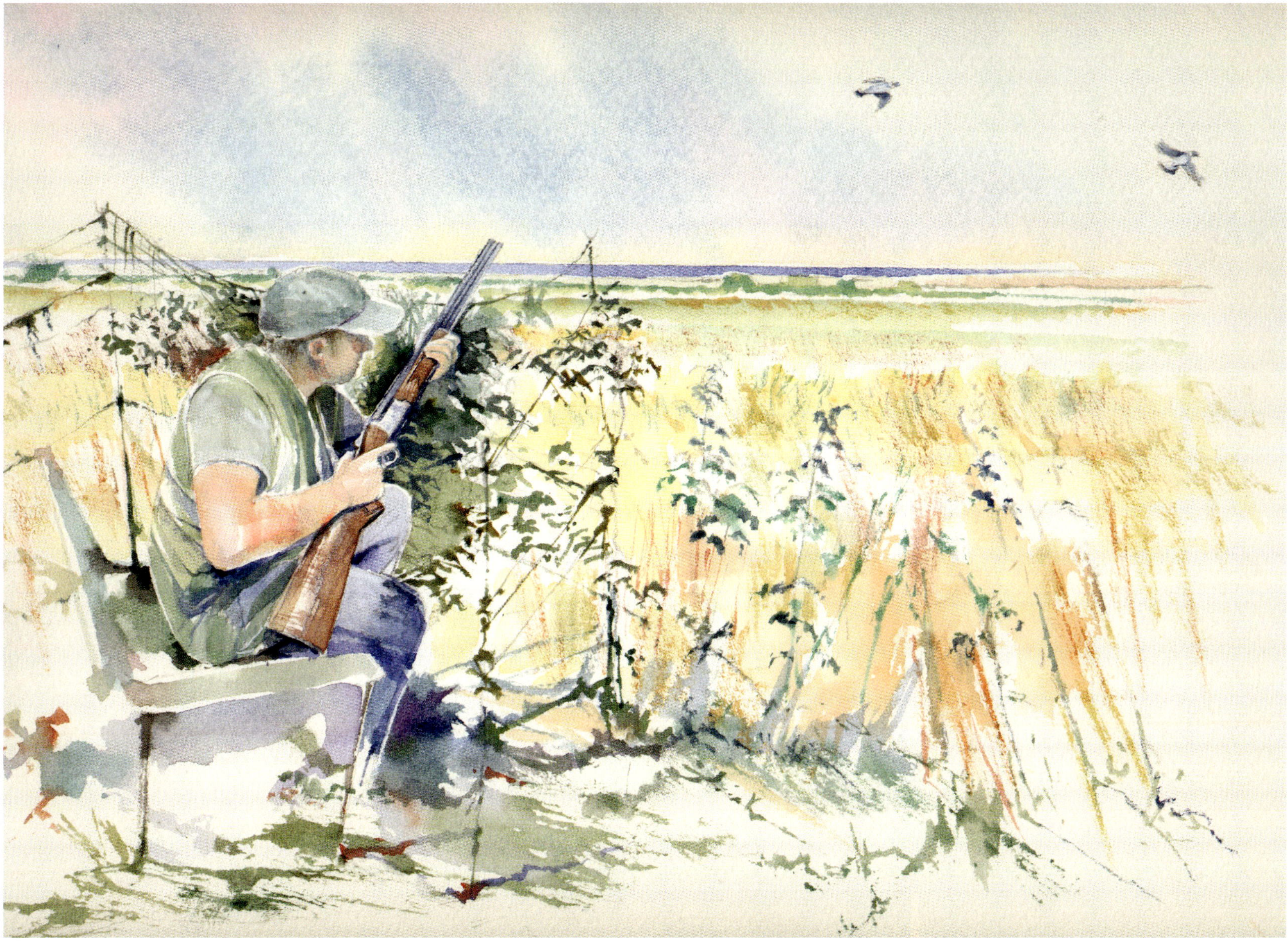

Pigeons over Laid Barley

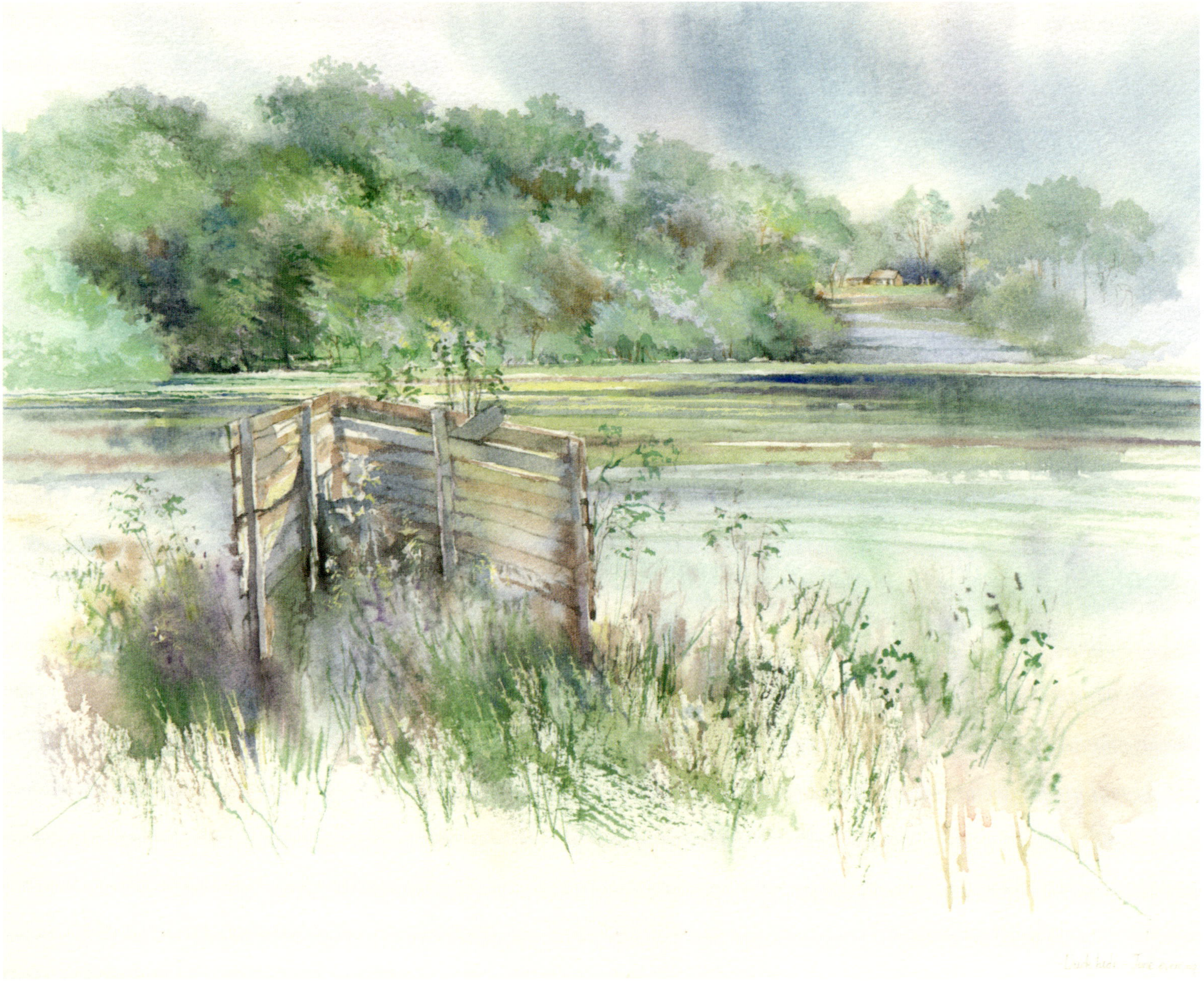

Duck Hide

A series of interlinked ponds may be found secreted amidst dense woodland to the south-east of Kelling Hall, once used for duck flighting and fishing by the Deterding family. It is here that Ronald Deterding encountered an otter and swam after a lost dog, as recorded in his game diaries. Today the area is a haven for wildlife. The distant building was named Mull by Shirley Deterding, who used it as her artist's studio for many years.

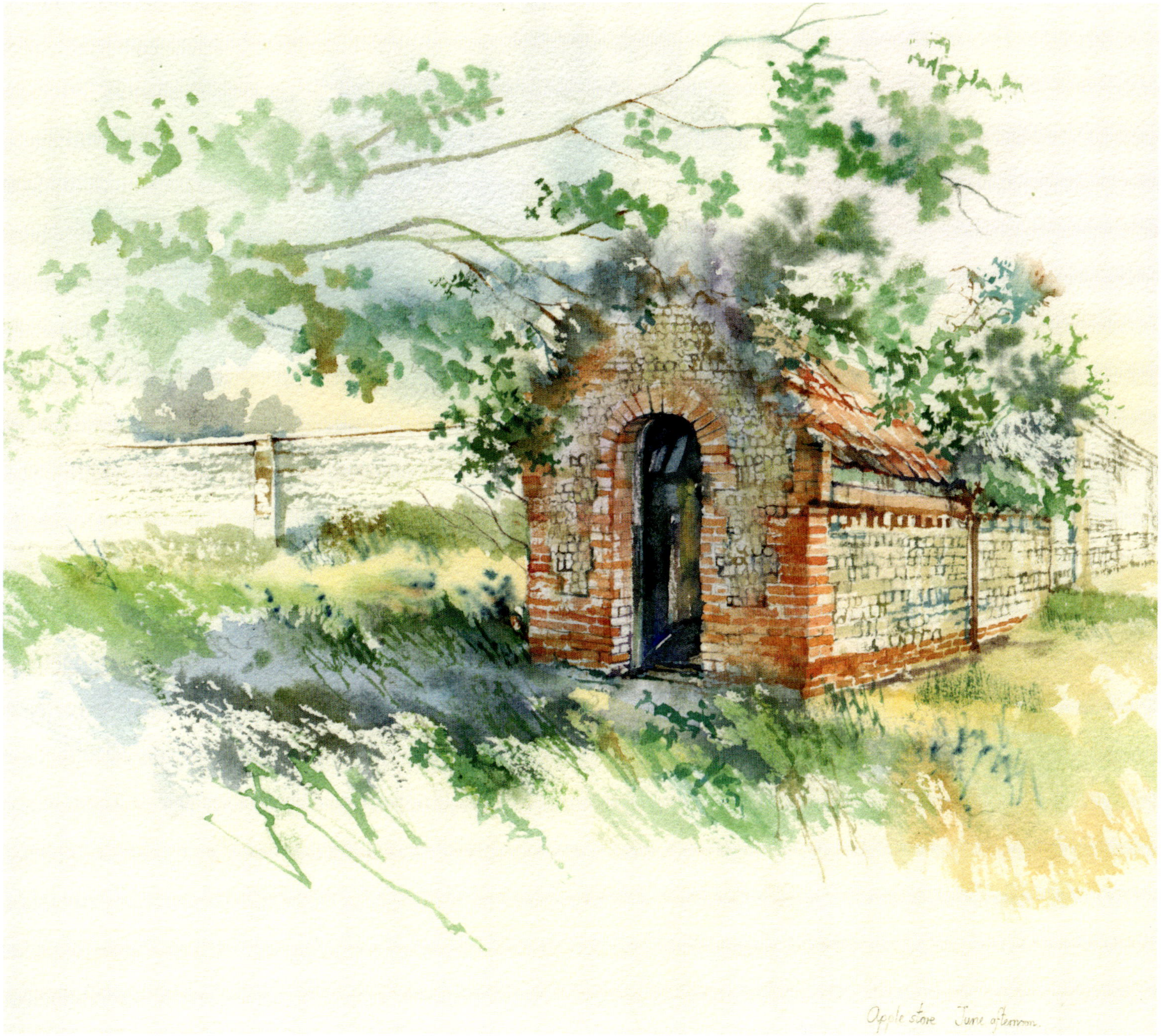

Apple Store

When I first discovered this unusual building, half hidden by a cloak of ivy my first thoughts were 'ice house', having seen them previously by the lakes of great estates. Not so apparently, for this is the kitchen garden apple store with a well insulated interior lined with lathe and plaster.

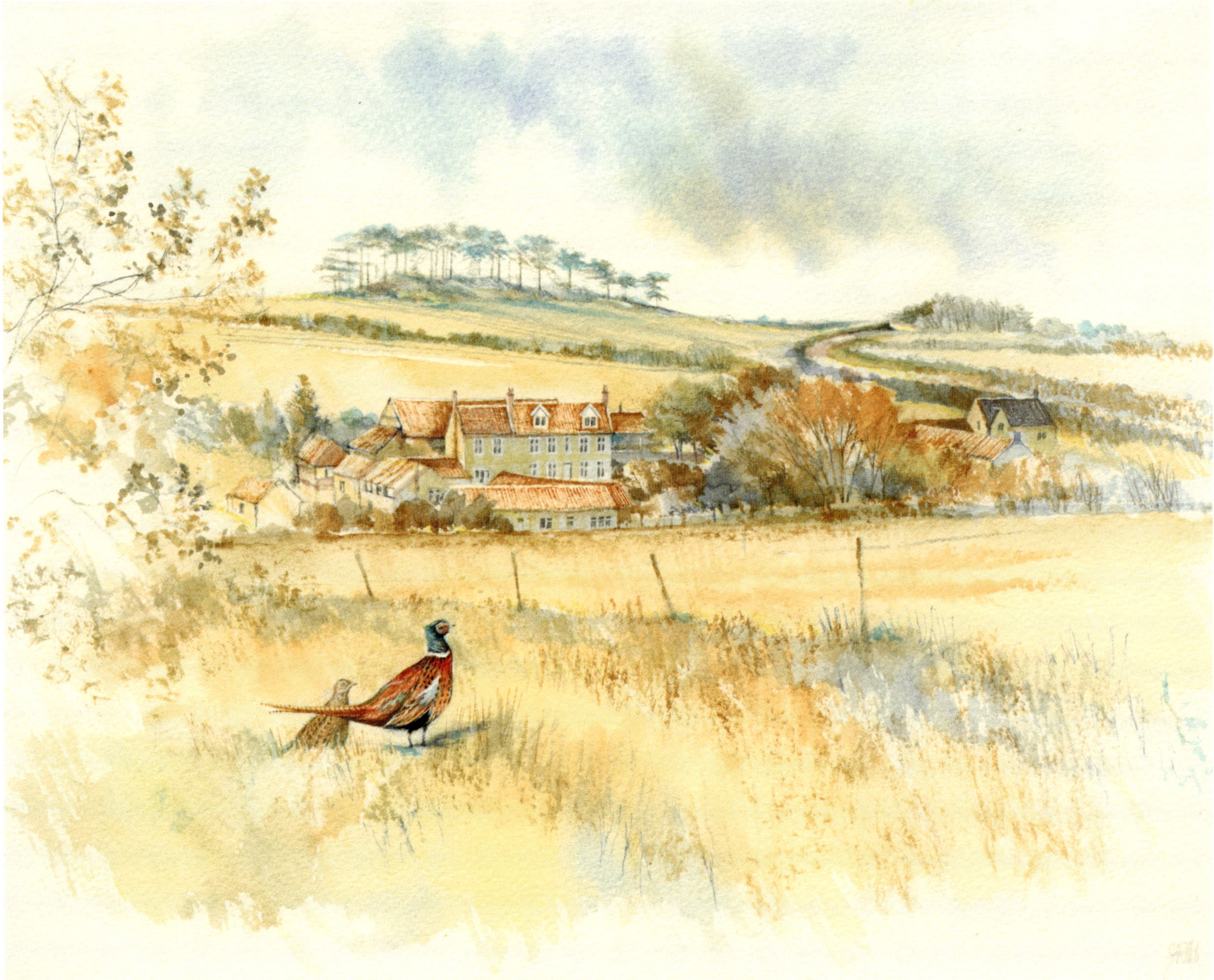

Beck House

From high ground at Broomhill Brecks one is able to look in a north-westerly direction and see Kelling village nestled in the valley below. You may pick out Beck House, Dutch in design and the original home of Sir Henry Deterding who resided there while the hall was being built. The distant clump of pines, which form a prominent landmark stand on Warborough Hill.

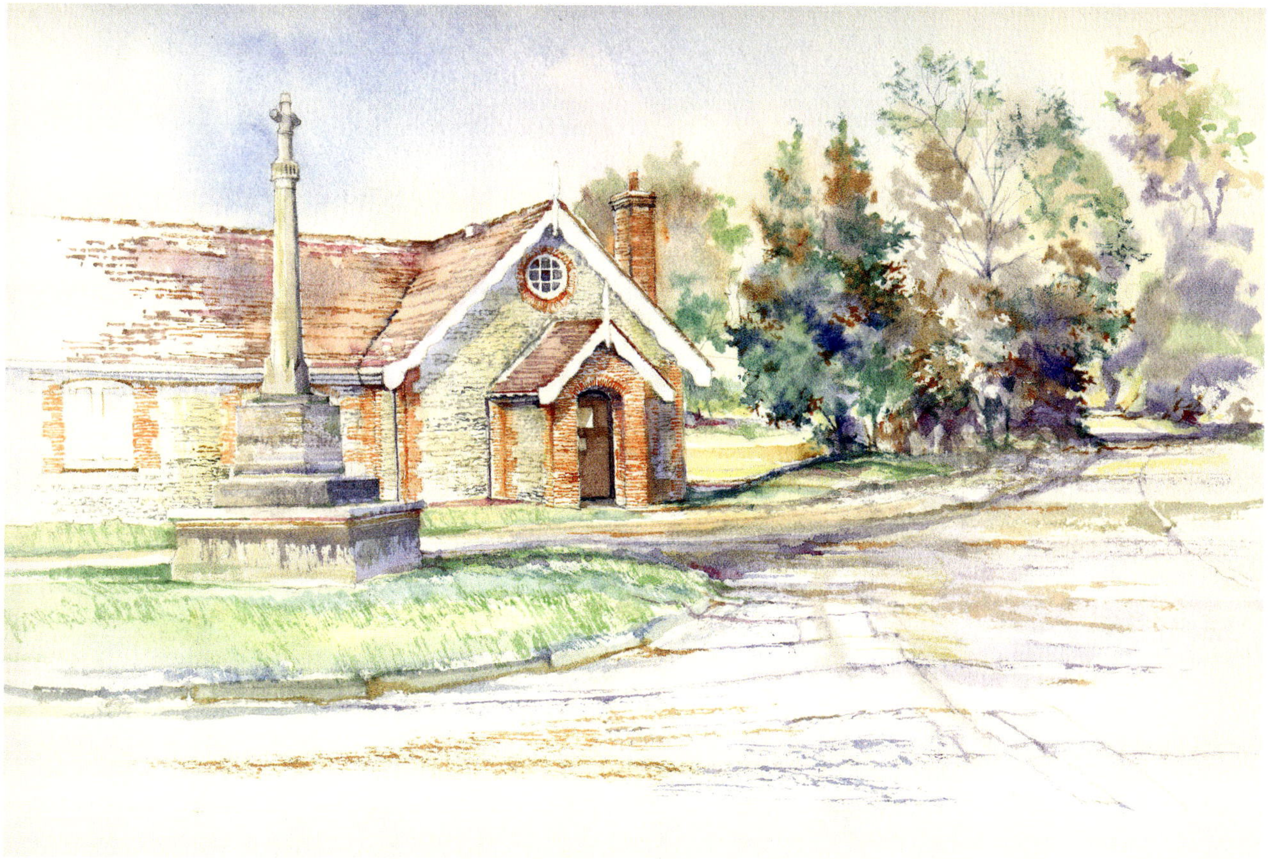

The Reading Room

1941-1942	Bags halved by lack of keepers, beaters and constant poaching by the Army and the RAF.
Dec 1942	No beaters at all.
18th Jan 1943	Jim killed his first pheasant in Green Plantation with .410.
Jan 1943	Drive badly disturbed by search light party.
29th Dec 1943	Jim killed his first woodcock.
4th Oct 1944	Brigadier's spaniel got its foot stuck in willows, Lowes Pond. Had to climb out to it - half stripped as I expected a ducking but managed to get out and back again with dry shirt. Dog none the worse.
1944	Pheasants eggs stolen by Italian prisoners of war at work on sugar beet.
22nd Nov 1944	Birds ran out of Sheringham Poor Land (military had pinched undergrowth for firewood).
2nd Jan 1945	Bill killed first woodcock on Bodham Rough.
Feb 1947	Deep snow. Sharp frost day and night. Flighted ducks to corn stacks as they were pulling them to pieces.
12th Feb 1947	Howling blizzards with north easterly gale. Snow waist high. Took 50 minutes to walk home - had to help dogs out of drifts several times.

AUTHOR'S NOTE: *One of the coldest winter's in living memory with north easterly gales and cutting blizzards between the 26th January and the 8th March 1947.*

19th Feb 1947	Went into a snowdrift and sank up to the armpits. Had rather a job to get out. Sweated like a pig in spite of 22° of frost. Woodcock could hardly fly, starved.
6th Oct 1947	Usual Salthouse gangsters snooping up and down Bix's Lane.
23rd Jan 1948	W.D.M. showed us how to cross a marsh by going in twice. Never a dull moment.

1947-1948 Season-Food shortage. Pheasants went up to 20/- each wholesale. These naturally all went on the black market. Court still fining poachers paltry sums which have no deterrent effect. Caught Cypriot spivs at Barningham working to and fro between London and Cromer. J. Mann (keeper) retired after 32 years of excellent service.

13th Oct 1949	Morning entirely ruined by fog - beaters too noisy. I'll strangle the next man who shouts, "Hold em up!"
22nd Oct 1951	Ford van seized up in reverse - had to come home backwards the whole way from Beckham pylons. Nearly disconnected my neck by looking over my shoulder for all that distance.
22nd Nov 1951	Saw heron trying to swallow a trout of well over one pound. Got a packet of no. 5's to help his digestion.
Jan 1952	F. Smith (keeper) retired after 41 years of excellent service.
31st Jan 1953	That night at 7.30 pm the wind increased to well over 100mph and with the high tide Cley, Salthouse and Blakeney were flooded. Sea bank broke at The Old Breach Hole between Cley East Bank and Salthouse.

AUTHOR'S NOTE: *Ronald Deterding's last diary entry was 1st February 1957. His last day pheasant shooting was mid December 1957 when he shot 16 out of 17 pheasants on the Broomhill drive. He died several days later.*

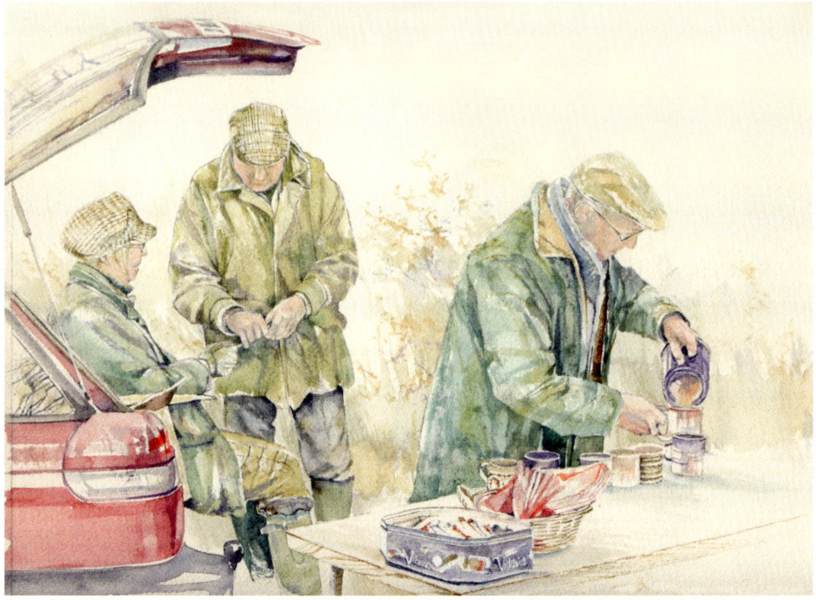

Soup Break on the Shoot

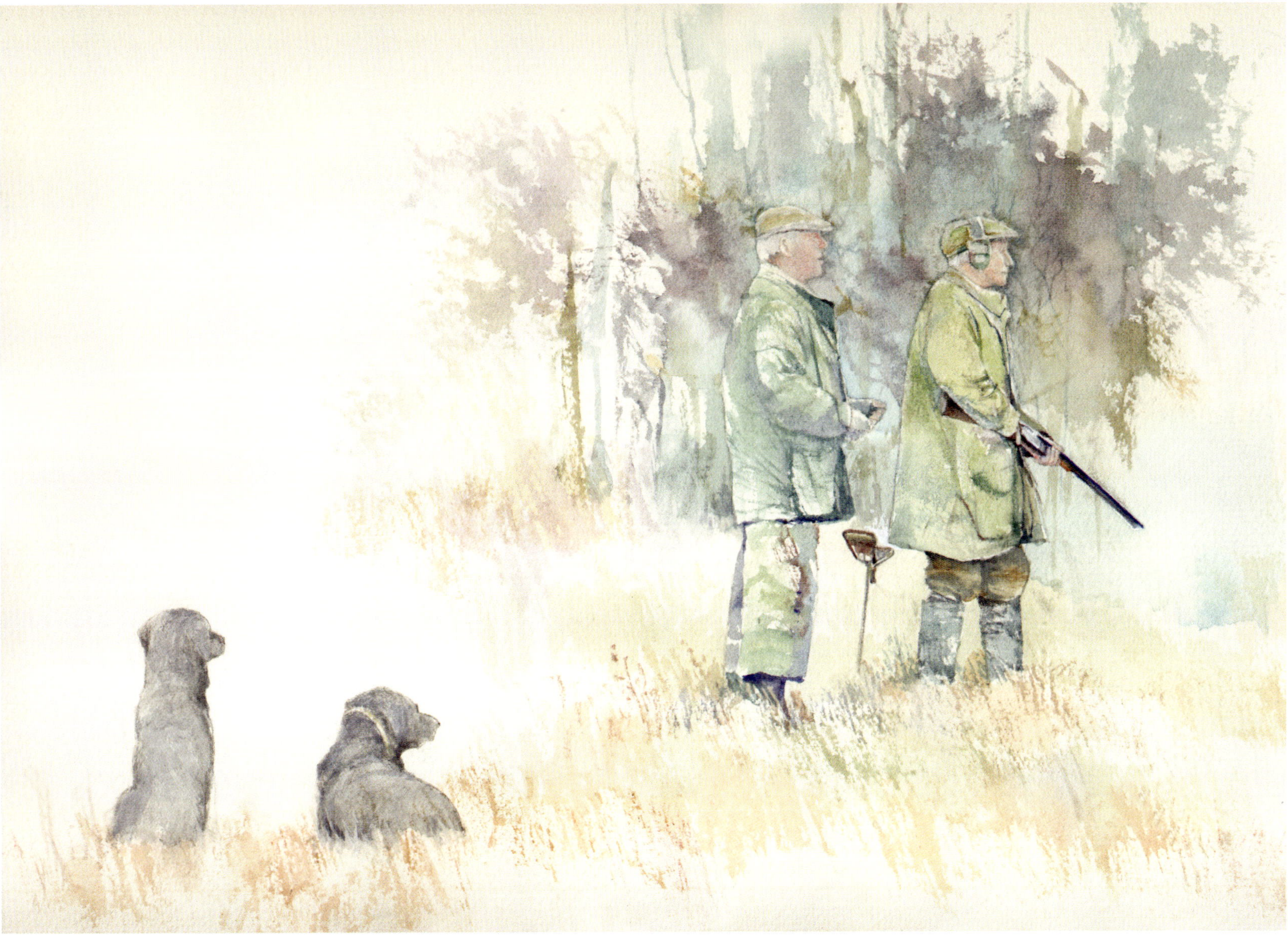

Jim Deterding, The Last Drive.
His first pheasant at Kelling was
on the 18th January 1943. His
last one was in December 2008.

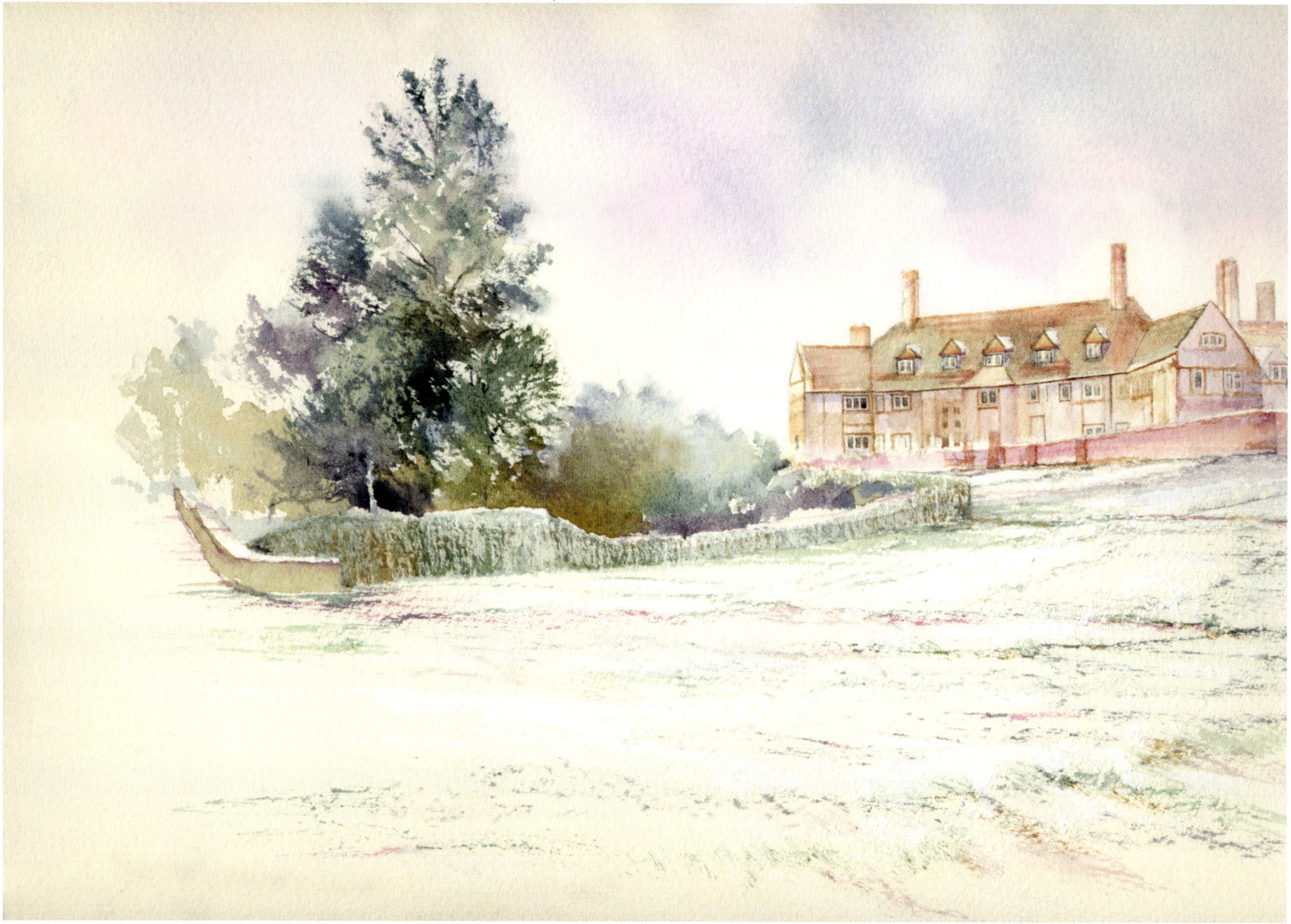

Snow at Kelling Hall

Unlike 1947, heavy snow seems very rare on the North Norfolk coast and so as my year of painting here drew to a close, its occurrence was a great surprise and challenge. In these studies, form is brought into sharp focus by the monochrome effect of snow on the landscape. By using pure, unwashed pigments a transformation of the palette took place as I strove to record deep pools, reflections and stark conifers.

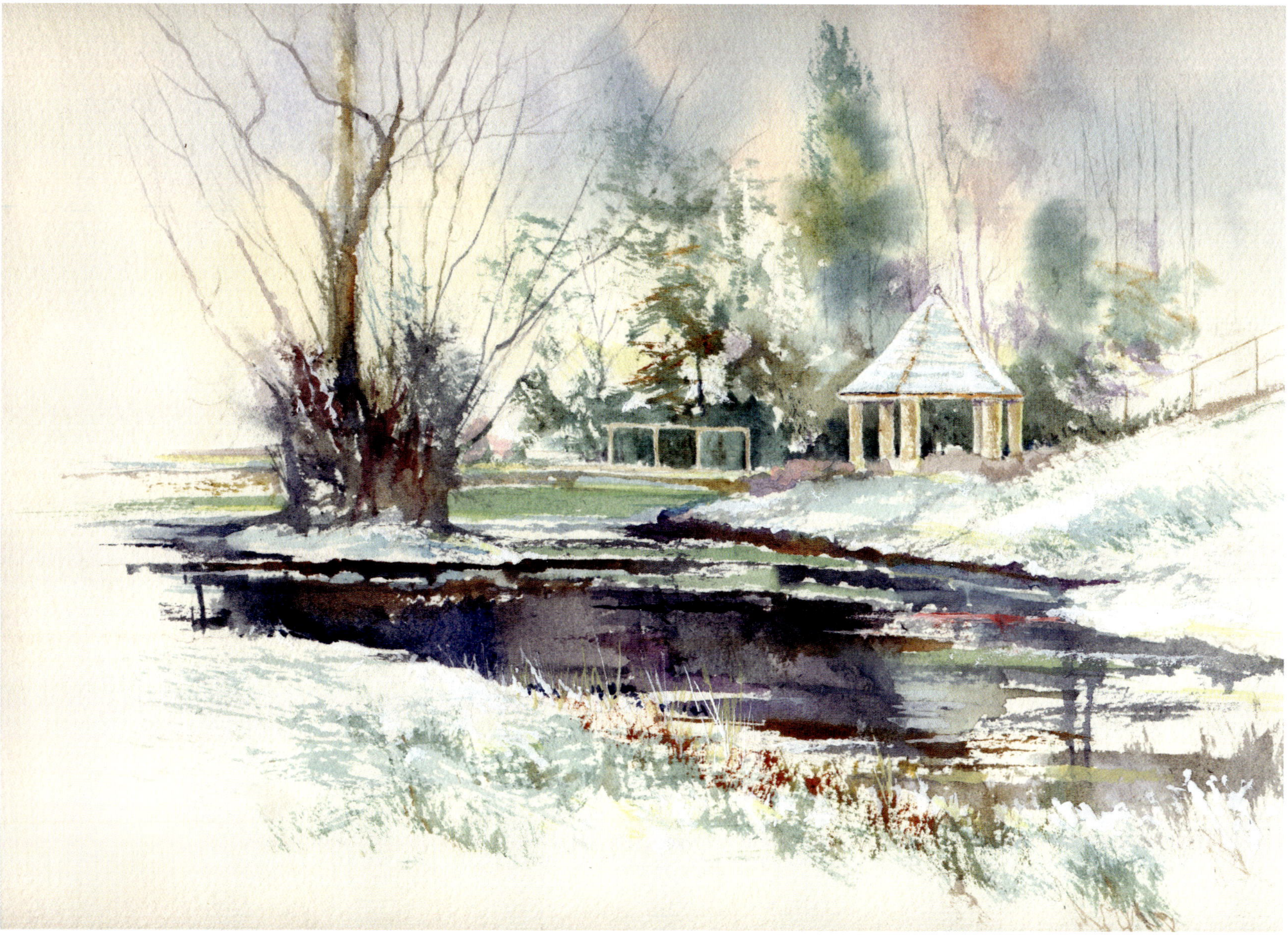

Temple in the Snow

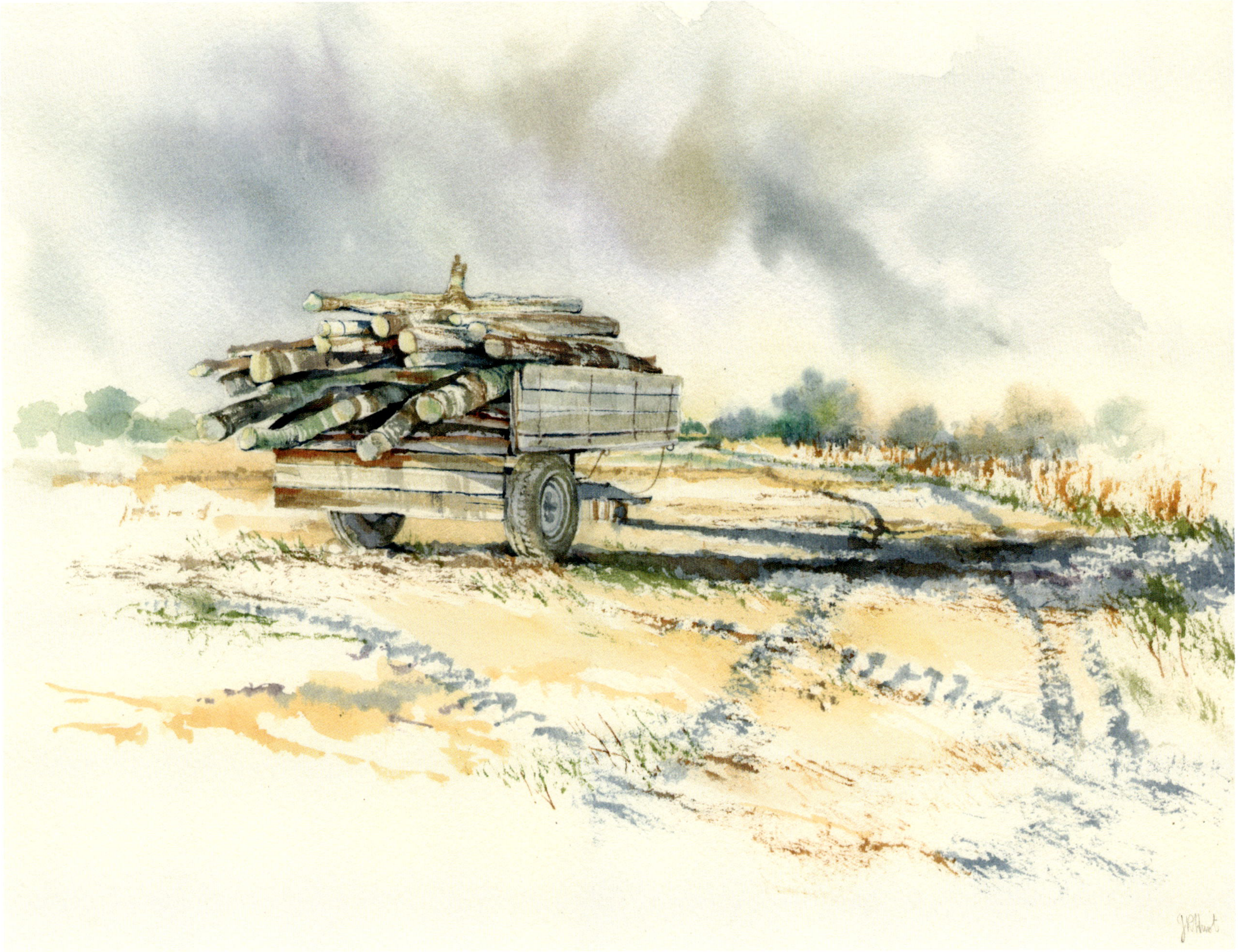

Log Trailer

As days shorten, the aroma of wood-smoke hangs by estate houses. The sound of a saw echoes from the ancient woods as fuel for the next winter is gathered. I traced the logs from this trailer to a subterranean wood-store deep beneath the hall, where in this shadowy cellar a primitive cleaver lay discarded.

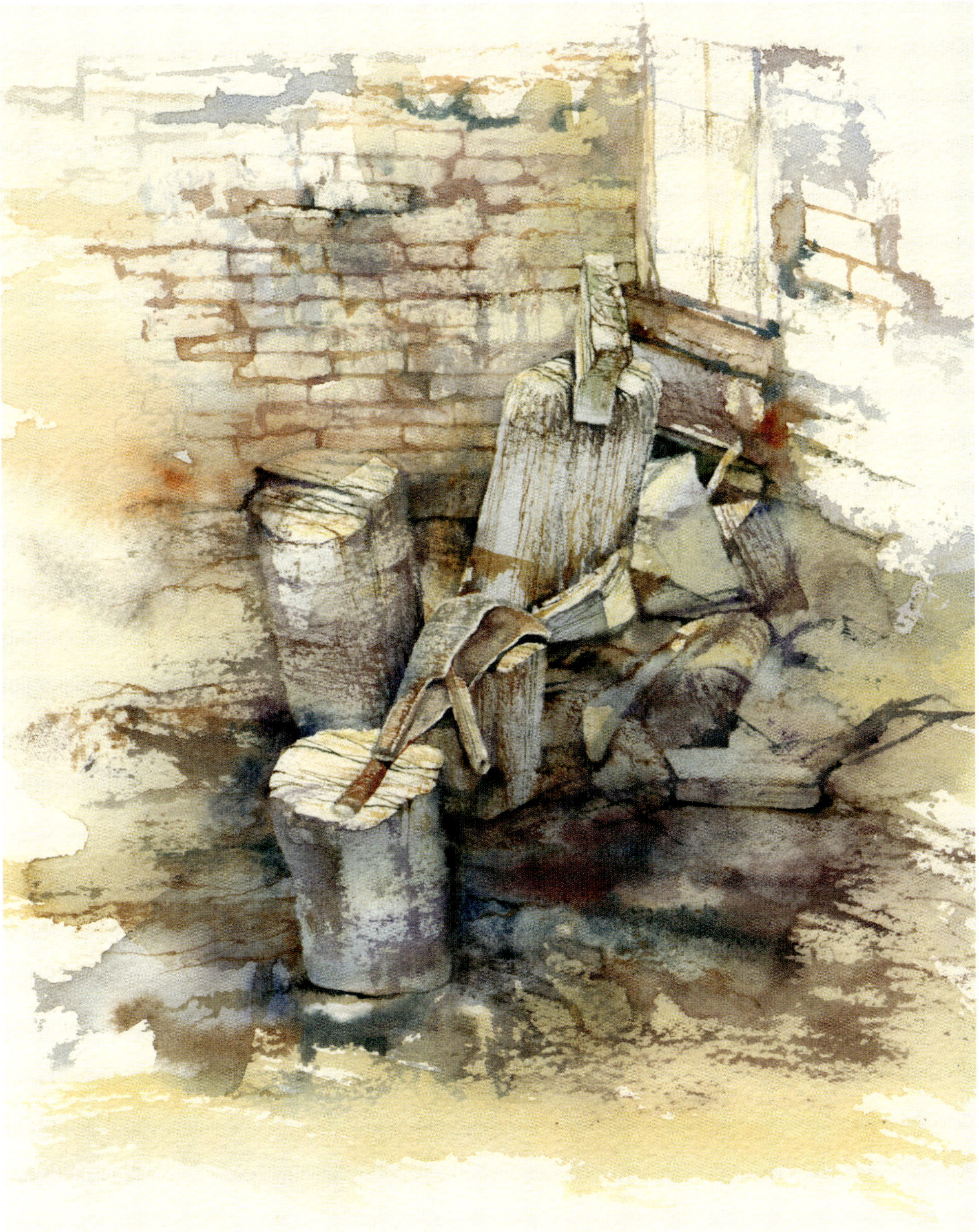

Wood Cellar

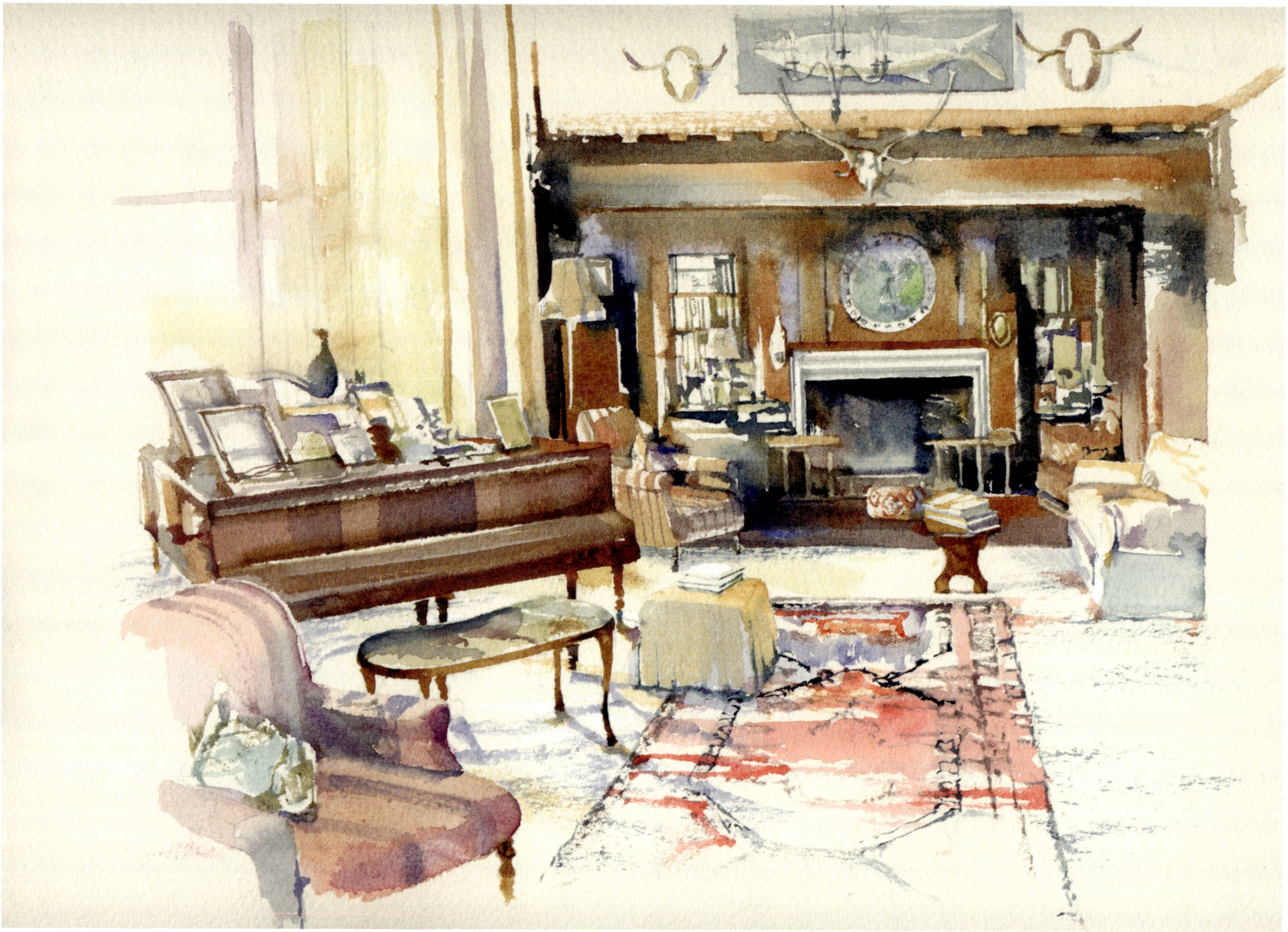

The Library

The original library at Kelling Hall was my favourite room, for here the logs found their final resting place on a roaring fire. One was surrounded by sporting trophies from far and distant lands; the enormous tarpon caught by rod and line on the Panuco River, Mexico, pristine game birds and the head of a Newfoundland elk, all of which evoked epic stories and challenges against the elements.

Above the fireplace is a beautifully painted dial designed to indicate wind direction and operated by a vane that once protruded from a chimney. It is a fact that the boys Jimmy and Bill used it as a dartboard (the holes are still evident) and Jimmy is quoted as saying, "My brother and I ate our meals off the mantelpiece for some considerable time - we couldn't sit down – oh, it did hurt!"

The dial ceased to work over fifty years ago because the vane disappeared.

"I think it fell down the chimney," said Jimmy.

"I thought your uncle knocked it off with his plane," replied Shirley.

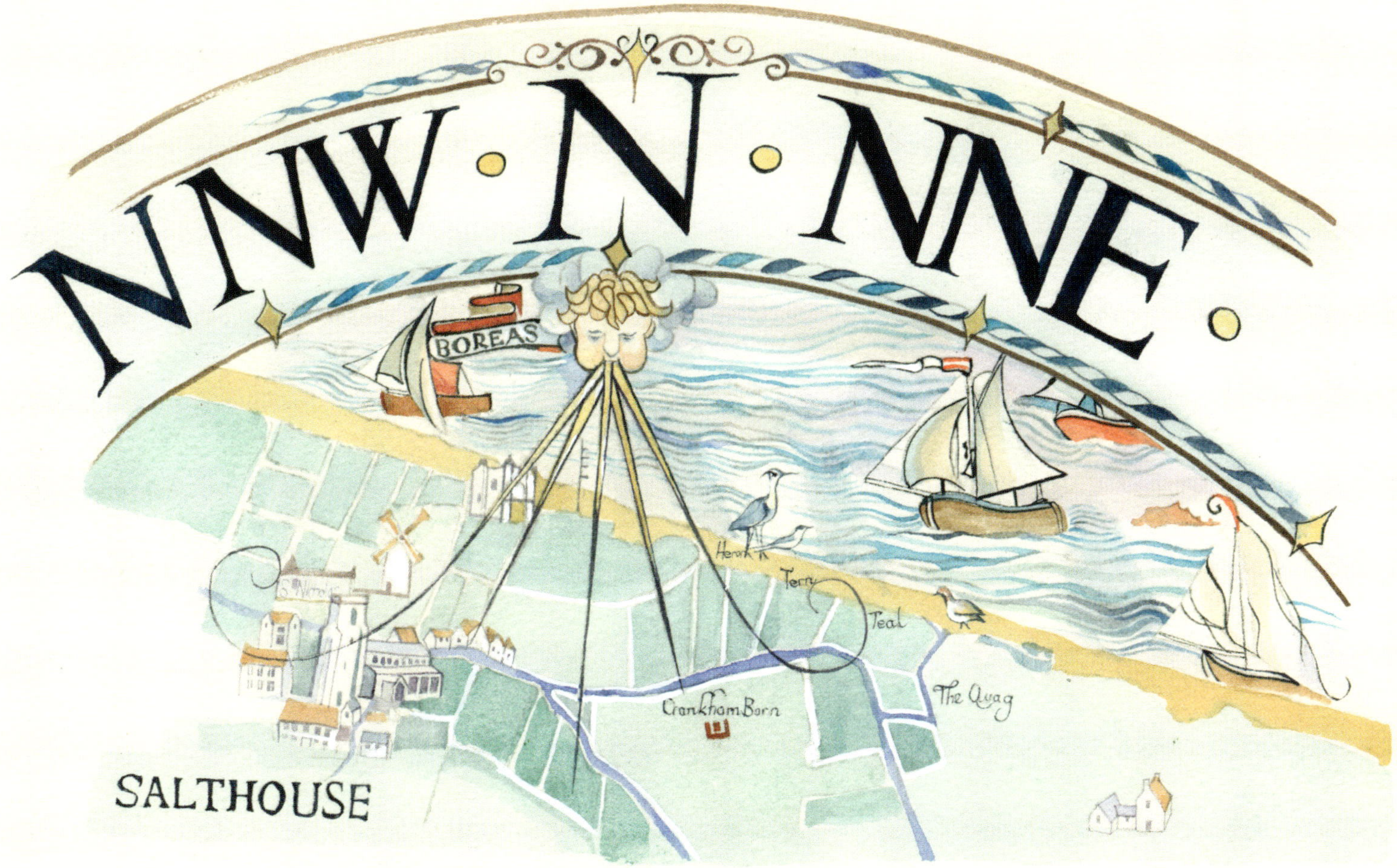

Weather Vane Detail

CLIFFS AND CRABS

Weybourne and Sheringham

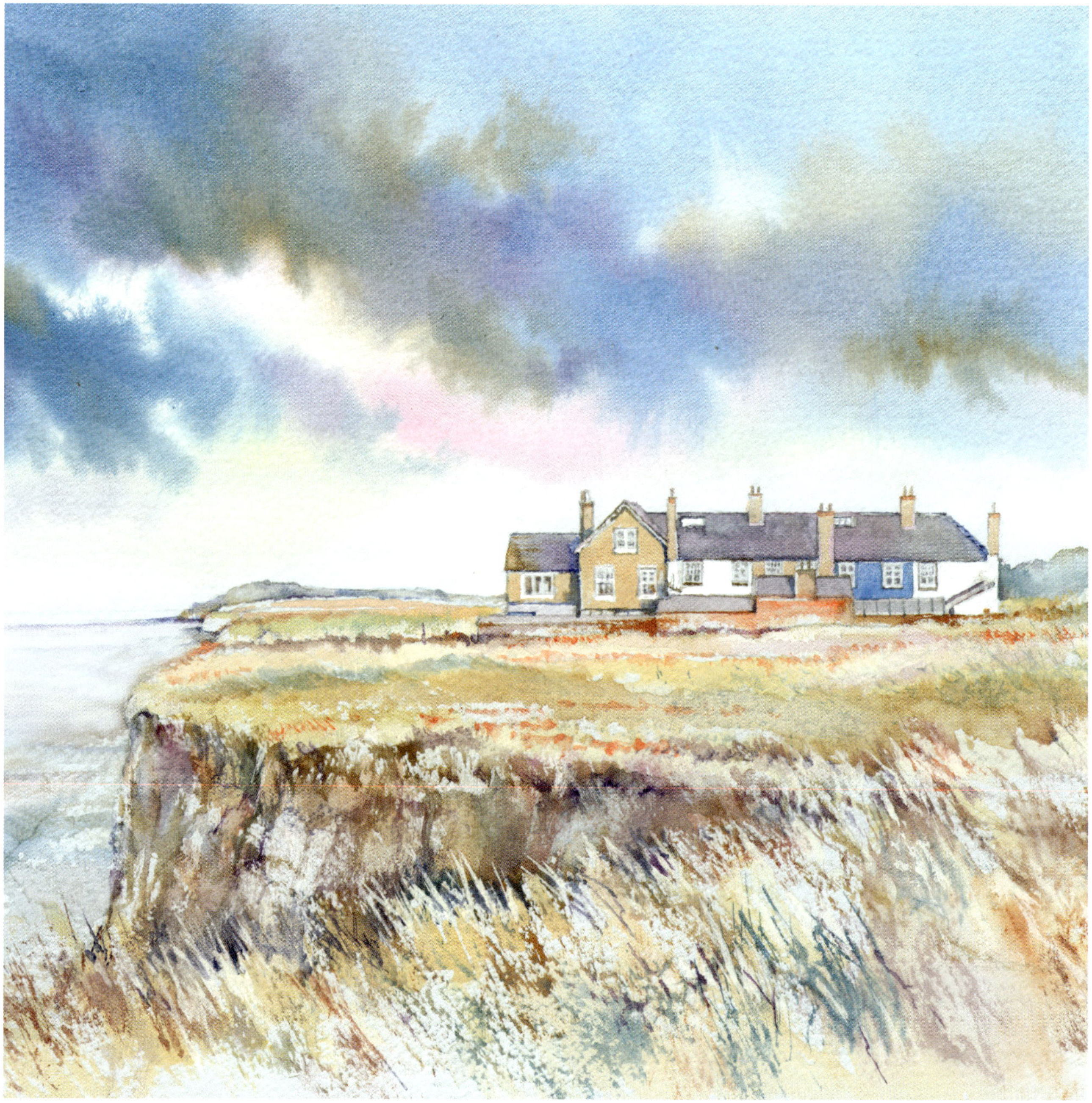

Close to the Edge,
Weybourne Coastguard Cottages
220mm x 220mm

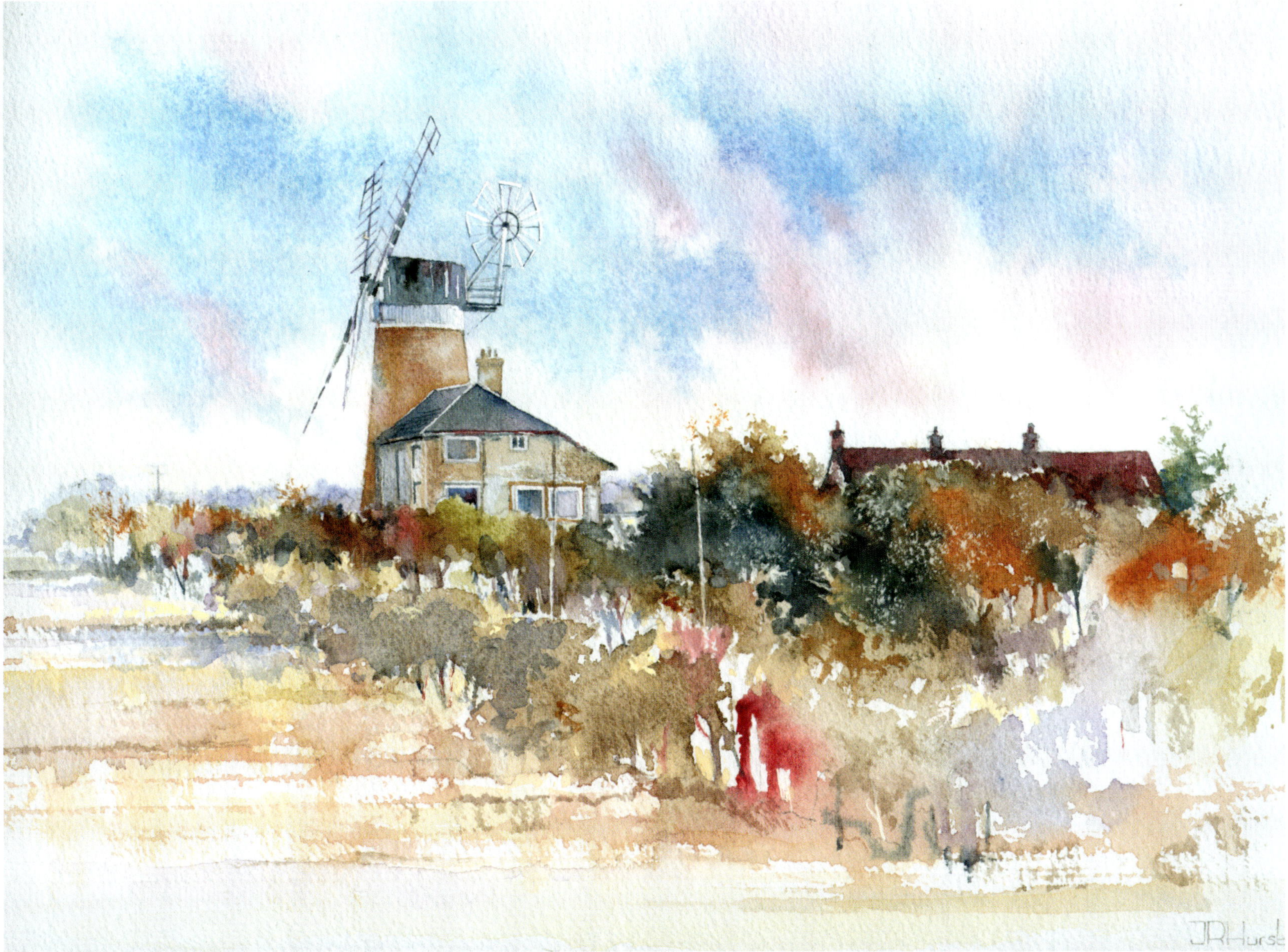

The Mill, Weybourne
300mm x 230mm

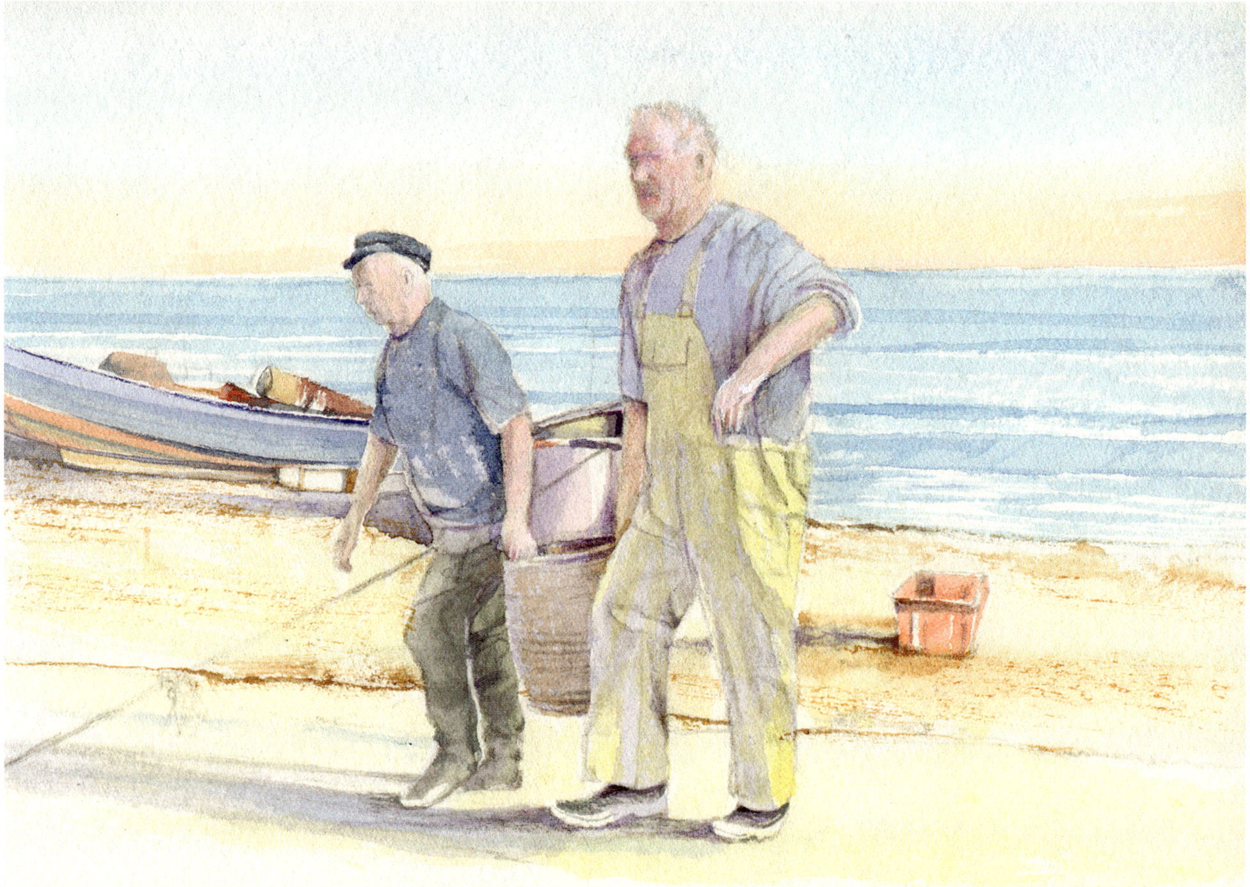

Sharing the Load, Sheringham
130mm x 130mm

There are four full time crabbing boats each hauling seventy pots a day out of Sheringham's West End. Known formerly as 'The Cowboys', they would compete with their East End counterparts 'The Redskins' of which there are now none working professionally. The boats have also changed dramatically within living memory from large three men 'hovellers' to the single-handed nineteen foot 'Orkney' and 'Tactile' class of crab boat. The former were timber boats used not only for crabbing but also long lining and whelking, often splitting as they baked on the hot Sheringham shingle yet healing up when returned to the sea.

The modern boats are moulded replicas of the old styles known fondly as 'Tupperware Skiffs' by the locals due to their lightness, manoeuvrability and disposable qualities. These qualities are ideal for the Sheringham fishermen who rely upon each other for departure and landing on the steep shingle beach. Each day if there is a tidal swell they launch one hour after high water, helping each other out and leaving the lightest boat until last. My time with the Middleton family ably supported by Messrs Holsey and Ayres was not only informative but also very amusing.

"Do you know?" said 'Fuzz' Middleton. "A crab tagged here turned up off Bridlington!"

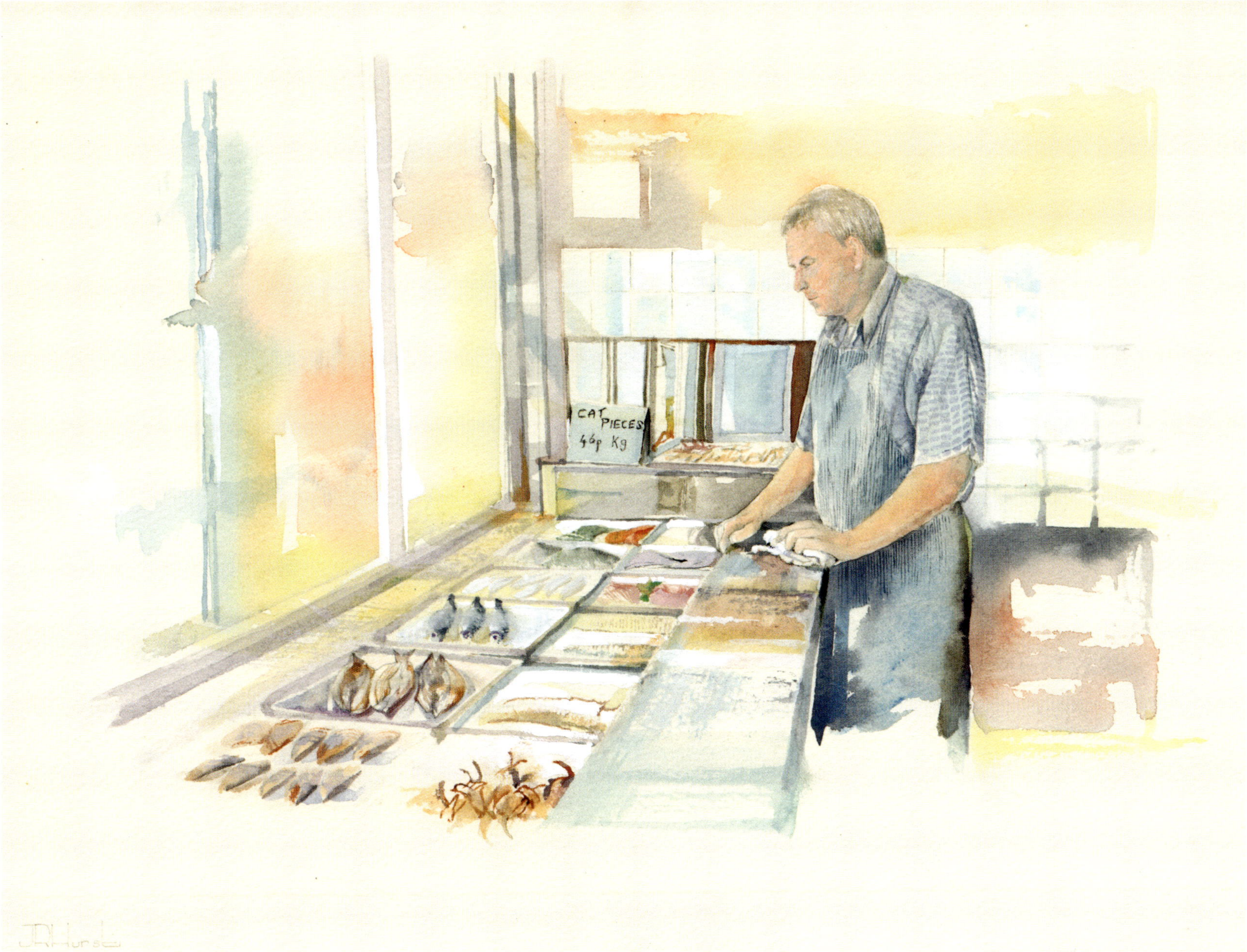

The Seafood Counter
350mm x 290mm

We often buy our fresh fish from P and J Scotters on Station Road in Sheringham or, if in Holt, from the aptly named Mr Finn at Spencer's Plaice. Here is a sketch of Ted Wood overseeing a fine array of kippers, haddock, skate, plaice and Dover sole. Sheringham crabs take pride of place of course.

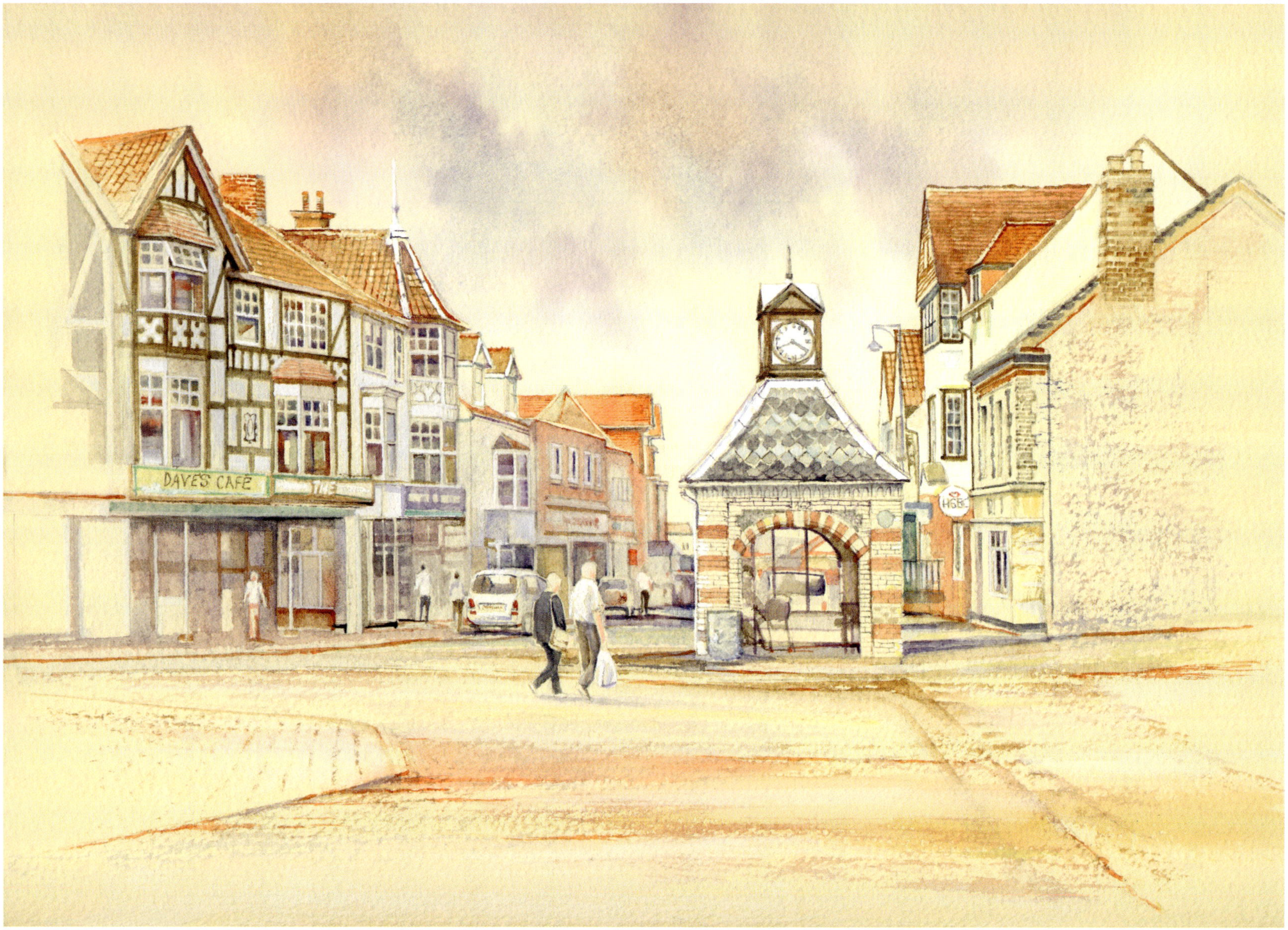

Sheringham Clock Tower
330mm x 240mm

A focal point for locals and visitors alike, the Clock Tower in Sheringham acts as a meeting place, shelter and timepiece. From here the High Street leads to the Promenade past a tempting selection of businesses including bakers, fish and chip shops, amusement arcades, public houses and a shellfish bar to name but a few.

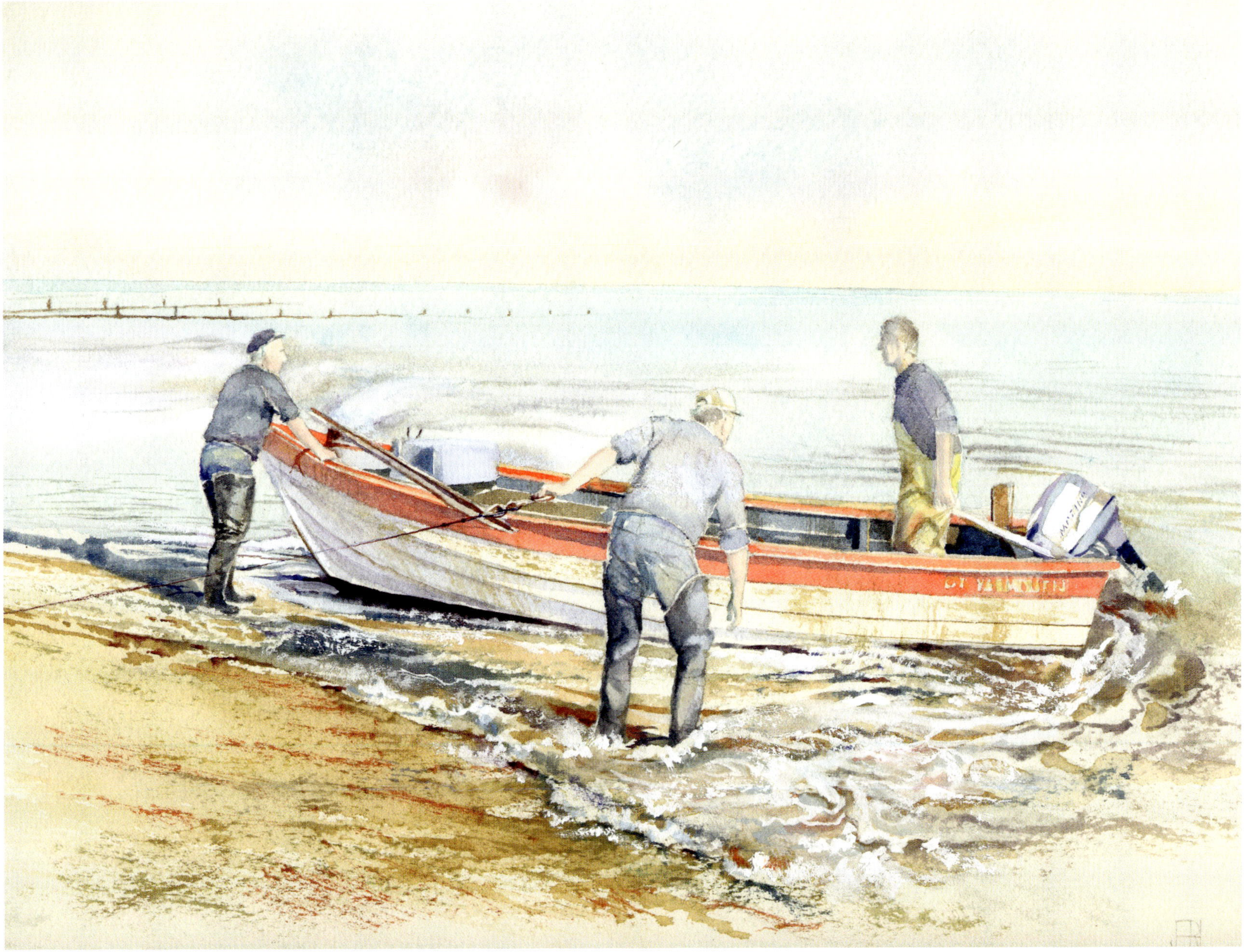

Crab Boat Ashore, Sheringham
273mm x 210mm

DAYS BY THE SEA

Cromer and Overstrand

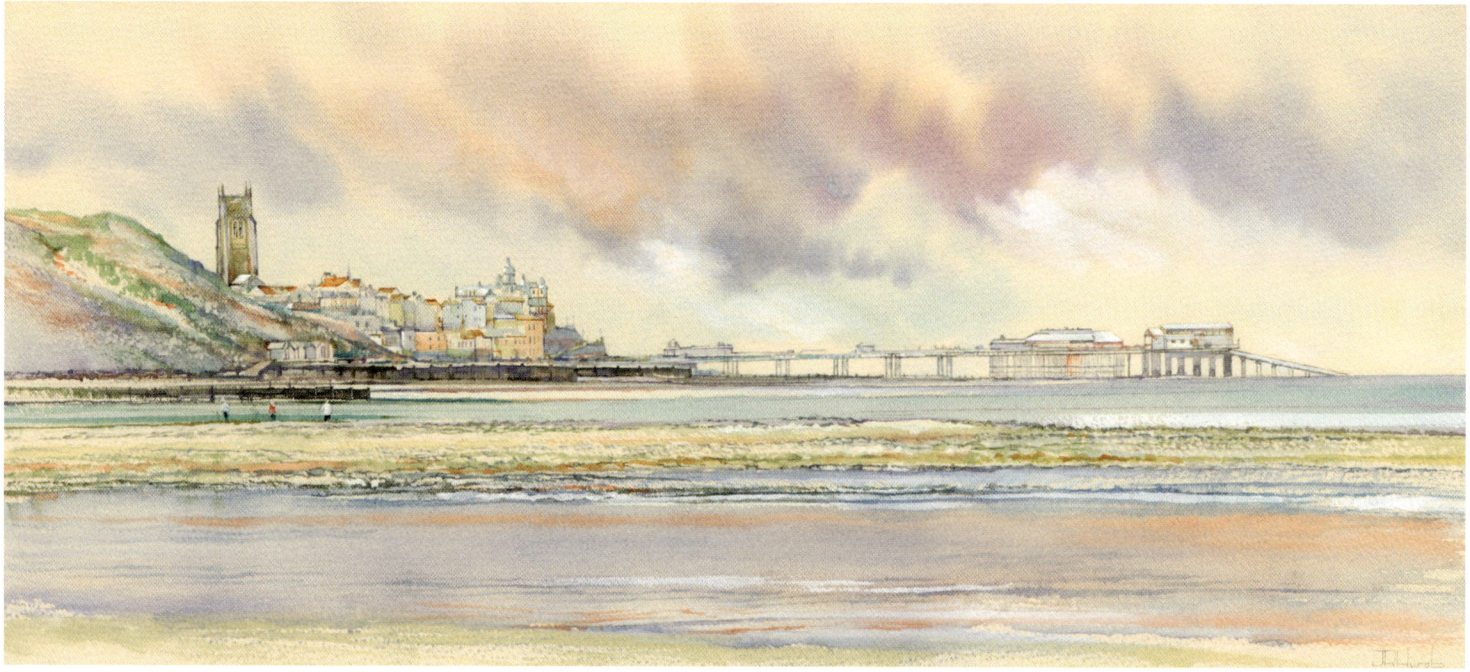

Cromer from Overstrand
510mm x 230mm

When one walks along the beach at very low tide in an easterly direction from Overstrand, the eye is drawn towards the great span of ironwork that is Cromer pier. Sparkling in afternoon sun a pastel roofscape made up of towers, domes and pantiles, creates a Mediterranean feel to this seaside resort.

The town of Cromer has an interesting history, resulting from its popularity with Victorian railway excursionists who wished to 'take the water'. This transformed a small fishing village into a sophisticated resort.

Between 1881 and 1901 the population of Cromer doubled from fifteen hundred to three thousand, rudimentary dirt roads became 'car paved streets' and the famous pier enjoyed two official openings. The promenade became the place to be seen, illuminated by gaslights and later somewhat erratic electric replacements. London papers arrived promptly each day by 10.00am and in 1895 the first deckchairs appeared. The resultant building boom gave the town its unique character. Japanese bungalows, Italian villas and eclectic design still visible today, represent the grandeur and extravagance of the late Victorian and Edwardian age. A prominent building in my study, noticeable by its dome, is the Hotel de Paris. Founded in 1830 and formerly the summer residence of Lord Suffield, it was previously called Marine Villa.

Other interesting features of Cromer's golden age are the bench seats below Jetty Cliff and the cast railings on The Gangway, installed between 1890 and 1901.

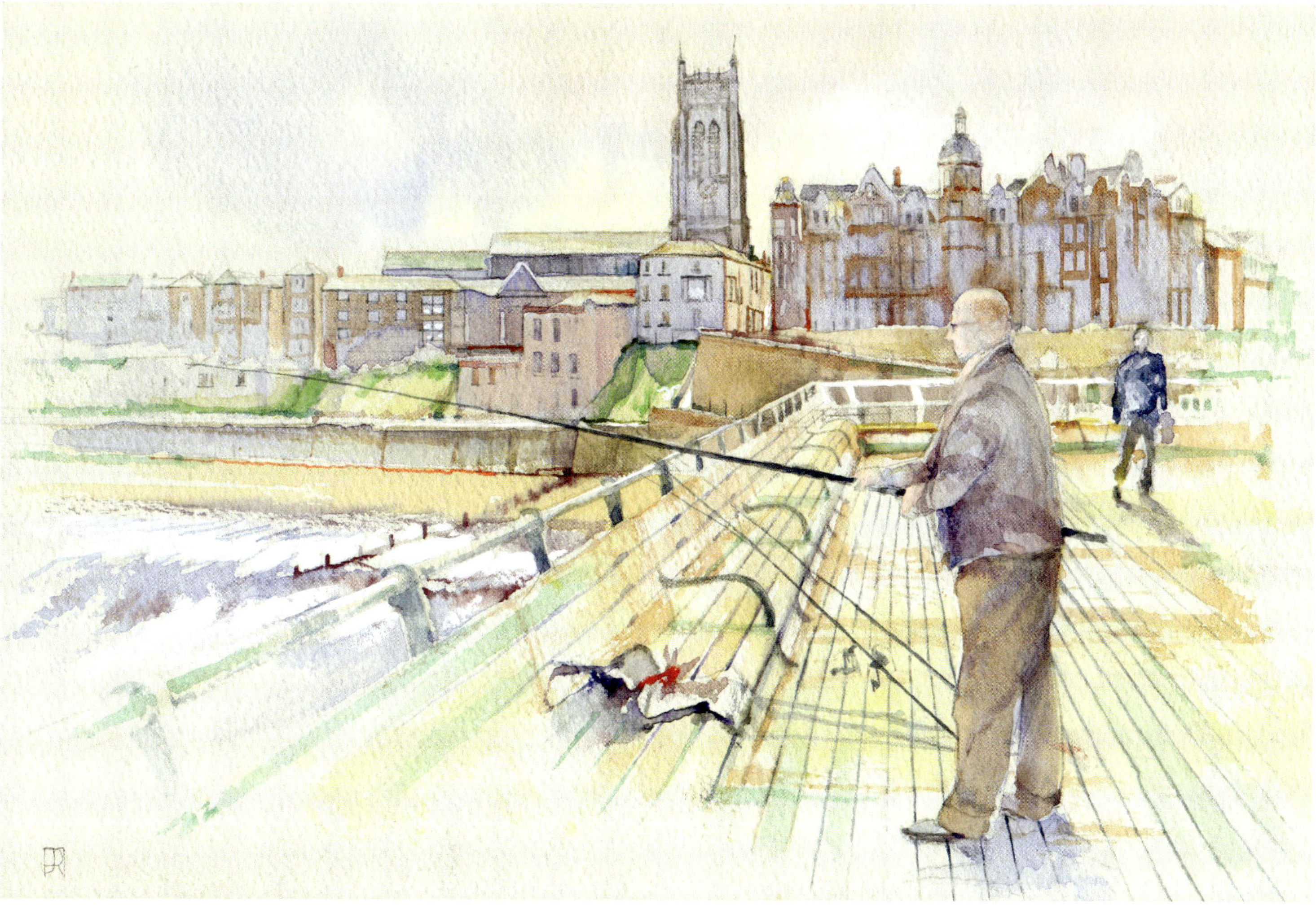

Cromer Pier Fisher
250mm x 170mm

Silhouetted by the noon summer sun, Cromer church and the Hotel de Paris towered over 'Goochie' Gooch and 'Sugar' Smith as they fished the flood tide for bass and flounder. Their benches on the pier were strewn with tackle and rancid newspapers, each revealing lugworm, peeler crab, squid and mackerel. They ingeniously attached worms to hooks by threading them along the hook shaft with remnants of soft shell crab being made secure by invisible tape. Below us the continuous roar of breakers swept relentlessly under the pier making rod tips quiver in anticipation whilst above, billowing cumulus clouds floated lazily inland.

"What time do you start fishing the pier each day?" I naively asked.

"When the bar opens!" replied Sugar, raising his local ale in salute.

These sketchbook studies were composed on Cromer beach at 6.00am on a hot, still morning in July. There are lifelong opportunities for an artist to record the crab fishers here, who kindly permitted me to encroach upon their working day.

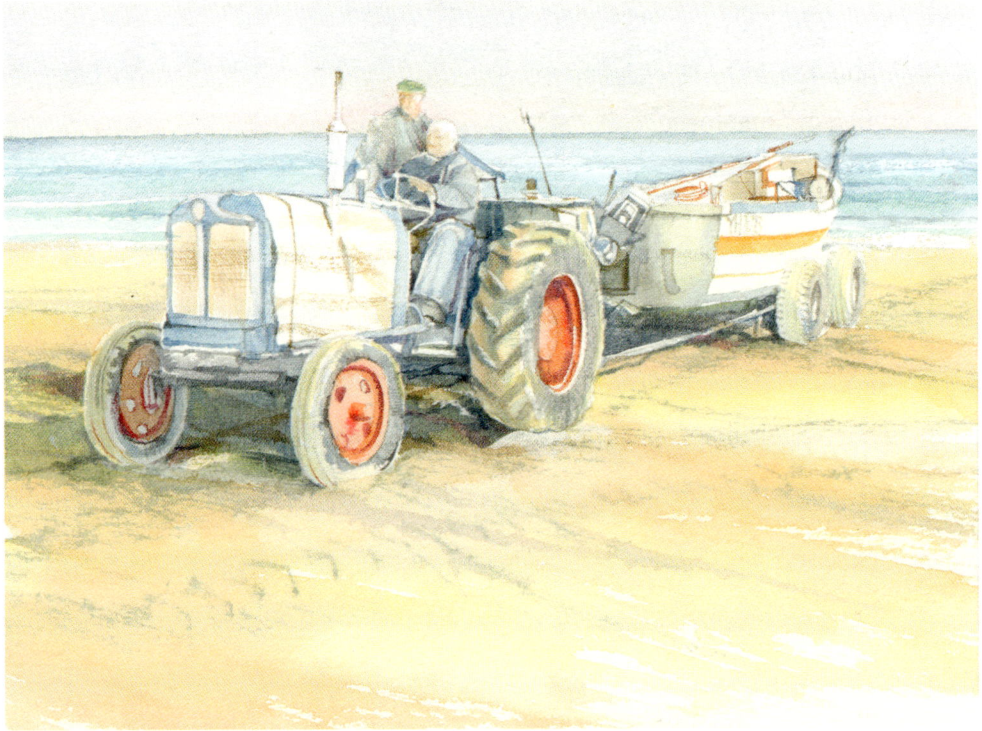

Boat Hauling, Cromer
160mm x 130mm

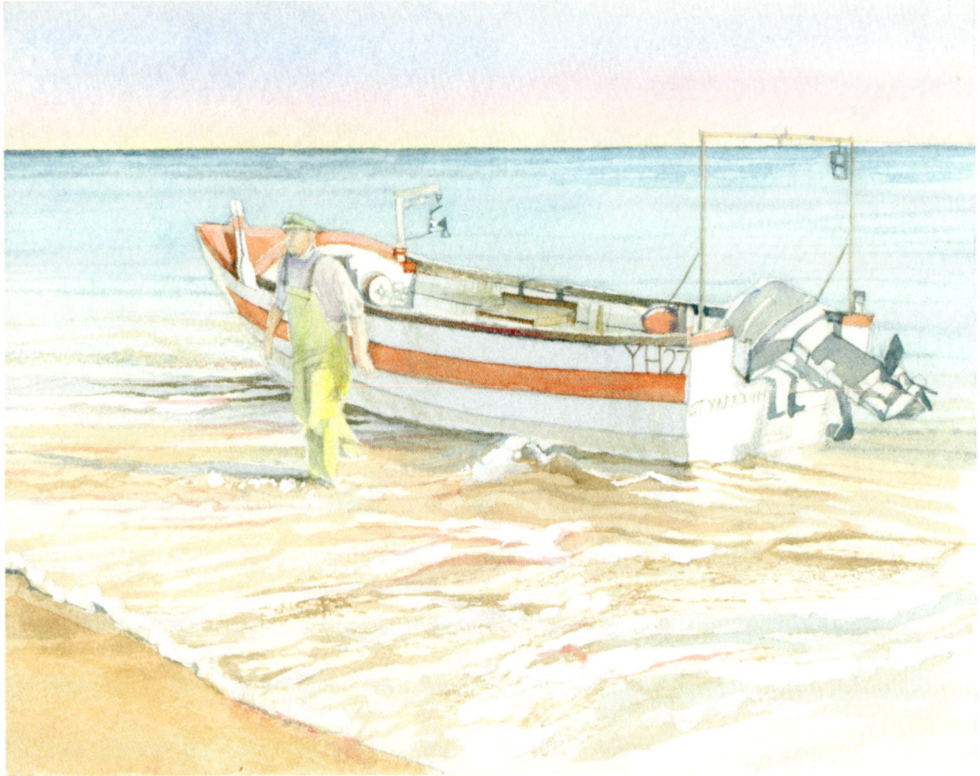

Cromer Crab Landing
160mm x 130mm

The Norfolk Wildlife Trust arranges a rock pool event each year at West Runton, these being the only accessible rock pools on the North Norfolk coast. A suggestion to my grandchildren that we might go there prompted an immediate response from the five year old.

"Rock pools are exciting but a little scary because the crabs might nip your toes. Oh, and don't run or you might slip and bang your head."

Finally the elder of the two said, "Be sure not to hurt the animals and release them after you have studied them."

Accompanied by these young marine biologists and briefed in both Health and Safety and ecological good sense, we set off on our adventure.

The assembled crowd of chattering children and apprehensive adults were expertly briefed by the event leaders and soon to yells of success and delight, shrimps, tiny crabs and a somewhat battered lobster ended up in their buckets. Then we saw it. Secreted in a crevice with angry bubbles appearing at its mouthparts, lodged the biggest crab imaginable.

"Get it out Grandad!" came an urgent plea. Eventually it was extricated from its cavern to cries of, "What a beauty," "my word" and "wicked."

When held up for close examination it immediately twisted around and nipped the leader's finger with one almighty crunch. As this monster of the deep was released, a tiny voice whispered, "Let's call it Claws!"

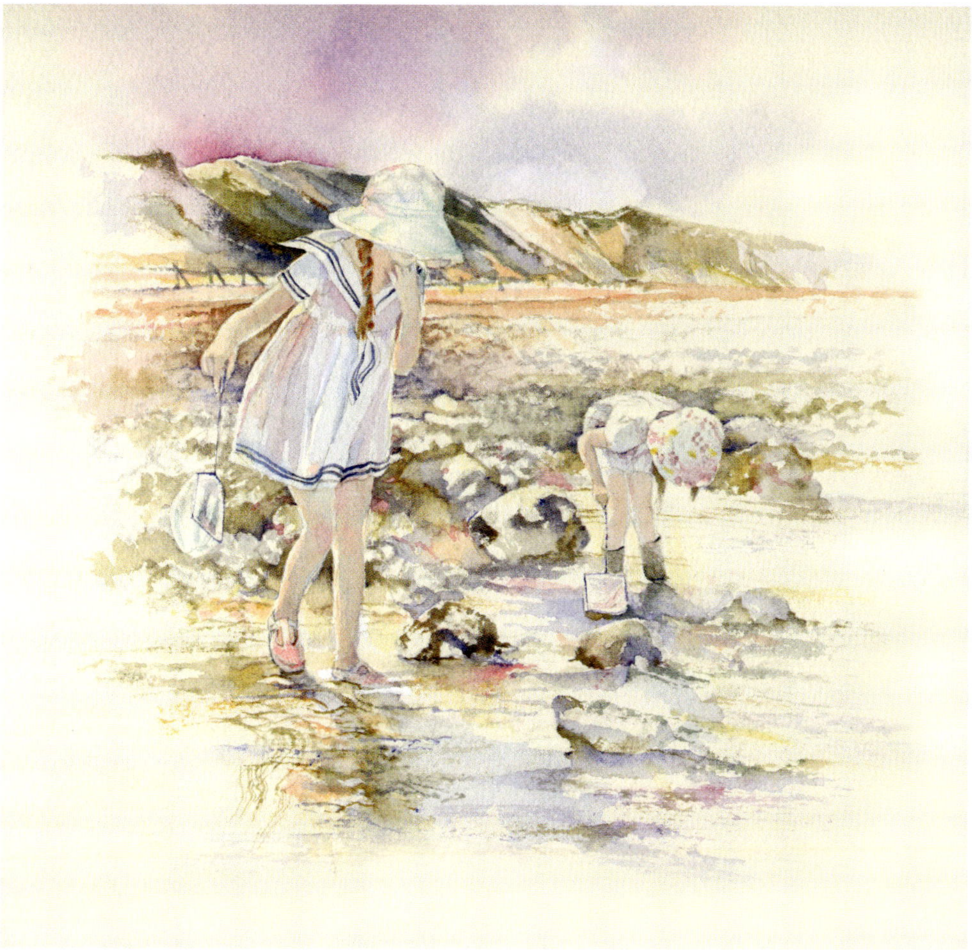

Rock Pool Children
250mm x 260mm

No collection of Coastal Colours would be complete without reference to Clement Scott, celebrated English theatre critic, playwright and travel writer who immortalised the area around Overstrand and Sidestrand by his fond naming of it as Poppyland. Scott wrote a series of articles in the *Daily Telegraph* after staying at the miller's house in Sidestrand during 1883. His influence upon the theatrical world ensured that a number of wealthy people subsequently bought land and had homes built in the area. Cyril Flower, later to become Lord Battersea, was one such enthusiast who purchased two semi-detached cottages made into one dwelling and thirty acres of land in 1888 as part of Lord Suffield's sale of the Overstrand estate. The cottages were to become integrated into a house 'full of clever tricks, eccentricities and touches of Art Noveau' by the prominent architect Edwin Lutyens and named The Pleasaunce, a now obsolete word used to define an area of garden designed for the sole purpose of sensual pleasure. Not all was plain sailing for the young architect however, for in her published reminiscences, Constance Battersea, in true Rothschild form, had shown her indignance at the building of an inappropriately-placed wall. She writes 'in spite of Sir Edwin Lutyen's orders, I threw bricks down on the terrace, to the ill-concealed amusement of the workmen'. I experienced 'The Pleasaunce' when stepping across herringbone patterns in the sunken garden and tracing flowing lines in the cloisters as they terminated in perfect perspective. Despite references to Lutyens' contemporary, Gertrude Jekyll as being the designer of the gardens, it appears that this may not be the case and credit for the design now goes to Lord and Lady Battersea. Prominent visitors to the house have included Queen Alexandra and her sister the Empress of Russia in 1911, whilst George Bernard Shaw and leading figures in the Fabian Society stayed in Overstrand in 1903. The Pleasaunce was aquired by Christian Endeavour Holiday Homes Ltd in 1936, who still maintain it today as a conference and retreat centre. Not only is the visitor enamoured by Lutyens' architectural splendour, secreted beneath the shady holm oaks within sight and smell of the sea there can be found the tiniest chapel I have ever seen and like other sanctuaries of constant prayer, a place of peace and tranquillity.

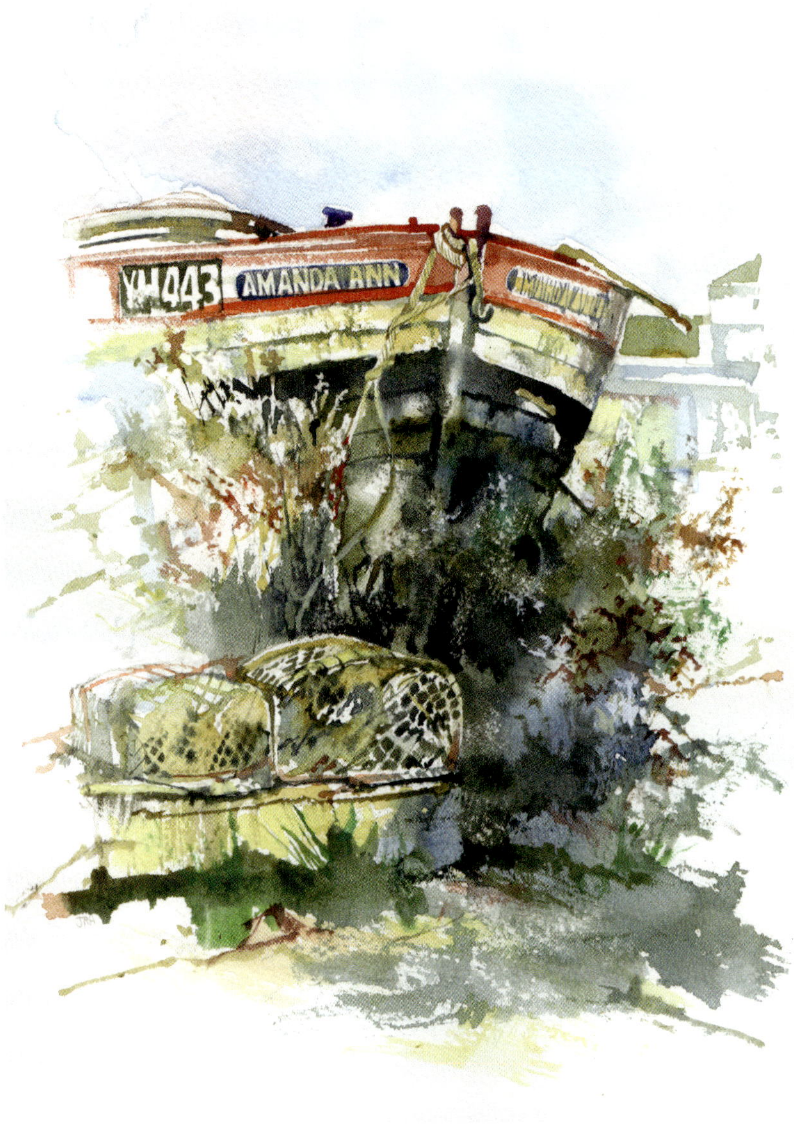

Overstrand Crab Boat
220mm x 270mm

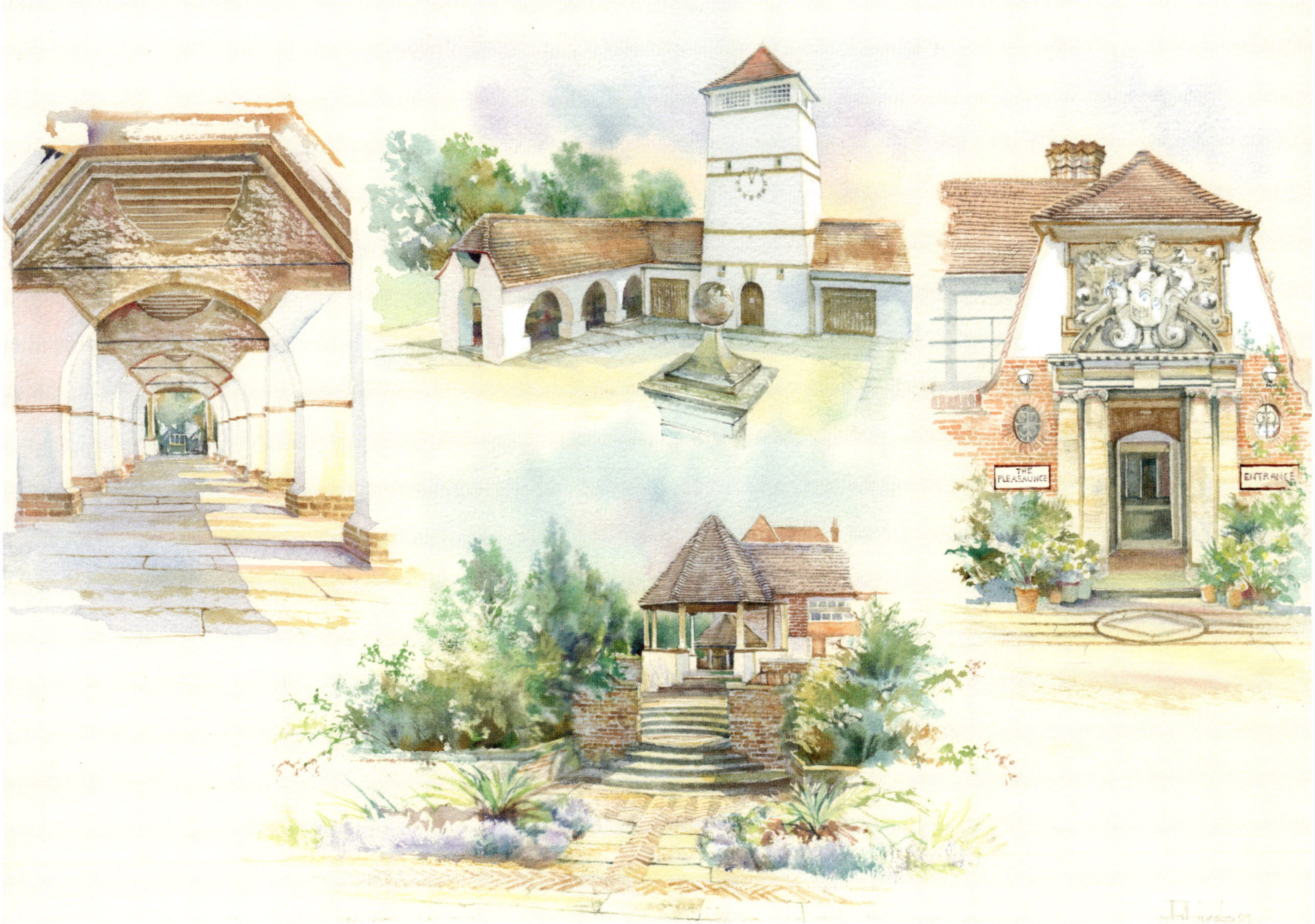

The Pleasaunce
410mm x 290mm

REEDS AND BREEZES

Broadland

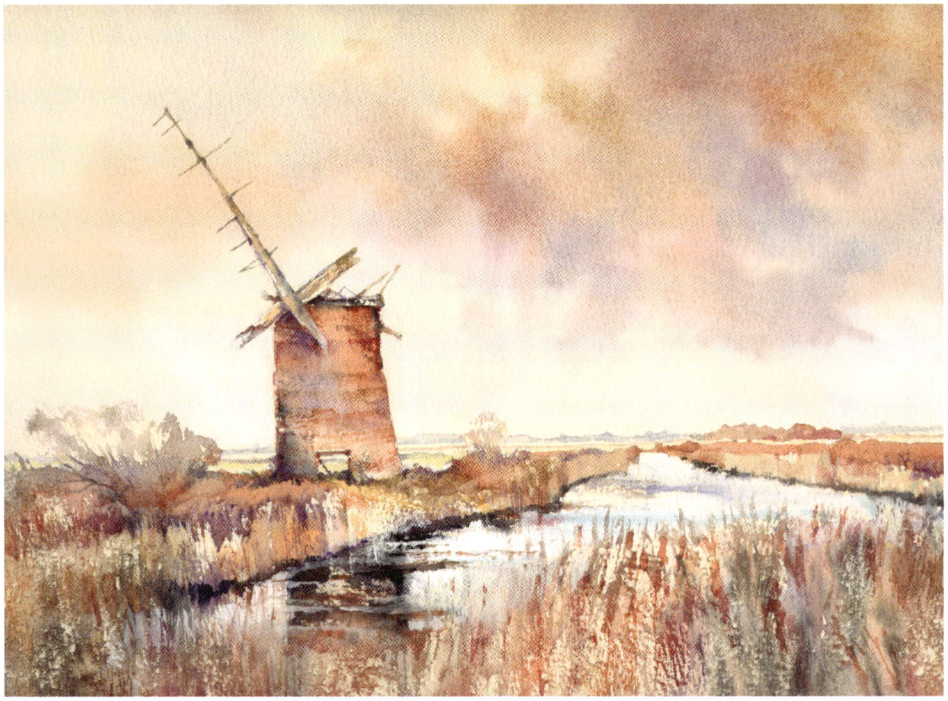

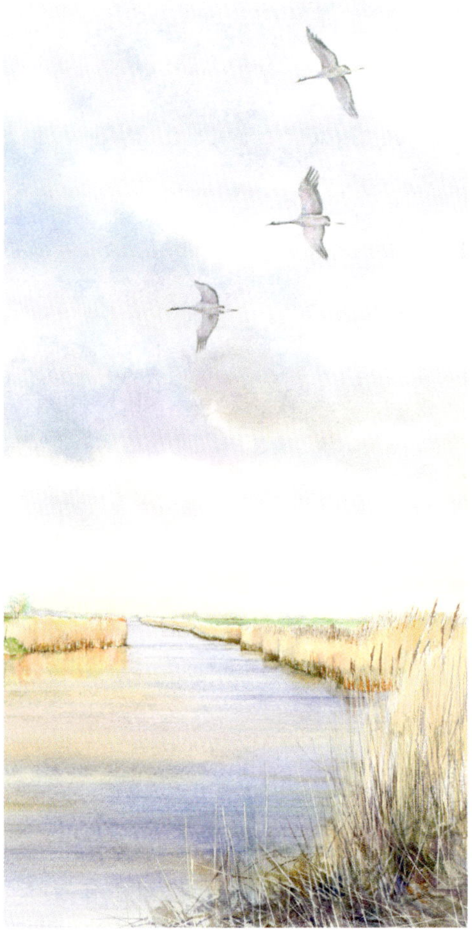

Brograve Mill
410mm x 220mm

Common Cranes near Horsey
130mm x 300mm

Sea breezes play tunes on the riverside reeds by Brograve Mill, barely two miles from the dune ridge at Waxham on the Norfolk coast. This viewpoint may be reached by walking from Horsey Mill round the broad on a well-worn path. I took such a walk in the early morning and witnessed a spectacle of spiralling cranes; their strange fluting calls now an integral part of the Norfolk Broads. This elegant bird has now established a fragile breeding population, centred on Hickling Broad. Often mistaken for sheep, they roam across the damp rushy meadows, much as they did in the mid nineteenth century, before intense persecution for plumage and food began to take its toll.

The drainage mill once moved water between field and dyke. Now solitary cormorants, their wings outstretched, perch on the one remaining sail and itinerant artists try to paint as I did, the earthy dampness of The Broads brushed by an ever fleeting sky.

This watercolour is one in a series showing how low winter light creates an atmosphere as shadows are formed across buildings and water. Skeletal trees add to the linear form of this composition, painted near a secluded mooring at Hickling Broad on a cold February morning.

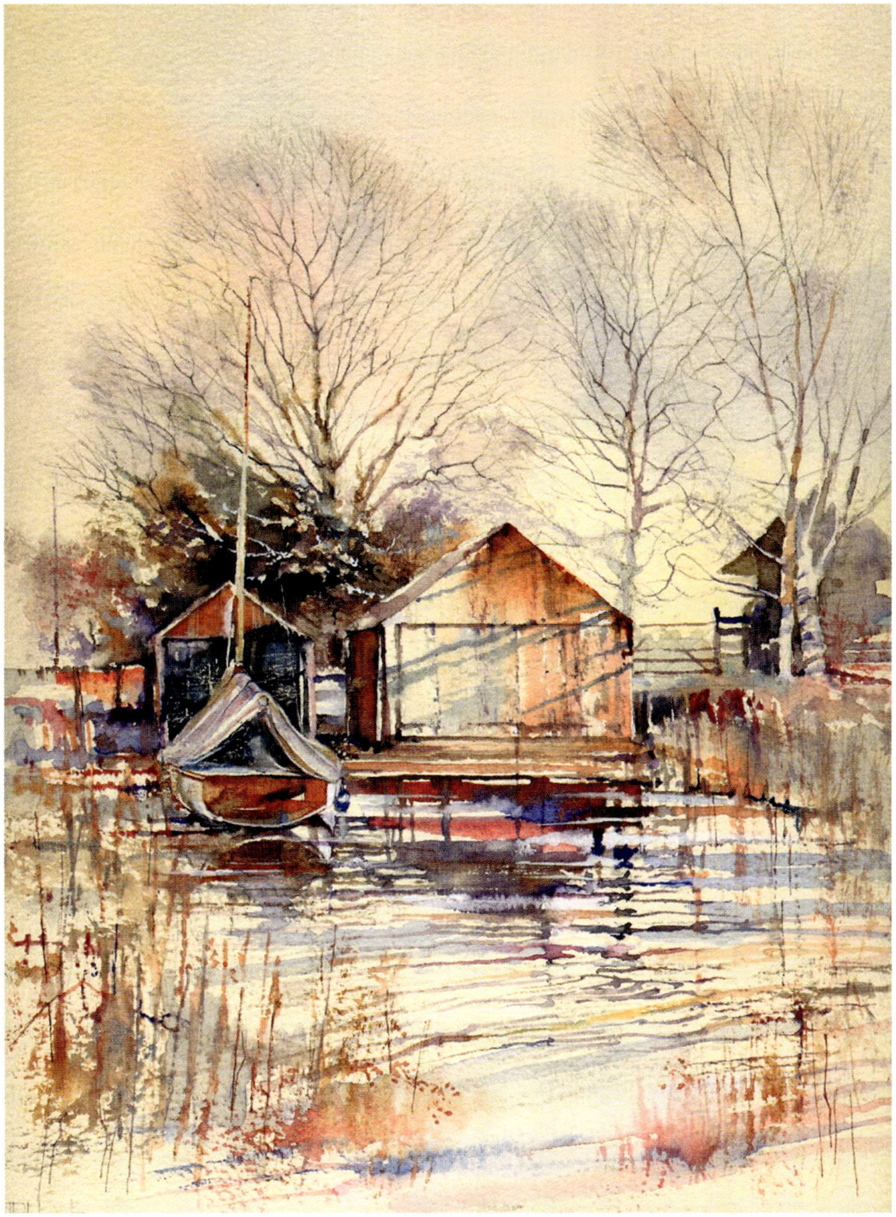

Boat Shed Shadows
230mm x 260mm

In addition to farming, my father was a dyking man who used his scythe to mow miles of fenland riverbanks in Lincolnshire. He arrived home one day with a small grass snake in his wellington boot and it was he who taught me to approach the lay of the grass sward in order to mow with greater ease. My family heritage and some knowledge of the scythe made my meeting with Eric Edwards MBE so much more enjoyable, although for this charismatic, inquisitive, self confessed 'people person', talking about marsh ways comes naturally.

Eric was born in 1940 at Lyng by the river Wensum and after a colourful life, which included playing football for Norfolk County, Kings Lynn and Yarmouth, he settled into the role of reed cutter and marshman in 1967, when appointed by Norfolk Education Authority and latterly the Broads Authority to work on Turf Fen by the River Ant. Inheriting some of the ancient marsh tools from his predecessor, Eric embarked upon a remarkable career in which he became the living ambassador of marshland heritage, recognised by the MBE bestowed upon him in 2004 with a citation that states, 'For services to Norfolk and Suffolk Broads'. Through his work Eric has met Margaret Thatcher and Prince Charles in addition to being featured in such television programmes as The Generation Game, (Eric always adds "three times, once with Bruce Forsythe and twice with Jim Davidson, he's a laugh!"), Go Fishing, Flog It, Songs of Praise, Rosie and Jim, and Highway. He speaks with great affection of Harry Secombe who presented the latter programme.

Swallowtail Butterfly
210mm x 210mm

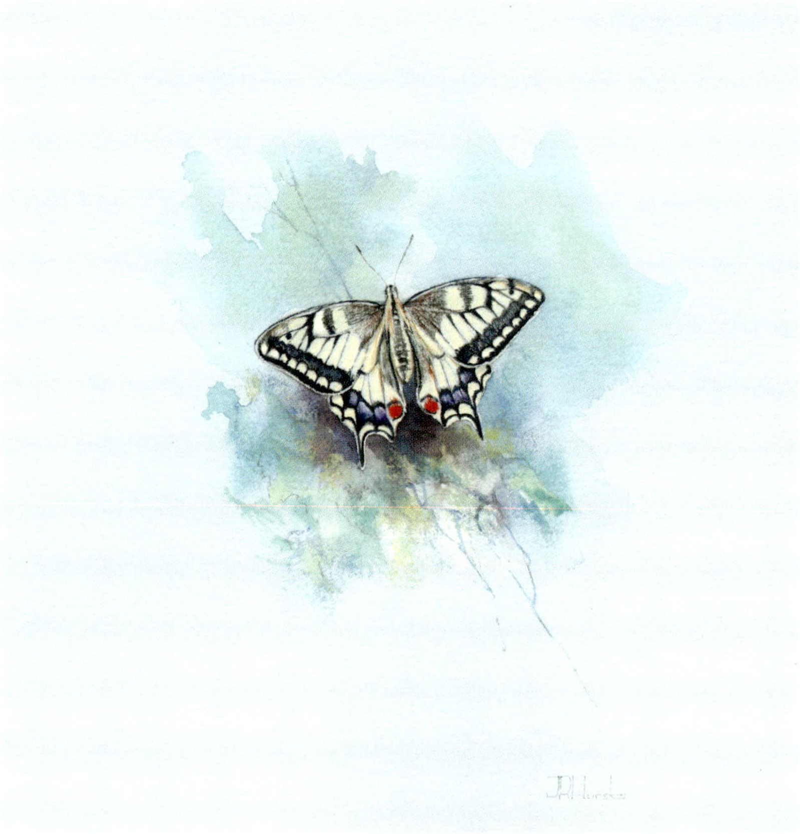

When Eric speaks in dialect about his collection of marshland artefacts, most of which he has personally used, there is a mass of information to assimilate. He calls the reed bundle a 'shuff', crosses the dyke on a 'ligger', scoops all manner of liquid ooze from the dykes with a 'dydle' and cuts underwater weed with a 'meag'. His trusty tool is the scythe, fashioned from an alder trunk, sourced many years ago by quanting a lighter boat upriver in winter and carefully selecting the scythe handle by eye. Eric's cherished possession is a pair of beautifully crafted leather fisherman's waders.

"When they weren't fishing they would be reed cutting" said Eric, adding "and all these tools are blacksmith made."

"What else is precious to you?" I asked.

Eric replied without a second thought, "My wife Ruby, the visit to the palace for my MBE, the beardies, bittern and swallowtail, and April when the colt is coming.

Eric is now employed by the How Hill Trust situated above Turf Fen by the river Ant, a private charity committed to sharing his world with both young and old. Eric was surrounded by attentive five year olds, as I departed, who constantly shot their hands in the air to ask questions.

AUTHOR'S NOTE: *'Beardies' are bearded tits. Colt are new reed shoots signalling the end of the cutting season. Ligger is a plank.*

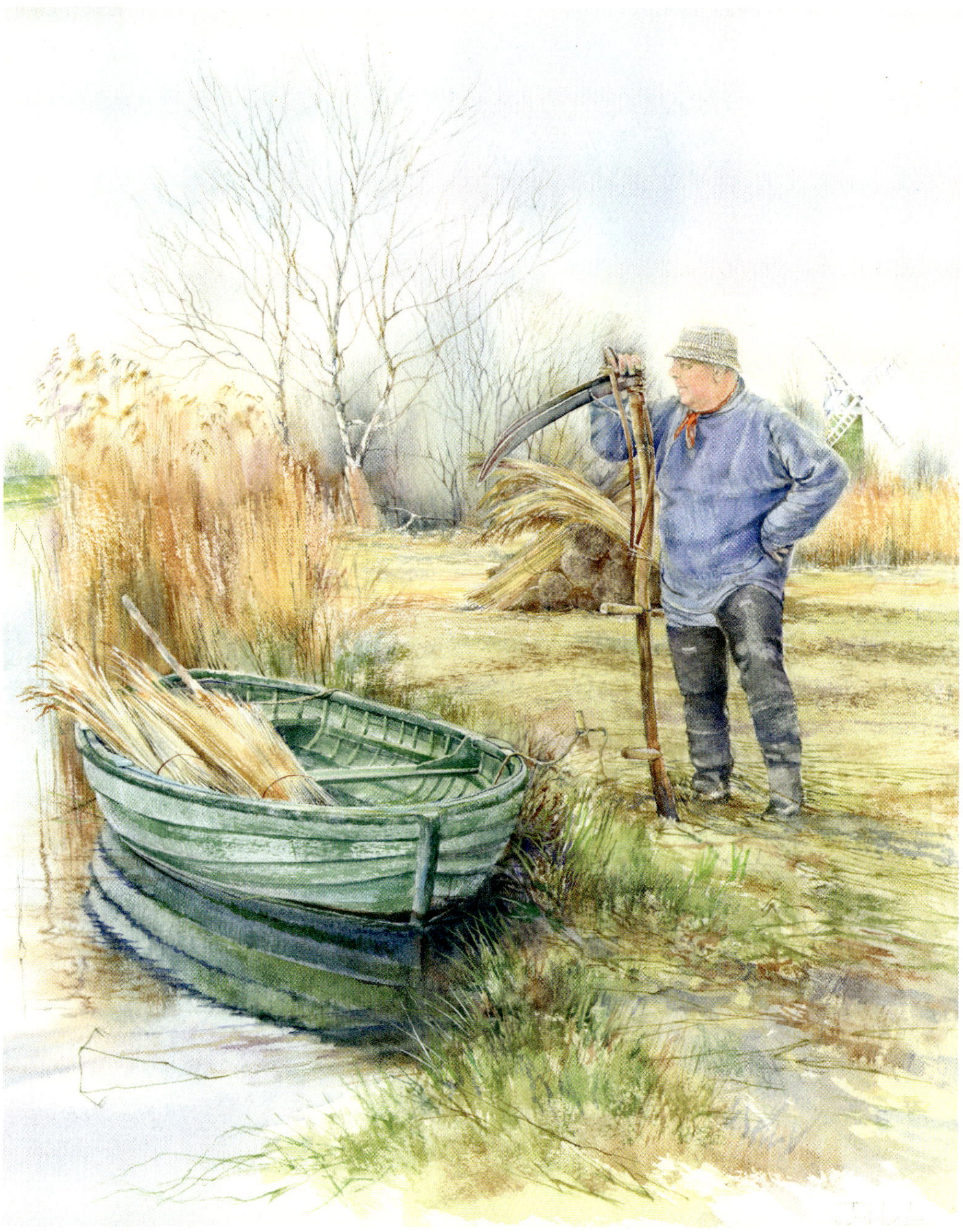

The Last Reed Cutter
300mm x 375mm

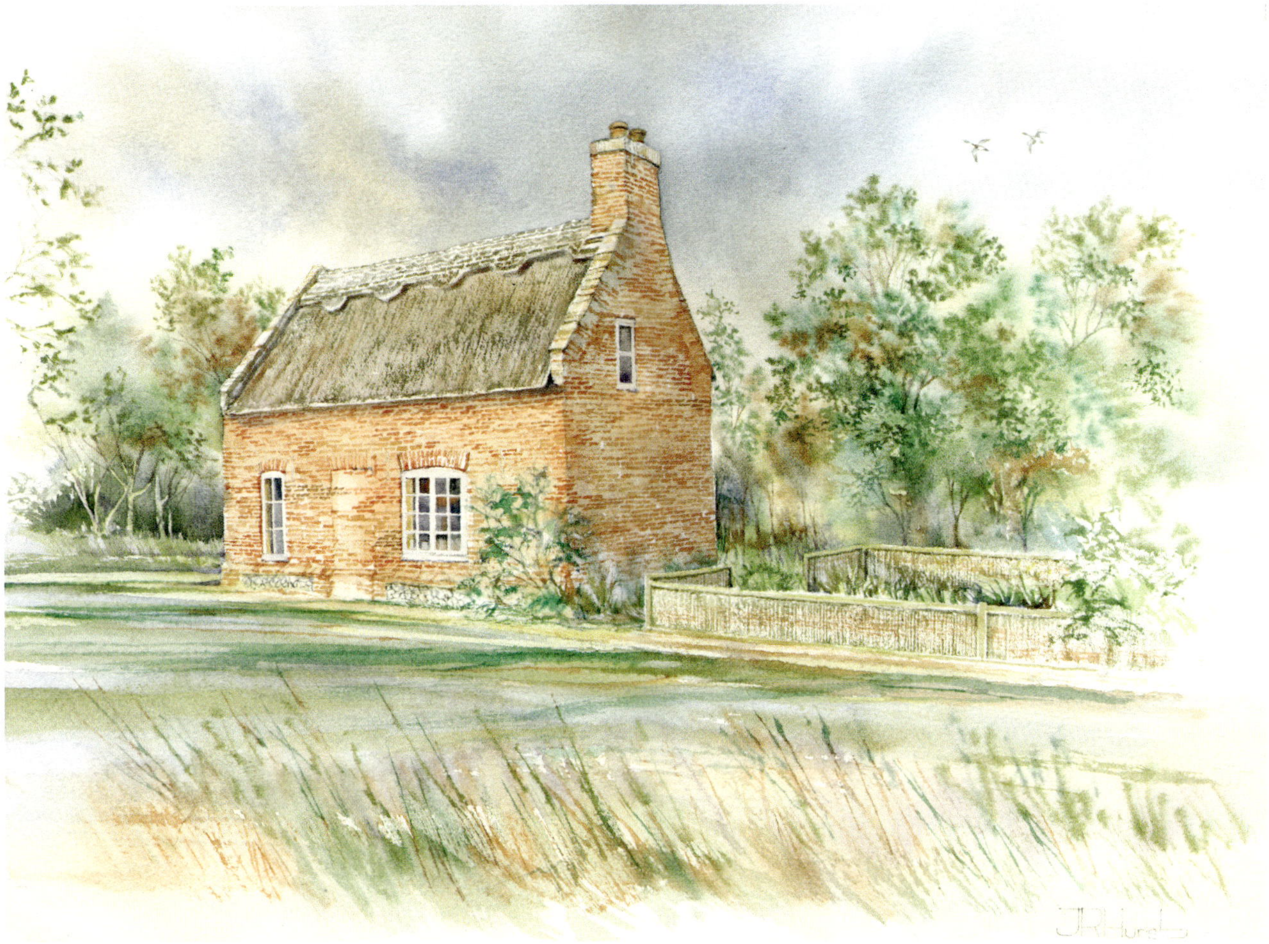

Marsh Cottage, How Hill
300mm x 230mm

The Norfolk Broads are Britain's largest protected wetland, an area of shallow lakes formed in medieval times when peat diggings became flooded due to rising sea levels. A fragile environment, combining open water with alder carr, fen and reed swamp, the Broads are either associated with the rivers Bure, Ant, Thurne, Yare and Waveney or completely isolated. Most are best viewed by boat although at Hickling and Ranworth there are accessible boardwalks and interpretive centres created by the Norfolk Wildlife Trust. Numerous surveys of the flora and fauna have taken place over the years resulting in many Sites of Special Scientific Interest culminating in the formation of the Broads Authority in 1989, its aim to conserve and enhance the natural beauty, wildlife and cultural heritage of the Broads.

A very fine example of this can be seen at How Hill where boating visitors to the River Ant may moor alongside the reserve and nearby Toad Hole Cottage Museum. Built between 1780 and 1820, the cottage was home for marsh families until 1900 when a local family, the Boardmans, bought the estate. Ben Curtis was one of the last people to live here, recorded in the annual census as an eel catcher although it was common knowledge that census titles given to a recipient often depended upon the task being performed on census day. The cottage museum represents marsh life in the late Victorian era including a cottage garden filled with vegetables, herbs and a medlar tree, well known for its bletted fruit made semi-rotten by frosts before being used in the most delicious jellies, fruit cheese or sauce for game.

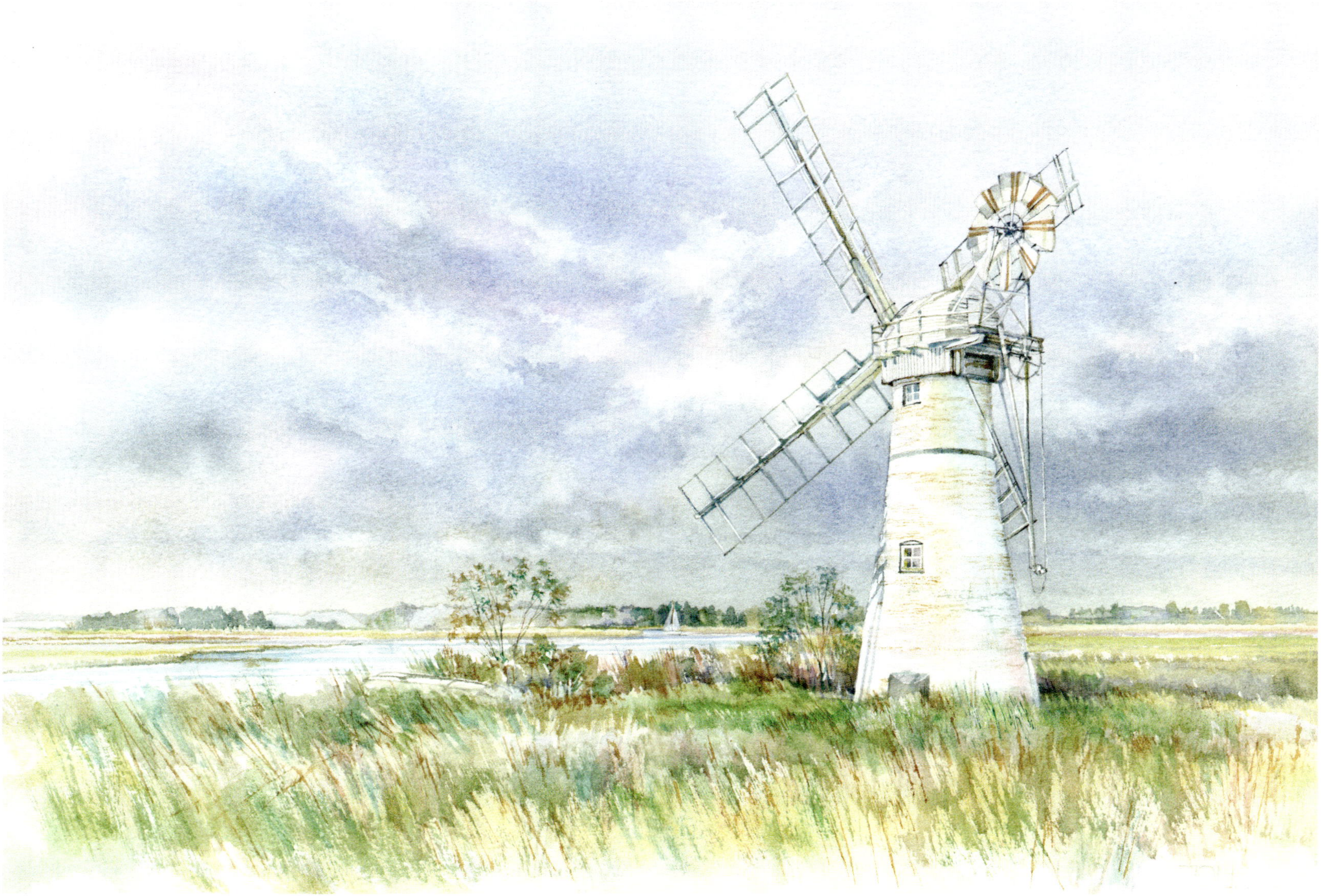

Thurne Dyke Drainage Mill
400mm x 240mm

My journey ends as it began, gazing at a vast Norfolk sky.

BIBLIOGRAPHY

The Birds of Blakeney Point, A. Stoddart & S. Joyner, Wren Publishing, 2005.
The Banville Diaries, Buxton, Virgo & Yaxley, Collins, 1986.
Guardian Spirit of The East Bank, M. Taylor, Wren Publishing, 2002.
Norfolk Coast Sketches, David Poole, Wilson – Poole, 1980.
The Unbroken Thread, Viscount Templewood, Collins, 1949.
Bird Sanctuary, Reginald Gaze, Faber & Faber.
Nature in Norfolk – A Heritage in Trust, Jarrold, 1976.
The Heritage of Cromer, A. D. Boyce, Cromer Preservation Society, 2009.
Hit & Miss, Lord Walsingham, Allan & Co, 1927.
Thornham – A Photographic History of A Norfolk Village and its People, Oliver, Thompson & Warham, Thornham History Society, 2006.
Hev Yew Gotta Loight Boy, Kieth Skipper, Countryside Books, 2001.
The Wild Flowers of Britain & Northern Europe, R. Fitter, A. Fitter, M. Blamey, Collins, 1974.
The Pleasaunce, Monica E. Sykes.
Toad Hole Cottage Remembers, The Broads Authority.
Joe Jordan – Guardian of The Marsh, Elizabeth Thomas, J. Baldwin Publishing Solutions, 2003.
Salthouse – The Story of A Norfolk Village, Val Fiddian, Salthouse History Group, 2003.
Reminiscences, Constance Battersea, Macmillan & Co, 1922.

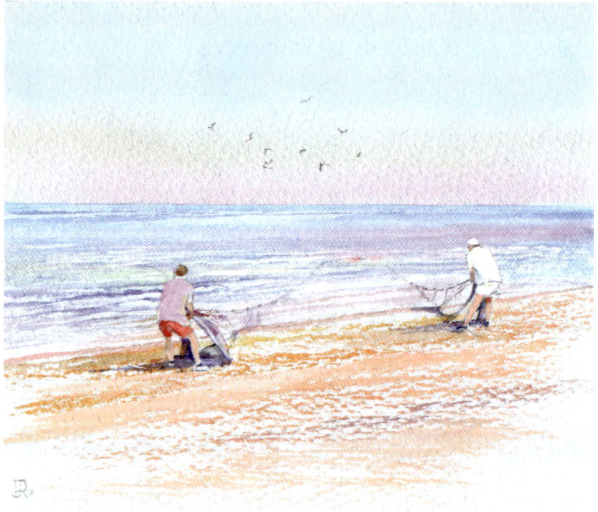

Netting Whitebait, Blakeney Point
Sketchbook Study
160mm x 170mm

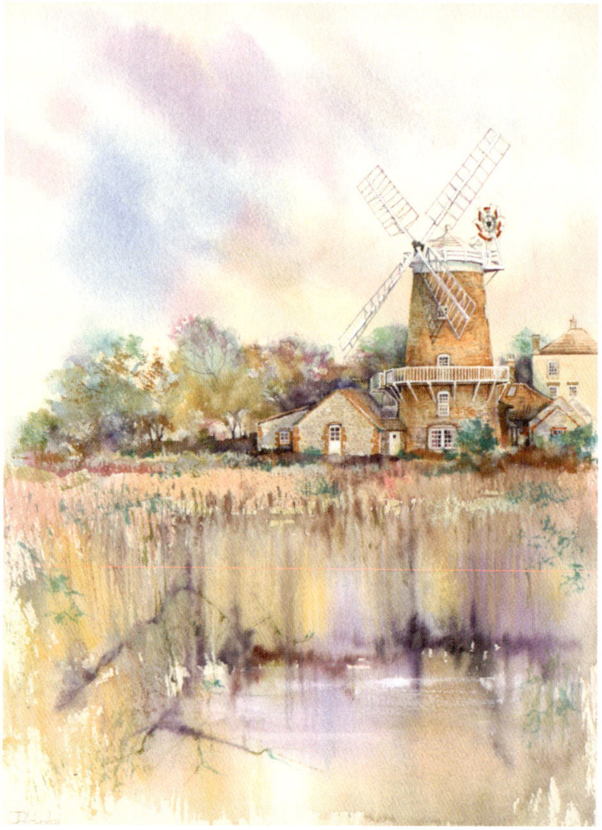

Cley Reed Bed
300mm x 500mm

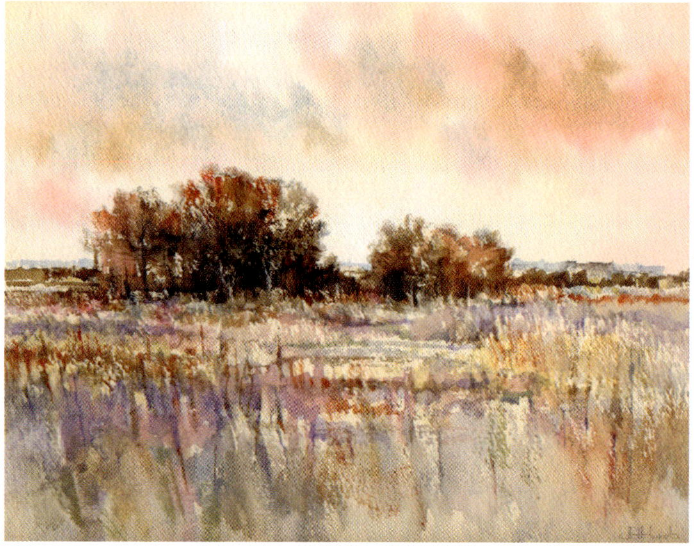

Blackthorn Copse
300mm x 250mm